AMERICA'S FAVORITE BRAND NAME

Baking

Publications International, Ltd.

Favorite Brand Name Recipes at www.fbnr.com

Pictured on the front cover *(clockwise from top left):* Peanut Butter Secrets *(page 114),* Lemon Crème Bars *(page 178),* Strawberry Rhubarb Pie *(page 282),* Chocolate Sour Cream Cheesecake *(page 254),* Arlington Apple Gingerbread Cake *(page 202)* and Sock-It-To-Me Cake *(page 216).*

Pictured on the back cover *(top to bottom):* Marble Cheesecake *(page 266)* and Cheddar-Apple Bread *(page 6).*

ISBN: 0-7853-3433-5

Library of Congress Catalog Card Number: 99-70120

Manufactured in China.

8 7 6 5 4 3 2 1

Microwave Cooking: Microwave ovens vary in wattage. Use the cooking times as guidelines and check for doneness before adding more time.

CONTENTS

BREADS & COFFEE CAKES

◆ Farmer-Style Sour Cream Bread ◆

1 cup sour cream,
   at room temperature
3 tablespoons water
2½ to 3 cups all-purpose
   flour, divided
1 package active dry yeast
2 tablespoons sugar

1½ teaspoons salt
¼ teaspoon baking soda
   Vegetable oil or nonstick
   cooking spray
1 tablespoon poppy or
   sesame seeds

Stir together sour cream and water in small saucepan. Heat over low heat until temperature reaches 120° to 130°F. *Do not boil.* Combine 2 cups flour, yeast, sugar, salt and baking soda in large bowl. Spread sour cream mixture evenly over flour mixture with rubber spatula. Stir until well blended. Turn out dough onto lightly floured surface. Knead 5 minutes or until smooth and elastic, gradually adding remaining flour to prevent sticking, if necessary.

Grease large baking sheet. Shape dough into ball; place on prepared sheet. Flatten into 8-inch circle. Brush with oil. Sprinkle with poppy seeds. Invert large bowl over dough and let rise in warm place 1 hour or until doubled in bulk.

Preheat oven to 350°F. Bake 22 to 27 minutes or until golden brown. Remove immediately from baking sheet. Cool completely on wire rack.

Makes 8 to 12 servings

Farmer-Style Sour Cream Bread

◆ Cheddar-Apple Bread ◆

2 cups all-purpose flour
2 teaspoons baking powder
1 teaspoon baking soda
¼ teaspoon salt
1 cup packed light brown
   sugar
½ cup margarine or butter,
   softened

2 eggs
1 teaspoon vanilla
1 cup sour cream
¼ cup milk
1½ cups diced dried apples
1 cup (4 ounces) shredded
   Cheddar cheese

Preheat oven to 350°F. Spray 9×5-inch loaf pan with nonstick cooking spray; set aside.

Combine flour, baking powder, baking soda and salt in small bowl. Beat sugar and margarine in large bowl with electric mixer at medium speed until light and fluffy. Beat in eggs and vanilla until blended. Add flour mixture to margarine mixture alternately with sour cream and milk, beginning and ending with flour mixture. Beat well at low speed after each addition. Stir in apples and cheese until blended. Spoon into prepared pan.

Bake 50 to 55 minutes or until toothpick inserted into center comes out clean. Cool in pan on wire rack 15 minutes. Remove from pan and cool completely on wire rack. *Makes 12 servings*

◆ Banana Cranberry Bread ◆

3 extra-ripe, medium DOLE®
   Bananas
2 cups DOLE® Fresh
   Cranberries
1½ cups sugar
2 tablespoons grated
   orange peel
3 eggs

1 cup vegetable oil
5 cups all-purpose flour
2 cups chopped walnuts
1 tablespoon baking soda
2 teaspoons ground
   cinnamon
¼ teaspoon salt
¼ teaspoon ground cloves

• Purée bananas in blender (1½ cups).

• Chop cranberries. Combine cranberries, sugar and orange peel in large bowl. Beat in bananas, eggs and oil.

• Combine flour, walnuts, baking soda, cinnamon, salt and cloves in small bowl. Beat flour mixture into banana mixture until blended.

• Turn into 2 greased 8½×4½-inch loaf pans. Bake at 350°F 50 to 60 minutes or until toothpick inserted comes out clean. Cool in pan 10 minutes. Turn onto wire rack to cool completely. *Makes 2 loaves*

Cheddar-Apple Bread

◆ Apricot-Almond Coffee Ring ◆

1 cup dried apricots, sliced
1 cup water
3½ teaspoons EQUAL® FOR
    RECIPES *or* 12 packets
    EQUAL® sweetener *or*
    ½ cup EQUAL®
    SPOONFUL™
⅛ teaspoon ground mace
1 loaf (16 ounces) frozen
    Italian bread dough,
    thawed

⅓ cup sliced or slivered
    almonds, divided
Skim milk
1 teaspoon EQUAL® FOR
    RECIPES *or* 3 packets
    EQUAL® sweetener *or*
    2 tablespoons EQUAL®
    SPOONFUL™

• Heat apricots, water, 3½ teaspoons Equal® for Recipes *or* 12 packets Equal® sweetener *or* ½ cup Equal® Spoonful™ and mace to boiling in small saucepan; reduce heat and simmer, covered, until apricots are tender and water is absorbed, about 10 minutes. Simmer, uncovered, until no water remains, 2 to 3 minutes. Cool.

• Roll dough on floured surface into 14×8-inch rectangle. Spread apricot mixture on dough to within 1 inch of edges; sprinkle with ¼ cup almonds. Roll dough up jelly-roll style, beginning with long edge; pinch edge of dough to seal. Place dough seam side down on greased cookie sheet, forming circle; pinch ends to seal.

• Using scissors, cut dough from outside edge almost to center, making cuts 1 inch apart. Turn each section cut side up so filling shows. Let rise, covered, in warm place until dough is double in size, about 1 hour.

• Brush top of dough lightly with milk; sprinkle with remaining almonds and 1 teaspoon Equal® for Recipes *or* 3 packets Equal® sweetener *or* 2 tablespoons Equal® Spoonful™. Bake coffee cake in preheated 375°F oven until golden, 25 to 30 minutes. Cool on wire rack.   *Makes about 12 servings*

Apricot-Almond Coffee Ring

◆ French Bread ◆

2 packages active dry yeast
1 tablespoon sugar
2½ cups warm water, 105° to
115°F, divided
6¾ to 7½ cups bread or all-
purpose flour, divided

2 teaspoons salt
2 tablespoons yellow
cornmeal
Water

To proof yeast, sprinkle yeast and sugar over ½ cup warm water in large bowl; stir until yeast is dissolved. Let stand 5 minutes or until mixture is bubbly. Add 2 cups flour, remaining 2 cups warm water and salt. Beat with electric mixer at low speed until blended, scraping down side of bowl once. Increase speed to medium; beat 2 minutes, scraping down side of bowl once. Stir in enough additional flour, about 4¾ cups, to make soft dough.

Turn out dough onto lightly floured surface; flatten slightly. Knead dough about 10 minutes or until smooth and elastic, adding remaining ¾ cup flour to prevent sticking if necessary. Shape dough into a ball; place in large greased bowl. Turn dough over so that top is greased. Cover with towel; let rise in warm place 1 to 1½ hours or until doubled in bulk.

Punch down dough. Knead dough in bowl 1 minute. Cover with towel; let rise in warm place about 1 hour or until doubled in bulk. Grease 2 (2-loaf) French bread pans or 2 large baking sheets. Sprinkle with cornmeal; set aside.

Punch down dough. Turn out dough onto lightly floured surface. Knead dough several times to remove air bubbles. Cut dough into 4 pieces. Cover with towel; let rest 10 minutes. Roll out each piece of dough back and forth, forming loaf about 14 inches long and 2 inches in diameter. Place loaves apart on prepared baking sheets. Cut 3 (¼-inch-deep) slashes into each loaf with tip of sharp knife. Brush loaves with water. Cover with towel; let rise in warm place about 35 minutes or until doubled in bulk.

Place small baking pan on bottom of oven. Preheat oven to 450°F. Place 2 ice cubes in pan on bottom of oven. Brush loaves with water; bake 10 minutes. Rotate pans top to bottom. Quickly spray loaves with cool water using spray mister. *Reduce heat to 400°F;* bake 10 to 15 minutes more or until loaves are golden brown. Immediately remove from pans; cool completely on wire racks. Serve warm.
Makes 4 loaves

French Bread

◆ Onion Dill Bread ◆

2 cups bread flour
1 cup whole wheat flour
½ cup instant nonfat dry milk
½ teaspoon salt
1 package active dry yeast
2 tablespoons sugar
1¼ cups water (110° to 115°F)
1 cup KELLOGG'S® ALL-BRAN® cereal

2 egg whites
¼ cup reduced-calorie margarine
¼ cup chopped green onions
¼ cup chopped red onion
1 tablespoon dill weed
1 tablespoon skim milk
2 tablespoons finely chopped white onion

1. Stir together flours, dry milk and salt.

2. In large electric mixer bowl, combine yeast, sugar and water. Stir in Kellogg's® All-Bran® cereal; let stand 2 minutes or until cereal is soft.

3. Add egg whites, margarine and ½ of flour mixture. Beat at medium speed for 2 minutes or about 200 strokes by hand.

4. Mix in green onions, red onion and dill weed. Stir in remaining flour mixture by hand to form stiff, sticky dough. Cover lightly. Let rise in warm place until double in volume (about 1 hour).

5. Stir down dough to original volume. Spoon into 2-quart round casserole or 9¼×5¼×2¾-inch loaf pan coated with nonstick cooking spray. Brush surface with milk and sprinkle evenly with white onion.

6. Bake at 350°F for 55 minutes or until loaf is golden brown and sounds hollow when lightly tapped. Place on wire rack; cool.   *Makes 1 loaf*

◆ Many Grains Bread ◆

2¾ to 3¼ cups all-purpose flour, divided
3 cups graham flour, divided
2 packages RED STAR® Active Dry Yeast or QUICK•RISE™ Yeast
4 teaspoons salt
3 cups water

½ cup dark molasses
¼ cup vegetable oil
½ cup buckwheat flour
½ cup rye flour
½ cup soy flour
½ cup yellow cornmeal
½ cup quick rolled oats
Butter

Combine 1½ cups all-purpose flour, 2 cups graham flour, yeast and salt in large bowl; mix well. Heat water, molasses and oil in large saucepan over medium heat until very warm (120° to 130°F). Add to flour mixture. Blend at low speed until moistened; beat 3 minutes at medium speed.

By hand, gradually stir in buckwheat, rye and soy flours, cornmeal, oats, remaining graham flour and enough remaining all-purpose flour to make a firm dough. Knead on floured surface 5 to 8 minutes. Place in large greased bowl, turning to grease top. Cover with clean kitchen towel; let rise in warm place about 1 hour or until double in bulk (about 30 minutes for Quick•Rise Yeast).

Punch down dough. Divide into 2 parts. On lightly floured surface, shape each half into round loaf. Place loaves on large greased baking sheet. Cover; let rise in warm place about 30 minutes or until double in bulk (15 minutes for Quick•Rise Yeast).

Preheat oven to 375°F. Make cross slash across top of each loaf. Bake 35 to 40 minutes or until bread sounds hollow when tapped. If bread starts to become too dark, cover loosely with foil during last 5 to 10 minutes of baking. Brush with butter; cool on wire racks.

Makes 2 round loaves

◆ French Twist Potato Bread ◆

1 **large Colorado russet variety potato, peeled and cut up**
5½ **to 6 cups bread flour or all-purpose flour, divided**
2 **packages active dry yeast**
1 **teaspoon salt**
1 **slightly beaten egg white**
1 **teaspoon coarse-grained (kosher) salt**
1 **teaspoon coarsely ground black pepper**
Cornmeal

In saucepan combine potato and 1 cup water. Bring to a boil; reduce heat. Cover and simmer about 15 minutes or until potato is very tender. Mash potato in liquid. Add additional water to make 2 cups. Cool liquid mixture to 120° to 130°F.

In large mixing bowl combine 1½ cups flour, yeast, 1 teaspoon salt and warm potato mixture. Beat on low speed to mix well; then beat on high speed 3 minutes, scraping side of bowl. Stir in as much of remaining flour as possible with spoon. Turn out onto floured surface and knead 8 to 10 minutes or until smooth and elastic. Place in greased bowl; let rise in warm place until doubled, about 1 hour.

Combine egg white and 1 tablespoon water; set aside. Punch down dough. Turn out onto floured surface; cut into 4 pieces and let rest 5 minutes. Roll each piece into 12- to 14-inch rope. Brush ropes lightly with egg white mixture; sprinkle lightly with coarse salt and pepper. For each loaf, twist 2 ropes together to form 1 loaf. Place loaves on greased and cornmeal-coated baking sheets. Let rise in warm place until nearly doubled, about 35 to 40 minutes. Bake in 375°F oven 35 to 40 minutes. Brush loaves with remaining egg white about half way through baking time. Cool on wire rack.

Makes 2 loaves

Favorite recipe from **Colorado Potato Administrative Committee**

◆ Orange Marmalade Bread ◆

3 cups all-purpose flour, stirred before measuring
4 teaspoons baking powder
1 teaspoon salt
½ cup chopped walnuts

¾ cup SMUCKER'S® Sweet Orange Marmalade
¾ cup milk
¼ cup honey
2 eggs, lightly beaten
2 tablespoons oil

Grease 9×5×3-inch loaf pan. Combine flour, baking powder and salt into large bowl. Stir in nuts. Combine marmalade, milk, honey, eggs and oil; blend well. Add to flour mixture; stir only until dry ingredients are moistened (batter will be lumpy). Turn into prepared pan.

Bake at 350°F for 65 to 70 minutes or until lightly browned and toothpick inserted in center comes out clean. *Makes 8 to 10 servings*

◆ Focaccia with Dried ◆ Tomatoes and Fontina

1 tablespoon olive oil
1 loaf (1 pound) frozen bread dough, thawed according to package directions
1 jar (8 ounces) SONOMA® Marinated Dried Tomatoes, drained, 2 tablespoons oil reserved

4 cloves garlic, minced
⅔ cup sliced black olives
1 tablespoon dried basil
1 teaspoon dried oregano
1 teaspoon dried rosemary
2 cups grated fontina cheese

Preheat oven to 425°F. Oil 13×9×2-inch baking pan. Roll and stretch dough on lightly floured surface; fit dough into pan.

Combine reserved tomato oil with garlic; brush over dough. Sprinkle olives, basil, oregano and rosemary evenly over dough. Arrange tomatoes on top; cover with cheese.

Bake 35 to 40 minutes or until bread is springy to the touch and golden brown around edges. (Cover loosely with foil during last 10 minutes if becoming too brown.) Cut into squares while still warm. *Makes 16 squares*

Orange Marmalade Bread

◆ Southwest Sausage Bread ◆

1 cup water
1 package active dry yeast
1 tablespoon sugar
1¾ to 2¼ cups all-purpose flour, divided
1½ cups whole wheat flour, divided
1 egg
2 tablespoons vegetable oil

¼ teaspoon salt
1 medium onion, finely chopped
4 ounces dry chorizo or pepperoni sausage, chopped
1 cup (4 ounces) shredded Monterey Jack cheese

Heat water in saucepan over low heat until water reaches 105° to 110°F. Sprinkle yeast and sugar over heated water in large bowl; stir until dissolved. Let stand 5 minutes or until bubbly. Add 1 cup all-purpose flour, 1 cup whole wheat flour, egg, oil and salt. Beat until blended. Beat at medium speed 3 minutes. Stir in remaining whole-wheat flour and enough all-purpose flour, about ¾ cup, to make soft dough.

Turn out dough onto all-purpose floured surface; flatten. Knead 5 to 8 minutes or until smooth and elastic; gradually add remaining ½ cup all-purpose flour to prevent sticking, if necessary. Shape into ball; place in lightly greased bowl. Turn dough over. Cover; let rise in warm place 1 hour or until doubled. Cook onion and sausage in skillet over medium heat 5 minutes or until onion is tender. Drain on paper towels.

Punch down dough. Knead on floured surface 1 minute. Cover; let rest 10 minutes. Spray 9×5-inch loaf pan with nonstick cooking spray. Roll dough into 24×11-inch rectangle. Sprinkle sausage mixture and cheese over dough. Roll up dough jelly-roll style from short end. Pinch seam and ends to seal. Cut dough lengthwise into halves. With cut sides facing up, twist halves together. Pinch ends to seal. Place in pan, cut sides up. Let rise 1 hour or until doubled.

Preheat oven to 375°F. Bake 30 minutes or until loaf sounds hollow when tapped. Remove immediately from pan. Cool 30 minutes on wire rack.

Makes 12 servings

Southwest Sausage Bread

◆ Cherry-Coconut-Cheese Coffee Cake ◆

2½ cups all-purpose flour
¾ cup sugar
½ teaspoon baking powder
½ teaspoon baking soda
2 packages (3 ounces each)
  cream cheese,
  softened, divided
¾ cup milk

2 tablespoons vegetable oil
2 eggs, divided
1 teaspoon vanilla
½ cup flaked coconut
¾ cup cherry preserves
2 tablespoons margarine or
  butter

Preheat oven to 350°F. Grease and flour 9-inch springform pan. Combine flour and sugar in large bowl. Reserve ½ cup flour mixture; set aside. Stir baking powder and baking soda into remaining flour mixture. Cut in 1 package cream cheese with pastry blender or 2 knives until mixture resembles coarse crumbs; set aside.

Combine milk, oil and 1 egg in medium bowl. Add to cream cheese mixture; stir just until moistened. Spread batter on bottom and 1 inch up side of prepared pan. Combine remaining package cream cheese, remaining egg and vanilla in small bowl; stir until smooth. Pour over batter, spreading to within 1 inch of edge. Sprinkle coconut over cream cheese mixture. Spoon preserves evenly over coconut.

Cut margarine into reserved flour mixture with pastry blender or 2 knives until mixture resembles coarse crumbs. Sprinkle over preserves. Bake 55 to 60 minutes or until brown and toothpick inserted into crust comes out clean. Cool in pan on wire rack 15 minutes. Remove side of pan; serve warm.

Makes 10 servings

◆ Savory French Bread ◆

1 large loaf French bread
¼ cup butter or margarine,
  softened
½ teaspoon dried basil
  leaves
½ teaspoon dried dill weed

½ teaspoon chopped dried
  chives
½ teaspoon TABASCO®
  brand Pepper Sauce
¼ teaspoon garlic powder
¼ teaspoon paprika

Preheat oven to 400°F. Slice bread diagonally, but do not cut through bottom crust of loaf. Mix remaining ingredients in small bowl. Spread between bread slices; wrap bread in aluminum foil and heat in oven for 15 to 20 minutes. Serve warm.

Makes 6 to 8 servings

Cherry-Coconut-Cheese Coffee Cake

◆ Brunch-Time Zucchini-Date Bread ◆

1 cup chopped, pitted
   dates
1 cup water
1 cup whole wheat flour
1 cup all-purpose flour
2 tablespoons granulated
   sugar
1 teaspoon baking powder
½ teaspoon baking soda
½ teaspoon salt
½ teaspoon ground
   cinnamon
¼ teaspoon ground cloves

2 eggs
1 cup shredded zucchini,
   pressed dry with paper
   towels

CHEESE SPREAD
1 package (8 ounces)
   nonfat cream cheese
¼ cup powdered sugar
1 tablespoon vanilla
⅛ teaspoon ground
   cinnamon
Dash ground cloves

1. Preheat oven to 350°F. Spray 8×4×2-inch loaf pan with nonstick cooking spray.

2. Combine dates and water in small saucepan. Bring to a boil over medium-high heat. Remove from heat; let stand 15 minutes.

3. Combine flours, granulated sugar, baking powder, baking soda, salt, ½ teaspoon cinnamon and ¼ teaspoon cloves in large bowl. Beat eggs in medium bowl; stir in date mixture and zucchini. Stir egg mixture into flour mixture just until dry ingredients are moistened. Pour batter evenly into prepared pan.

4. Bake 30 to 35 minutes or until toothpick inserted into center comes out clean. Cool 5 minutes. Remove from pan. Cool completely on wire rack.

5. Meanwhile, to prepare cheese spread, combine cream cheese, powdered sugar, vanilla, ⅛ teaspoon cinnamon and dash cloves in small bowl. Beat until smooth. Cover and refrigerate until ready to use.

6. Cut bread into 16 slices. Serve with cheese spread. *Makes 16 servings*

Brunch-Time Zucchini-Date Bread

◆ Corn Bread ◆

⅓ cup CRISCO® Oil*, divided
1 cup yellow cornmeal
1 cup all-purpose flour
3 tablespoons granulated
   sugar

1 tablespoon baking
   powder
¼ teaspoon salt
1 cup milk
1 egg, lightly beaten

*Any Crisco® Oil can be used.

1. Heat oven to 425°F. Coat 8 or 9-inch square pan with 1 tablespoon Crisco® Oil.

2. Combine cornmeal, flour, sugar, baking powder and salt in mixing bowl. Combine milk, egg and remaining 5 tablespoons oil.

3. Heat oiled pan at 425°F for 3 minutes. Stir liquids into dry ingredients. Mix well with wooden spoon. Scrape batter into hot pan. Spread evenly.

4. Return pan to oven. Bake 20 to 25 minutes or until toothpick inserted into center comes out clean. Cut into serving pieces. Serve immediately.

Makes 6 to 8 servings

Preparation Time: 5 minutes
Total Time: 30 to 35 minutes

◆ Roman Meal® Homemade Bread ◆

2 cups ROMAN MEAL®
   Cereal
⅔ cup nonfat dry milk
1 tablespoon salt
2 packages active dry yeast
5½ cups all-purpose flour,
   divided

2½ cups very warm water
   (115° to 120°F)
⅓ cup honey
¼ cup vegetable oil
1 tablespoon molasses

In large bowl blend cereal, dry milk, salt, yeast and 3 cups flour. Add water, honey, oil and molasses. Stir to mix; beat 60 strokes. Blend in remaining 2½ cups flour. On lightly floured board, knead dough until it feels springy (about 5 minutes), adding just enough flour to hands and board to prevent sticking. Grease bowl; return dough to bowl, turning once to grease top. Cover and let rise in warm place until doubled (about 1 hour). Punch down dough and turn over. Cover and let rise 30 minutes. Form into 2 loaves and place in well-greased 9×5×3-inch loaf pans. Grease tops of loaves; cover and let rise until doubled (about 45 minutes). Bake at 400°F for about 40 minutes. Remove from pans and cool on racks.

Makes 2 loaves

Corn Bread

◆ Blueberry Coffee Cake ◆

2⅓ cups all-purpose flour
1⅓ cups plus 2 tablespoons granulated sugar, divided
½ teaspoon salt
¾ CRISCO® Stick or ¾ cup CRISCO® all-vegetable shortening
¾ cup milk
3 eggs, divided
2 teaspoons baking powder

1 teaspoon vanilla
1 cup ricotta cheese
1 tablespoon finely grated fresh lemon peel
1 cup fresh or frozen blueberries
½ cup chopped walnuts
⅓ cup packed brown sugar
1 teaspoon cinnamon
Confectioners' Sugar Icing (recipe follows)

1. Heat oven to 350°F. Grease 13×9×2-inch baking pan. Set aside.

2. Combine flour, 1⅓ cups granulated sugar and salt in bowl. Cut in Crisco® with pastry blender or 2 knives until crumbly. Reserve 1 cup mixture for topping. Add milk, 2 eggs, baking powder and vanilla to remaining mixture. Beat at medium speed 2 minutes, scraping bowl. Spread in prepared pan.

3. Combine remaining 2 tablespoons sugar, remaining egg, ricotta cheese and lemon peel in bowl. Mix well. Sprinkle blueberries over batter in pan. Spoon cheese mixture over berries. Spread cheese mixture gently and evenly.

4. Mix reserved crumb mixture, nuts, brown sugar and cinnamon. Sprinkle over cake. Bake at 350°F about 45 minutes or until toothpick inserted in center comes out clean. Cool slightly. Drizzle with Confectioners' Sugar Icing.

Makes 12 servings

Confectioners' Sugar Icing: Combine 1 cup confectioners' sugar, 1 tablespoon milk, orange juice or liqueur and ¼ teaspoon vanilla in small bowl. Stir in additional milk, 1 teaspoon at a time, until icing is of desired drizzling consistency.

Makes about ½ cup

◆ Golden Cheddar Batter Bread ◆

1 package active dry yeast
¾ cup warm water (110° to 115°F)
3 cups unsifted all-purpose flour, divided
1½ cups finely chopped Golden Delicious apples
1 cup shredded Cheddar cheese

2 large eggs, lightly beaten
2 tablespoons vegetable shortening
2 tablespoons sugar
1 teaspoon salt
Buttery Apple Spread (recipe follows)

1. In large bowl, combine yeast and water, stirring to dissolve yeast. Set aside until mixture begins to foam, about 5 minutes. Add 1½ cups flour, apples, cheese, eggs, shortening, sugar and salt to yeast mixture; beat with electric mixer at medium speed 2 minutes. Beat in remaining flour gradually with spoon. Cover with clean cloth and let rise 50 to 60 minutes or until doubled. Meanwhile, prepare Buttery Apple Spread.

2. Grease 9×5-inch loaf pan. Beat batter by hand 30 seconds. Spread batter evenly in prepared pan. Cover with cloth and let rise 40 minutes or until nearly doubled.

3. Heat oven to 375°F. Bake bread 45 to 55 minutes or until loaf sounds hollow when gently tapped. Remove from pan; cool on wire rack at least 15 minutes. Serve with Buttery Apple Spread. *Makes 1 loaf*

Buttery Apple Spread: Peel, core and slice 1 Golden Delicious apple; place in small saucepan with 1 tablespoon water. Cover tightly and cook over medium heat until apple is very tender. Mash apple with fork; cool completely. In small bowl, beat ½ cup softened butter with electric mixer until light and fluffy. Gradually add mashed apple; beat until well combined. Makes about 1 cup

Favorite recipe from **Washington Apple Commission**

◆ Dilly of a Batter Bread ◆

3¼ cups all-purpose flour, divided
2 packages RED STAR® Active Dry Yeast or QUICK•RISE™ Yeast
2 tablespoons sugar
1 tablespoon instant minced onion

2 teaspoons dill seed
1 teaspoon salt
1 carton (8 ounces) plain yogurt
½ cup water
2 tablespoons shortening
1 egg

In large mixer bowl, combine 1½ cups flour, yeast, sugar, onion, dill seed and salt; mix well. In small saucepan, heat yogurt, water and shortening until very warm (120° to 130°F; shortening does not need to melt). Add to flour mixture. Add egg. Blend at low speed until moistened; beat 3 minutes at medium speed. By hand, gradually stir in remaining flour to make stiff batter.

Spoon into greased 1½- or 2-quart casserole. Cover; let rise in warm place until light and double, about 1 hour (30 minutes for Quick•Rise Yeast). Bake at 375°F for 35 to 40 minutes or until golden brown. Remove from casserole; serve warm or cold. *Makes 1 round loaf*

◆ Marble Swirl Bread ◆

2¾ to 3¼ cups all-purpose
   flour, divided
¼ cup sugar
1 package active dry yeast
1 teaspoon salt
1⅓ cups plus 1 tablespoon
   water
¼ cup butter or margarine

1 whole egg
2 tablespoons molasses
2 teaspoons unsweetened
   cocoa powder
1 teaspoon instant coffee
   powder
1 to 1¼ cups rye flour
1 egg yolk

1. Combine 1½ cups all-purpose flour, sugar, yeast and salt in large bowl; set aside.

2. Combine 1⅓ cups water and butter in 1-quart saucepan. Heat over low heat until mixture is 120° to 130°F. (Butter does not need to completely melt.) Gradually beat water mixture into flour mixture with electric mixer at low speed. Increase speed to medium; beat 2 minutes.

3. Reduce speed to low; beat in 1 egg and ½ cup all-purpose flour. Increase speed to medium; beat 2 minutes. Reserve half of batter (about 1⅓ cups) in another bowl. Stir ¾ cup all-purpose flour into remaining batter to make stiff dough, adding remaining ½ cup all-purpose flour if necessary; set aside.

4. To make darker dough, stir molasses, cocoa, coffee powder and enough rye flour, about 1¼ cups, into reserved batter to make stiff dough. Cover doughs with clean kitchen towels; let rise in warm place about 1 hour or until doubled in bulk.

5. Punch down doughs. Knead doughs separately on lightly floured surface 1 minute. Cover with towels; let rest 10 minutes. Grease large baking sheet. Roll out lighter dough into 12×9-inch rectangle with lightly floured rolling pin; set aside.

6. Roll out darker dough into 12×8-inch rectangle; place on top of lighter dough. Starting with 1 (12-inch) side, roll up doughs jelly-roll style. Pinch seam and ends to seal. Place loaf, seam side down, on prepared baking sheet, tucking ends under. Cover with clean kitchen towel; let rise in warm place about 45 minutes or until doubled in bulk.

7. Preheat oven to 350°F. Add remaining 1 tablespoon water to egg yolk; beat until just combined. Make 3 (½-inch-deep) slashes across top of loaf with tip of sharp knife. Brush with egg yolk mixture.

8. Bake 35 to 40 minutes or until loaf is browned and sounds hollow when tapped. Immediately remove from baking sheet; cool completely on wire rack.

Makes 1 loaf

Marble Swirl Bread

◆ Irish Soda Bread ◆

4 cups all-purpose flour	1 tablespoon caraway seeds
¼ cup sugar	⅓ cup vegetable shortening
1 tablespoon baking powder	1 cup raisins or currants
1 teaspoon baking soda	1 egg
1 teaspoon salt	1¾ cups buttermilk*

Or, substitute soured fresh milk. To sour milk, place 2 tablespoons lemon juice plus enough milk to equal 1¾ cups in 2-cup measure. Stir; let stand 5 minutes before using.

1. Preheat oven to 350°F. Grease large baking sheet; set aside.

2. Sift flour, sugar, baking powder, baking soda and salt into large bowl. Stir in caraway seeds. Cut in shortening with pastry blender or 2 knives until mixture resembles coarse crumbs. Stir in raisins. Beat egg in medium bowl. Add buttermilk; beat until well combined. Add buttermilk mixture to flour mixture; stir until mixture forms soft dough that clings together and forms a ball.

3. Turn dough out onto well-floured surface. Knead dough gently 10 to 12 times. Place dough on prepared baking sheet. Pat dough into 7-inch round. Score top of dough with tip of sharp knife, making an "x" about 4 inches long and ¼ inch deep.

4. Bake 55 to 60 minutes or until toothpick inserted in center comes out clean. Immediately remove from baking sheet; cool on wire rack.** Bread is best eaten the day it is made. *Makes 12 servings*

**For a sweet crust, combine 1 tablespoon sugar and 1 tablespoon water in custard cup. Brush over hot loaf.

◆ Roman Meal® Cream of Rye Bread ◆

1¼ teaspoons yeast	2 teaspoons caraway seeds
2 cups flour	1 tablespoon honey
⅔ cup ROMAN MEAL® Cream of Rye Cereal	2 teaspoons molasses
2 tablespoons nonfat dry milk	2 tablespoons shortening
1 teaspoon salt	1 cup water

Bread Machine Method

Pour yeast to one side of inner pan. Add remaining ingredients in order. Select white bread and push "start." *Makes 1 loaf*

Irish Soda Bread

◆ Honey-Pecan Coffee Cake ◆

⅔ cup milk

6 tablespoons margarine or butter, softened

9 tablespoons honey, divided

2½ to 3½ cups all-purpose flour, divided

1 package active dry yeast

¾ teaspoon salt

3 eggs, divided

1¼ cups toasted coarsely chopped pecans, divided

3 tablespoons brown sugar

1½ tablespoons margarine or butter, melted

1 tablespoon ground cinnamon

1 teaspoon water

Heat milk, softened margarine and 3 tablespoons honey in small saucepan over low heat until temperature reaches 120° to 130°F. Combine 2¼ cups flour, yeast and salt in large bowl. Slowly add heated milk mixture to flour mixture. Beat 2 eggs in small bowl; add to flour mixture. Stir with rubber spatula 2 minutes or until mixture is well blended. Scrape down side of bowl once. Gradually add more flour until soft but rough dough forms.

Turn out dough onto lightly floured surface. Knead 5 to 8 minutes or until smooth and elastic, gradually adding remaining flour to prevent sticking, if necessary. Shape dough into ball; cover with inverted bowl. Let rise in warm place 35 to 40 minutes or until dough has increased in size by one third. Punch down dough; turn out onto lightly floured surface. Roll out into 14×8-inch rectangle using lightly floured rolling pin.

Combine 1 cup pecans, sugar, melted margarine, cinnamon and 3 tablespoons honey in small bowl. Spread evenly over dough; press in gently with fingertips. Starting from one long end, roll up tightly, jelly-roll style. Pinch seams lightly; turn seam side down. Flatten slightly. Twist dough 6 to 8 turns. Grease 9-inch cake pan. Place dough in pan in a loose spiral starting in center and working to the side. Tuck outside end under dough; pinch to seal. Loosely cover with lightly greased sheet of plastic wrap. Let rise in warm place 60 to 75 minutes or until doubled in bulk.

Preheat oven to 375°F. Place pan on cookie sheet. Beat remaining egg with 1 teaspoon water in small bowl; brush on dough. Drizzle remaining 3 tablespoons honey evenly over top; sprinkle with remaining ¼ cup pecans. Bake 40 to 45 minutes or until deep golden brown. Turn pan and tent with sheet of foil halfway through baking time to prevent burning. Remove foil for last 5 minutes of baking. Cool in pan on wire rack 5 minutes. Remove from pan. Cool completely on wire rack. *Makes 12 servings*

Honey-Pecan Coffee Cake

◆ Swedish Limpa Bread ◆

1¾ to 2 cups all-purpose flour, divided
½ cup rye flour
1 package active dry yeast
1 tablespoon sugar
1½ teaspoons grated orange peel
1 teaspoon salt
½ teaspoon fennel seeds, crushed
½ teaspoon caraway seeds, crushed

¾ cup plus 4 teaspoons water, divided
4 tablespoons molasses, divided
2 tablespoons margarine or butter
1 teaspoon instant coffee granules
¼ teaspoon whole fennel seeds
¼ teaspoon whole caraway seeds

Combine 1½ cups all-purpose flour, rye flour, yeast, sugar, orange peel, salt and crushed seeds in large bowl. Heat ¾ cup water, 3 tablespoons molasses and margarine in small saucepan over low heat until temperature reaches 120° to 130°F. Stir in coffee. Stir water mixture into flour mixture with rubber spatula to form soft but sticky dough. Gradually add more all-purpose flour to form rough dough.

Turn out dough onto lightly floured surface. Knead 2 minutes or until soft dough forms, gradually adding remaining flour to prevent sticking, if necessary. Cover with inverted bowl; let rest 5 minutes. Continue kneading 5 to 8 minutes until smooth and elastic. Shape dough into ball; place in large greased bowl. Turn dough over so top is greased. Loosely cover with lightly greased sheet of plastic wrap. Let rise in warm place 75 minutes or until almost doubled in bulk.

Punch down dough. Grease 8½×4½-inch loaf pan. Roll dough into 12×7-inch rectangle. Starting with one short end, roll up tightly, jelly-roll style. Pinch seams and ends to seal. Place seam side down in prepared pan. Cover loosely with plastic wrap. Let rise in warm place 1 hour or until doubled in bulk.

Preheat oven to 350°F. Stir remaining 1 tablespoon molasses and 4 teaspoons water in small bowl; set aside. Uncover loaf; make 3 diagonal slashes on top of dough using sharp knife. Bake 40 to 45 minutes or until loaf sounds hollow when tapped. Brush top with molasses mixture and sprinkle with whole fennel and caraway seeds halfway through baking time. Brush again with molasses mixture about 10 minutes before removing loaf from oven. Cool in pan on wire rack 5 minutes. Remove from pan. Cool completely on wire rack.

Makes 12 servings

Swedish Limpa Bread

◆ Banana Brunch Coffee Cake ◆

2 ripe, medium DOLE®
   Bananas
1 package (18.25 ounces)
   yellow cake mix
1 package (3.4 ounces)
   instant vanilla pudding
   mix (4 servings)
½ cup vegetable oil
4 eggs

1 teaspoon vanilla extract
½ cup chopped DOLE®
   Almonds
⅓ cup packed brown sugar
1 teaspoon ground
   cinnamon
½ teaspoon ground nutmeg

• Purée bananas in blender (1 cup). Combine bananas, cake mix, pudding mix, oil, eggs and vanilla in large mixing bowl. Mix well and beat at medium speed 8 minutes, scraping side of bowl occasionally.

• Combine almonds, brown sugar, cinnamon and nutmeg. Pour one-half cake batter into greased 3-quart Bundt pan. Sprinkle with sugar mixture. Cover with remaining batter. Insert knife in batter and swirl in figure eight patterns through layers. (Be sure not to over mix the layers.)

• Bake at 300°F 55 to 60 minutes. Cool in pan on wire rack 10 minutes. Invert onto rack to complete cooling. Dust with powdered sugar when cool, if desired. Garnish with sliced bananas, raspberries and fresh mint, if desired.

Makes 12 servings

Prep Time: 15 minutes
Bake Time: 60 minutes

◆ Cajun Bubble Bread ◆

¼ cup (½ stick) unsalted
   butter
2 green onions, finely
   chopped
2 cloves garlic, minced
2 teaspoons Cajun
   seasoning spice blend*
4 tablespoons FRANK'S®
   REDHOT® Hot Sauce
¼ cup chopped almonds,
   divided

2 pounds thawed frozen
   bread dough
⅔ cup (3 ounces) shredded
   Monterey Jack-Cheddar
   cheese blend, divided
2 tablespoons grated
   Parmesan cheese,
   divided

If Cajun seasoning is unavailable, substitute ¾ teaspoon each Italian seasoning and chili powder, and ½ teaspoon celery seed.

1. Melt butter in small saucepan. Add onions, garlic and Cajun spice; cook over medium-low heat 3 minutes or just until tender. Remove from heat; stir in REDHOT sauce.

2. Grease 10-inch tube pan or 12-cup Bundt pan**. Sprinkle bottom of tube pan with 1 tablespoon almonds. Cut bread dough into 24 (1-inch) pieces; shape into balls. Dip dough balls, one at a time, into butter mixture. Place in single layer in bottom of tube pan. Sprinkle with ¼ cup Monterey Jack-Cheddar cheese, 1 tablespoon almonds and 2 teaspoons Parmesan cheese.

3. Repeat layers twice with remaining ingredients. Cover with plastic wrap; let rise in warm place 1½ hours or until doubled in size.

4. Preheat oven to 375°F. Bake 35 minutes or until golden brown. (Loosely cover with foil during last 15 minutes if bread browns too quickly.) Loosen bread from sides of pan. Invert immediately onto serving plate; serve warm.

Makes 8 servings

**You may substitute 2 (8×4-inch) loaf pans.

Prep Time: 30 minutes
Rise Time: 1½ hours
Cook Time: 35 minutes

◆ Quick Crumb Coffee Cake ◆

2 cups all-purpose flour
1½ cups sugar
2 teaspoons baking powder
¼ teaspoon salt
¾ CRISCO® Stick *or*
　　¾ cup CRISCO® all-vegetable shortening

2 eggs
½ cup milk
1 teaspoon vanilla
½ cup chopped pecans

1. Heat oven to 350°F. Grease two 8×1½-inch round cake pans; set aside.

2. Combine flour, sugar, baking powder and salt in a medium mixing bowl. Cut in Crisco® until crumbly. Reserve 1 cup crumb mixture for topping.

3. Stir together eggs, milk and vanilla. Add to remaining crumb mixture. Stir just until moistened. (Batter will be slightly lumpy.) Spread batter evenly in prepared pans.

4. Combine reserved crumbs and chopped nuts. Sprinkle evenly over batter. Bake at 350°F about 25 minutes or until edges are lightly browned and toothpick inserted in center comes out clean. Cool on wire rack. Serve warm or cool.

Makes 16 servings

Sour Cream Coffee Cake with
◆ Brandy-Soaked Cherries ◆

Streusel Topping (recipe
   follows)
3¼ cups all-purpose flour,
   divided
1 cup dry sweet or sour
   cherries
½ cup brandy
1½ cups sugar

¾ cup butter or margarine
3 eggs
1 container (16 ounces)
   sour cream
1 tablespoon vanilla
2 teaspoons baking powder
2 teaspoons baking soda
¼ teaspoon salt

1. Prepare Streusel Topping; set aside.

2. Preheat oven to 350°F. Grease 10-inch tube pan with removable bottom. Sprinkle ¼ cup flour into pan, rotating pan to evenly coat bottom and sides of pan. Discard any remaining flour.

3. Bring cherries and brandy to a boil in small saucepan. Cover; remove from heat. Let stand 20 to 30 minutes or until cherries are tender. Drain; discard any remaining brandy.

4. Beat sugar and butter in large bowl with electric mixer at medium speed until light and fluffy, scraping down side of bowl once. Add eggs, 1 at a time, beating until thoroughly incorporated. Beat in sour cream and vanilla.

5. Add remaining 3 cups flour, baking powder, baking soda and salt. Beat with electric mixer at low speed until just blended. Stir in cherries.

6. Spoon ½ of batter into prepared tube pan. Sprinkle with ½ of Streusel Topping. Repeat with remaining batter and Streusel Topping. Bake 1 hour or until wooden skewer inserted into center comes out clean.

7. Cool in pan on wire rack 10 minutes. Remove from pan. Serve warm or at room temperature. Garnish as desired. *Makes 16 servings*

Streusel Topping

1 cup chopped walnuts or
   pecans
½ cup packed brown sugar
1 teaspoon ground
   cinnamon

½ teaspoon ground nutmeg
2 tablespoons melted
   butter or margarine

Combine nuts, brown sugar, cinnamon and nutmeg in small bowl. Drizzle mixture with butter and toss with fork until evenly mixed.

*Sour Cream Coffee Cake with
Brandy-Soaked Cherries*

◆ Onion-Zucchini Bread ◆

1 large zucchini
(¾ pound), shredded

2½ cups all-purpose flour*

1⅓ cups FRENCH'S® French Fried Onions

⅓ cup grated Parmesan cheese

1 tablespoon baking powder

1 tablespoon chopped fresh basil *or*
1 teaspoon dried basil leaves

½ teaspoon salt

¾ cup milk

½ cup (1 stick) butter or margarine, melted

¼ cup packed light brown sugar

2 eggs

You may substitute 1¼ cups whole wheat flour for 1¼ cups of all-purpose flour.

Preheat oven to 350°F. Grease 9×5×3-inch loaf pan.

Drain zucchini in colander. Combine flour, French Fried Onions, cheese, baking powder, basil and salt in large bowl.

Combine milk, butter, brown sugar and eggs in medium bowl; whisk until well blended. Place zucchini in kitchen towel; squeeze out excess liquid. Stir zucchini into milk mixture.

Stir milk mixture into flour mixture, stirring just until moistened. Do not overmix. (Batter will be very stiff and dry.) Pour batter into prepared pan. Run knife down center of batter.

Bake 50 to 65 minutes or until toothpick inserted in center comes out clean. Cool in pan on wire rack 10 minutes. Remove bread from pan to wire rack; cool completely. Cut into slices to serve.**   *Makes 10 to 12 servings*

**For optimum flavor, wrap bread overnight and serve the next day.*

Prep Time: 20 minutes
Cook Time: about 1 hour

Onion-Zucchini Bread

◆ Walnut-Chocolate Quick Bread ◆

1½ cups milk
1 cup sugar
⅓ cup vegetable oil
1 egg, beaten
1 tablespoon molasses
1 teaspoon vanilla
3 cups all-purpose flour
3 tablespoons unsweetened
 cocoa powder

2 teaspoons baking soda
2 teaspoons baking powder
1 teaspoon salt
1 cup chocolate chips
½ cup walnuts, coarsely
 chopped

1. Preheat oven to 350°F. Grease four 5×3-inch loaf pans; set aside.

2. Combine milk, sugar, oil, egg, molasses and vanilla in medium bowl. Stir until sugar is dissolved; set aside.

3. Whisk together flour, cocoa, baking soda, baking powder and salt in large bowl. Add chocolate chips, nuts and milk mixture; stir just until combined. Pour into prepared pans.

4. Bake 30 minutes or until toothpick inserted near center of loaf comes out clean. Cool in pan 15 minutes. Remove from pan and cool on wire rack.

Makes 4 loaves

Muffin Variation: *Preheat oven to 375°F. Spoon batter into 12 greased muffin cups. Bake 20 minutes or until toothpick inserted near center of muffin comes out clean.*

◆ Oatmeal-Almond Bread ◆

½ cup BLUE DIAMOND®
 sliced natural almonds
1½ cups sifted flour
2 teaspoons baking powder
1 teaspoon salt
1 cup uncooked oats
¾ cup sugar

½ cup dark seedless raisins
1 tablespoon grated
 orange peel
½ cup milk
½ cup orange juice
⅓ cup salad oil
1 egg

Spread almonds in shallow pan and toast at 350°F for 5 minutes. Sift flour with baking powder and salt into large mixing bowl. Stir in oats, sugar, toasted almonds, raisins and orange peel. All at once add milk, orange juice, oil and egg; mix just until dry ingredients are moistened. Pour batter into greased and floured 8½×4½- or 9×5-inch loaf pan; bake at 350°F for 50 to 60 minutes or until toothpick inserted in center of loaf comes out clean. Cool 10 minutes in pan; remove from pan and cool completely.

Makes 1 loaf

Walnut-Chocolate Quick Bread

◆ Whole Wheat Herb Bread ◆

⅔ cup water
⅔ cup fat-free (skim) milk
2 teaspoons sugar
2 envelopes active dry
    yeast
3 egg whites, lightly
    beaten
3 tablespoons olive oil

1 teaspoon salt
½ teaspoon dried basil
    leaves
½ teaspoon dried oregano
    leaves
4 to 4½ cups whole wheat
    flour

1. Bring water to a boil in small saucepan. Remove from heat; stir in milk and sugar. When mixture is warm (110° to 115°F), add yeast. Mix well; let stand 10 minutes or until bubbly.

2. Combine egg whites, oil, salt, basil and oregano in large bowl until well blended. Add yeast mixture; mix well. Add 4 cups flour, ½ cup at a time, mixing well after each addition, until dough is no longer sticky. Knead about 5 minutes or until smooth and elastic, adding more flour if dough is sticky. Form into ball. Cover and let rise in warm place about 1 hour or until doubled in bulk.

3. Preheat oven to 350°F. Punch down dough and place on lightly floured surface. Divide into 4 pieces and roll each piece into ball. Lightly spray baking sheet with nonstick cooking spray. Place dough balls on prepared baking sheet. Bake 30 to 35 minutes or until golden brown and loaves sound hollow when tapped.

Makes 24 slices

◆ Banana Walnut Bread ◆

⅔ cup sugar
⅓ cup butter or margarine
¾ teaspoon grated lemon
    peel
1 egg
1¼ cups all-purpose flour

¾ cup ground Walnuts
1½ teaspoons baking powder
¼ teaspoon baking soda
1⅓ cups mashed ripe
    bananas (about 3)
½ cup chopped Walnuts

In mixing bowl cream sugar, butter and lemon peel. Beat in egg. Combine flour, ground walnuts, baking powder and baking soda. Add to sugar mixture alternately with bananas, blending thoroughly after each addition. Stir in chopped walnuts. Pour batter into greased 8½×4½-inch loaf pan. Bake in 350°F oven 50 to 55 minutes or until golden brown and toothpick inserted in center comes out clean. Remove from pan. Cool on rack before slicing.

Makes 1 loaf (10 slices)

Favorite recipe from **Walnut Marketing Board**

Whole Wheat Herb Bread

Sour Cream Coffee Cake
◆ with Chocolate and Walnuts ◆

¾ cup butter or margarine,
    softened
1½ cups packed light brown
    sugar
3 eggs
2 teaspoons vanilla
3 cups all-purpose flour
2 teaspoons baking powder
2 teaspoons ground
    cinnamon

1½ teaspoons baking soda
½ teaspoon ground nutmeg
¼ teaspoon salt
1½ cups sour cream
½ cup semisweet chocolate
    chips
½ cup chopped walnuts
    Powdered sugar

Preheat oven to 350°F. Grease and flour 12-cup Bundt pan or 10-inch tube pan. Beat butter in large bowl with electric mixer on medium speed until creamy. Add brown sugar; beat until light and fluffy. Beat in eggs and vanilla until well blended. Combine flour, baking powder, cinnamon, baking soda, nutmeg and salt in large bowl; add to butter mixture on low speed alternately with sour cream, beginning and ending with flour mixture until well blended. Stir in chocolate and walnuts. Spoon into prepared pan.

Bake 45 to 50 minutes or until toothpick inserted near center comes out clean. Cool in pan 15 minutes. Remove from pan to wire rack; cool completely. Store tightly covered at room temperature. Sprinkle with powdered sugar before serving.
Makes 1 (10-inch) coffee cake

◆ Savory Cheddar Bread ◆

2 cups all-purpose flour
1 cup (4 ounces)
    SARGENTO® Fancy
    Shredded Mild or Sharp
    Cheddar Cheese
4 teaspoons baking powder
1 tablespoon sugar
½ teaspoon onion salt

½ teaspoon dried oregano
    leaves, crushed
¼ teaspoon dry mustard
1 cup milk
1 egg, beaten
1 tablespoon butter or
    margarine, melted

In large bowl, stir together flour, cheese, baking powder, sugar, onion salt, oregano and dry mustard. In separate bowl, combine milk, egg and butter; add to dry ingredients, stirring just until moistened. Spread batter in greased 8×4-inch loaf pan. Bake at 350°F 45 minutes or until wooden pick inserted in center comes out clean. Cool 10 minutes on wire rack. Remove from pan.
Makes 16 slices

Sour Cream Coffee Cake with Chocolate and Walnuts

◆ Kahlúa® Pecan-Pear Bread ◆

2 cups all-purpose flour
2 teaspoons baking soda
½ teaspoon salt
½ teaspoon ground
   cinnamon
¼ teaspoon ground nutmeg
½ cup (8 tablespoons)
   butter, at room
   temperature

½ cup sugar
2 eggs
½ cup KAHLÚA® Liqueur
1 large pear, peeled, cored
   and diced
¾ cup chopped pecans
   Spicy Kahlúa® Butter
   (recipe follows)

Sift flour, baking soda, salt, cinnamon and nutmeg into medium bowl; set aside. In large bowl of electric mixer, beat butter and sugar until light and fluffy. Beat in eggs, 1 at a time; beat in Kahlúa®. (Mixture may appear curdled.) Add flour mixture and beat on low speed just until blended. Stir in pear and pecans to distribute evenly. Pour batter into greased and floured 8½×4-inch loaf pan. Bake at 350°F about 1 hour 15 minutes or until toothpick inserted in center comes out clean. Cool in pan 10 minutes. Turn out onto wire rack and cool completely. Serve with Spicy Kahlúa® Butter. *Makes 1 loaf*

Spicy Kahlúa® Butter: In food processor or blender, combine ½ cup butter, 1 tablespoon Kahlúa® Liqueur, ½ teaspoon ground cinnamon and ¼ teaspoon nutmeg. Process until well blended. Makes ½ cup

◆ Oatmeal Pumpkin Bread ◆

1 cup quick-cooking oats
1 cup hot low-fat milk
¾ cup cooked or canned
   pumpkin
2 eggs, beaten
¼ cup margarine, melted
2 cups all-purpose flour
1 cup sugar

1 tablespoon baking
   powder
1 teaspoon ground
   cinnamon
¼ teaspoon ground nutmeg
¼ teaspoon salt
1 cup raisins
½ cup chopped pecans

Preheat oven to 350°F. In large bowl, combine oats and milk; allow to stand about 5 minutes. Stir in pumpkin, eggs and margarine. In separate bowl, mix together flour, sugar, baking powder, cinnamon, nutmeg and salt. Gradually add dry ingredients to oatmeal mixture; stir in raisins and nuts and mix well. Place in greased 9×5-inch loaf pan. Bake 55 to 60 minutes or until done. Cool on wire rack. *Makes 1 loaf (16 slices)*

Favorite recipe from **The Sugar Association, Inc.**

◆ Raspberry Crumb Coffee Cake ◆

COFFEE CAKE

1 (18.25-ounce) package deluxe white cake mix
1 cup all-purpose flour
1 package (¼-ounce) active dry yeast
⅔ cup warm water
2 eggs

1½ cups (18-ounce jar) SMUCKER'S® Red Raspberry Preserves
¼ cup granulated sugar
1 teaspoon cinnamon
6 tablespoons butter or margarine

TOPPING

1 cup powdered sugar
1 tablespoon corn syrup

1 to 3 tablespoons milk

Grease 13×9-inch pan. Reserve 2½ cups dry cake mix. Combine remaining cake mix, flour, yeast, water and eggs. Mix by hand 100 strokes. Spread batter in greased pan. Spoon preserves evenly over batter.

Combine reserved cake mix, granulated sugar and cinnamon; cut in butter with fork until fine particles form. Sprinkle over preserves.

Bake at 375°F for 30 to 35 minutes or until golden brown.

Combine all topping ingredients, adding enough milk for desired drizzling consistency. Drizzle over warm or cooled coffee cake.

Makes 12 to 16 servings

◆ Hot Pepper Cheddar Loaf ◆

2½ cups all-purpose flour
1 tablespoon baking powder
½ teaspoon salt
¼ teaspoon fresh ground black pepper
2 large eggs
1 cup skim milk

1 tablespoon vegetable oil
2 teaspoons TABASCO® brand Pepper Sauce
8 ounces shredded sharp Cheddar cheese
1 teaspoon chopped jalapeño pepper (optional)

Preheat oven to 350°F. Grease 9×5-inch loaf pan.

Combine flour, baking powder, salt and pepper in large bowl. Combine eggs, milk, oil and TABASCO® Sauce in medium bowl. Add egg mixture to dry ingredients just until blended. Stir in cheese and jalapeño pepper.

Spoon batter into prepared pan and place on rack in center of oven. Bake 45 to 50 minutes or until lightly browned and firm. *Makes 1 loaf (10 servings)*

◆ Anadama Bread ◆

7¾ to 8¼ cups all-purpose
flour, divided
2 packages (¼ ounce each)
active dry yeast
1½ teaspoons salt

2¾ cups water
¾ cup molasses
¼ cup butter or margarine
1¼ cups yellow cornmeal

1. Combine 4 cups flour, yeast and salt in large bowl; set aside. Combine water, molasses and butter in 2-quart saucepan. Heat over low heat until mixture is 120° to 130°F. (Butter does not need to completely melt.)

2. Gradually beat water mixture into flour mixture with electric mixer at low speed. Increase speed to medium; beat 2 minutes, scraping down side of bowl once.

3. Beat in cornmeal and 2 cups flour at low speed. Increase speed to medium; beat 2 minutes, scraping down side of bowl once.

4. Stir in enough additional flour, about 1¾ cups, with wooden spoon to make soft dough. Turn out dough onto floured surface; flatten slightly. Knead dough 8 to 10 minutes or until smooth and elastic, adding remaining ½ cup flour to prevent sticking if necessary.

5. Shape dough into a ball; place in large greased bowl. Turn dough over so that top is greased. Cover with towel; let rise in warm place about 1 hour or until doubled in bulk.

6. Punch down dough. Knead dough on well-floured surface 1 minute. Cut dough into halves. Cover with towel; let rest 10 minutes.

7. Grease 2 (1½-quart) soufflé or casserole dishes or 2 (9×5-inch) loaf pans. For soufflé dishes, shape each half of dough into a ball; place in prepared pans. For loaf pans, roll out one half of dough into 12×8-inch rectangle with well-floured rolling pin. Starting with one 8-inch side, roll up dough jelly-roll style. Pinch seam and ends to seal. Place loaf, seam side down, in prepared pan, tucking ends under. Repeat with remaining dough.

8. Cover loaves with towel. Let rise in warm place about 40 minutes or until doubled in bulk.

9. Preheat oven to 375°F. Bake 35 to 40 minutes or until loaves are browned and sound hollow when tapped. Immediately remove from soufflé dishes; cool on wire racks.
Makes 2 loaves

Anadama Bread

◆ Sour Cream Coffee Cake ◆

Streusel Topping (recipe
    follows)
¾ cup sugar
6 tablespoons butter
2 eggs
1 cup sour cream
1½ teaspoons vanilla
1 tablespoon grated lemon
    peel

1½ cups all-purpose flour
1½ teaspoons ground
    cardamom
1 teaspoon baking powder
1 teaspoon baking soda
⅛ teaspoon salt

1. Prepare Streusel Topping. Set aside. Grease and flour bottom and side of 8-inch springform pan.

2. Preheat oven to 350°F. Beat sugar and butter in large bowl with electric mixer at medium speed until light and fluffy. Beat in eggs, 1 at a time, until well blended. Beat in sour cream, vanilla and lemon peel. Add flour, cardamom, baking powder, baking soda and salt; beat at low speed just until blended.

3. Spoon half of batter into prepared pan. Sprinkle half of streusel over batter. Repeat layers ending with streusel. Bake 50 to 60 minutes or until toothpick inserted in center comes out clean. Cool in pan on wire rack 15 minutes.

4. Run long slender knife around edge of pan to loosen cake. Unhinge side; lift off. Cool until cake is just warm to touch. Slide long slender knife under cake; rotate cake to loosen from bottom. Slide off onto serving plate. Wrap in plastic wrap. Store at room temperature up to 1 week. *Makes 10 servings*

Streusel Topping

¾ cup chopped walnuts or
    pecans
⅓ cup packed light brown
    sugar
2 tablespoons all-purpose
    flour
½ teaspoon ground
    cardamom

½ teaspoon ground nutmeg
½ teaspoon ground
    cinnamon
3 tablespoons butter or
    margarine, melted

Combine walnuts, sugar, flour, cardamom, nutmeg and cinnamon in small bowl. Stir in butter until well blended. *Makes about ¾ cup*

Sour Cream Coffee Cake

◆ Southern Spoon Bread ◆

4 eggs, separated
3 cups milk
1 cup yellow cornmeal
3 tablespoons margarine or
  butter
1 teaspoon salt

¼ teaspoon black pepper *or*
  ⅛ teaspoon ground red
  pepper
1 teaspoon baking powder
1 tablespoon grated
  Parmesan cheese

Preheat oven to 375°F. Spray 2-quart round casserole with nonstick cooking spray; set aside. Beat egg yolks in small bowl; set aside.

Heat milk almost to a boil in medium saucepan over medium heat. Gradually beat in cornmeal using wire whisk. Cook 2 minutes, stirring constantly. Whisk in margarine, salt and pepper. Beat about ¼ cup cornmeal mixture into egg yolks. Beat egg yolk mixture into remaining cornmeal mixture; set aside.

Beat egg whites in large bowl with electric mixer at high speed until stiff peaks form. Stir baking powder into cornmeal mixture. Stir about ¼ cup egg whites into cornmeal mixture. Gradually fold in remaining egg whites. Pour into prepared casserole; sprinkle with cheese.

Bake 30 to 35 minutes or until golden brown and toothpick inserted into center comes out clean. Serve immediately. *Makes 6 servings*

◆ Apple Country® Bread ◆

1 cup sugar
½ cup shortening
2 eggs
1 teaspoon vanilla
2 cups all-purpose flour
1 teaspoon baking powder

1 teaspoon baking soda
½ teaspoon salt
2 cups chopped peeled
  apples
½ cup chopped nuts
⅓ cup dried cherries

TOPPING
1 tablespoon sugar

¼ teaspoon ground
  cinnamon

Preheat oven to 350°F. Grease and flour 9×5×3-inch pan.

Mix 1 cup sugar, shortening, eggs and vanilla in large bowl. Stir in flour, baking powder, baking soda and salt until smooth. Stir in apples, nuts and dried cherries. Spread in prepared pan. Mix 1 tablespoon sugar and cinnamon. Sprinkle over batter. Bake until toothpick inserted in center comes out clean (50 to 60 minutes). Immediately remove from pan. Cool completely before slicing. Store tightly covered. *Makes 1 loaf*

Favorite recipe from **New York Apple Association, Inc.**

Southern Spoon Bread

◆ Plum Honey Tea Bread ◆

2 cups all-purpose flour
1 teaspoon baking powder
1 teaspoon baking soda
1 teaspoon ground
    cinnamon
½ teaspoon salt
¼ teaspoon ground nutmeg

¾ cup buttermilk
½ cup honey
2 tablespoons vegetable oil
1 egg, beaten
3 plums, pitted and
    chopped
½ cup chopped walnuts

Combine flour, baking powder, baking soda, cinnamon, salt and nutmeg in large bowl; mix well. Combine buttermilk, honey, oil and egg in small bowl; mix until blended. Stir buttermilk mixture into flour mixture until just moistened. Fold in plums and walnuts. Pour into greased 9×5×3-inch loaf pan. Bake at 325°F 50 to 55 minutes or until wooden pick inserted near center comes out clean. During baking, cover top with foil after 25 minutes to prevent overbrowning.   *Makes 8 servings*

Muffin Variation: *Prepare batter as directed above. Fill 12 greased muffin cups ¾ full. Bake at 325°F about 20 minutes or until wooden pick inserted near centers comes out clean.*

Favorite recipe from **National Honey Board**

◆ Boston Brown Bread ◆

1 cup whole wheat flour
1 cup rye flour
1 cup yellow cornmeal
1½ teaspoons baking powder
1 teaspoon salt

½ teaspoon baking soda
2 cups buttermilk
¾ cup molasses
2 tablespoons CRISCO® Oil*
1 cup dark seedless raisins

*Any Crisco® Oil can be used.

1. Mix flours, cornmeal, baking powder, salt and baking soda in large bowl. Stir in buttermilk, molasses, oil and raisins until well mixed.

2. Spoon batter into 4 well-greased 1-pound vegetable or fruit cans. Cover with aluminum foil and tie with string.

3. Place cans on a rack in Dutch oven or large saucepan. Pour boiling water to come halfway up sides of cans. Cover and simmer for 2½ to 3 hours. Pour in more boiling water, if necessary, to keep cans in boiling water to the halfway point.

4. Remove from Dutch oven and remove foil. Cool in cans for 10 minutes on a rack. Invert loaves onto rack. Serve warm.   *Makes 4 loaves*

Plum Honey Tea Bread

MUFFINS, SCONES & BISCUITS

◆ Pineapple-Raisin Muffins ◆

¼ cup chopped pecans
¼ cup packed light brown
　　sugar
2 cups all-purpose flour
¼ cup granulated sugar
2½ teaspoons baking powder
¾ teaspoon salt
½ teaspoon ground
　　cinnamon

6 tablespoons cold butter
½ cup raisins
1 can (8 ounces) crushed
　　pineapple in juice,
　　undrained
⅓ cup unsweetened
　　pineapple juice
1 egg

1. Preheat oven to 400°F. Paper-line or grease 12 (2½-inch) muffin cups.

2. Combine pecans and brown sugar in small bowl; set aside. Combine flour, granulated sugar, baking powder, salt and cinnamon in large bowl. Cut in butter with pastry blender or 2 knives until mixture resembles fine crumbs. Stir in raisins.

3. Combine undrained pineapple, pineapple juice and egg in small bowl until blended; stir into flour mixture just until moistened. Spoon evenly into prepared muffin cups, filling ⅔ full. Sprinkle with pecan mixture.

4. Bake 20 to 25 minutes or until golden brown and toothpick inserted in center comes out clean. Immediately remove from pan; cool on wire rack 10 minutes. Serve warm or cold. *Makes 12 muffins*

Pineapple-Raisin Muffins

◆ Dill Sour Cream Scones ◆

2 cups all-purpose flour
2 teaspoons baking powder
½ teaspoon baking soda
½ teaspoon salt
4 tablespoons butter or
   margarine

2 eggs
½ cup sour cream
1 tablespoon chopped
   fresh dill or 1 teaspoon
   dried dill weed

Preheat oven to 425°F.

Combine flour, baking powder, baking soda and salt. Cut in butter with pastry blender or 2 knives until mixture resembles coarse crumbs. Beat eggs with fork in small bowl. Add sour cream and dill; beat until well combined. Stir into flour mixture until mixture forms soft dough that pulls away from side of bowl.

Turn out dough onto well-floured surface. Knead dough 10 times.* Roll out dough into 9×6-inch rectangle with lightly floured rolling pin. Cut dough into 6 (3-inch) squares. Cut each square diagonally in half, making 12 triangles. Place triangles 2 inches apart onto *ungreased* baking sheets.

Bake 10 to 12 minutes or until golden brown and toothpick inserted in center comes out clean. Cool on wire rack 10 minutes. Serve warm or cool completely.   *Makes 12 scones*

To knead dough, fold dough in half toward you and press dough away from you with heels of hands. Give dough a quarter turn and continue folding, pushing and turning.

◆ Apricot-Peanut Butter Muffins ◆

1¾ cups all-purpose flour
2½ tablespoons sugar
2½ teaspoons baking powder
¾ teaspoon salt
¼ cup shortening
¼ cup SMUCKER'S® Creamy
   Natural Peanut Butter
   or LAURA SCUDDER'S®
   Smooth Old-Fashioned
   Peanut Butter

¾ cup milk
1 egg, well beaten
2 tablespoons SMUCKER'S®
   Apricot Preserves

Grease 10 large muffin cups. Combine flour, sugar, baking powder and salt; cut in shortening and peanut butter. Mix milk and egg together and add all at once to dry ingredients. Stir only until dry ingredients are moistened. Fill muffin cups ⅔ full. Spoon about ½ teaspoon preserves in center of each muffin.

Bake at 400°F for 25 minutes or until done.   *Makes 10 muffins*

Dill Sour Cream Scones

◆ Herb Biscuits ◆

¼ cup hot water (130°F)
1½ teaspoons (½ package) fast-rising active dry yeast
2½ cups all-purpose flour
3 tablespoons sugar
1½ teaspoons baking powder
½ teaspoon baking soda
½ teaspoon salt
5 tablespoons cold margarine, cut into pieces

2 teaspoons finely chopped fresh parsley *or* ½ teaspoon dried parsley flakes
2 teaspoons finely chopped fresh basil *or* ½ teaspoon dried basil leaves
2 teaspoons finely chopped fresh chives *or* ½ teaspoon dried chives
¾ cup buttermilk

1. Preheat oven to 425°F. Spray cookie sheet with nonstick cooking spray.

2. Combine hot water and yeast in small cup; let stand 2 to 3 minutes. Combine flour, sugar, baking powder, baking soda and salt in medium bowl; cut in margarine using pastry blender or 2 knives until mixture resembles coarse crumbs. Mix in parsley, basil and chives. Stir in buttermilk and yeast mixture to make soft dough. Turn dough out onto lightly floured surface. Knead 15 to 20 times.

3. Roll to ½-inch thickness. Cut hearts or other shapes with 2½-inch cookie cutter. Place biscuits on prepared cookie sheet. Bake 12 to 15 minutes or until browned. Cool on wire racks. Serve immediately.   *Makes 18 biscuits*

◆ Banana Scotch Muffins ◆

1 ripe, large DOLE® Banana
½ cup sugar
1 egg, beaten
¼ cup milk
¼ cup vegetable oil
1 teaspoon vanilla
1 cup all-purpose flour

1 cup quick-cooking rolled oats
1 teaspoon baking powder
½ teaspoon baking soda
½ teaspoon salt
½ cup butterscotch chips

• Preheat oven to 400°F. Purée banana in blender (⅔ cup). In medium bowl, combine puréed banana, sugar, egg, milk, oil and vanilla.

• In large bowl, combine flour, oats, baking powder, baking soda and salt. Stir banana mixture and butterscotch chips into dry ingredients just until blended.

• Spoon into well-greased 2½-inch muffin cups. Bake 12 to 15 minutes. Remove from pan.   *Makes 12 muffins*

Herb Biscuits

◆ White Chocolate Chunk Muffins ◆

2½ cups all-purpose flour
1 cup packed brown sugar
⅓ cup unsweetened cocoa powder
2 teaspoons baking soda
½ teaspoon salt
1⅓ cups buttermilk

6 tablespoons butter or margarine, melted
2 eggs, beaten
1½ teaspoons vanilla
1½ cups chopped white chocolate

Preheat oven to 400°F. Grease 12 (3½-inch) large muffin cups; set aside. Combine flour, sugar, cocoa, baking soda and salt in large bowl. Combine buttermilk, butter, eggs and vanilla in small bowl until blended. Stir into flour mixture just until moistened. Fold in white chocolate. Spoon into prepared muffin cups, filling half full.

Bake 25 to 30 minutes or until toothpick inserted in center comes out clean. Cool in pan on wire rack 5 minutes. Remove from pan. Cool on wire rack 10 minutes. Serve warm or cool completely. *Makes 12 jumbo muffins*

◆ Cheesy Buttermilk Biscuits ◆

2 cups all-purpose flour
1 tablespoon baking powder
1 teaspoon salt
½ teaspoon baking soda
½ teaspoon red pepper flakes
⅓ cup vegetable shortening

2 tablespoons unsalted butter, at room temperature
¾ cup low fat buttermilk
1 cup (4 ounces) shredded ALPINE LACE® Reduced Fat Cheddar Cheese

1. Preheat the oven to 450°F. Spray a baking sheet with nonstick cooking spray. In a large bowl, stir together the flour, baking powder, salt, baking soda and red pepper flakes.

2. Using a pastry cutter or 2 knives, cut in the shortening and butter until coarse crumbs form. Using a wooden spoon, stir in the buttermilk and cheese just until a soft dough forms.

3. Turn the dough onto a lightly floured board and knead for about 30 seconds. Pat or roll the dough until it is 1 inch thick. Using a 2-inch biscuit cutter (preferably a fluted one), cut out 16 biscuits, re-rolling the scraps of dough as you go.

4. Place the biscuits 2 inches apart on the baking sheet and brush the tops with additional buttermilk, if you wish. Bake for 12 minutes or just until golden brown. *Makes 16 biscuits*

White Chocolate Chunk Muffins

◆ Cranberry Scones ◆

1½ **cups all-purpose flour**	¾ **cup dried cranberries**
½ **cup oat bran**	⅓ **cup milk**
¼ **cup plus 1 tablespoon sugar, divided**	1 **egg**
2 **teaspoons baking powder**	¼ **cup sour cream**
½ **teaspoon baking soda**	1 **tablespoon uncooked quick-cooking or old-fashioned oats (optional)**
½ **teaspoon salt**	
5 **tablespoons margarine or butter**	

Preheat oven to 425°F. Combine flour, oat bran, ¼ cup sugar, baking powder, baking soda and salt in large bowl. Cut in margarine with pastry blender or 2 knives until mixture resembles fine crumbs. Stir in cranberries. Lightly beat milk and egg in small bowl. Reserve 2 tablespoons milk mixture; set aside. Stir sour cream into remaining milk mixture. Stir into flour mixture until soft dough forms.

Turn out dough onto well-floured surface. Gently knead 10 to 12 times. Roll out into 9×6-inch rectangle. Cut dough into 6 (3-inch) squares using floured knife; cut diagonally into halves, forming 12 triangles. Place 2 inches apart on *ungreased* baking sheets. Brush triangles with reserved milk mixture. Sprinkle with oats, if desired, and remaining 1 tablespoon sugar.

Bake 10 to 12 minutes or until golden brown. Remove from baking sheets and cool on wire racks 10 minutes. Serve warm. *Makes 12 scones*

◆ Biscuits ◆

2 **cups sifted all-purpose flour**	⅓ **CRISCO® Stick or** ⅓ **cup CRISCO® all-vegetable shortening**
3 **teaspoons baking powder**	
1 **teaspoon salt**	¾ **cup milk**

1. Heat oven to 425°F. Combine flour, baking powder and salt in bowl. Cut in shortening using pastry blender (or 2 knives) until mixture resembles coarse meal. Add milk; stir with fork until blended.

2. Transfer dough to lightly floured surface. Knead gently 8 to 10 times. Roll dough ½ inch thick. Cut with floured 2-inch-round cutter.

3. Bake at 425°F 12 to 15 minutes. *Do not overbake.*

Makes 12 to 16 (2-inch) biscuits

Cranberry Scones

◆ Zesty Parmesan Biscuits ◆

4 cups all-purpose flour
½ cup grated Parmesan cheese
2 tablespoons baking powder
2 teaspoons sugar
1 teaspoon baking soda
6 tablespoons cold butter, cut into pieces
6 tablespoons cold solid vegetable shortening
1 cup plus 2 tablespoons buttermilk, divided
½ cup FRANK'S® REDHOT® Hot Sauce
Sesame seeds (optional)

1. Preheat oven to 450°F. Place flour, cheese, baking powder, sugar and baking soda in blender or food processor*. Cover; process 30 seconds. Add butter and shortening; process, pulsing on and off, until fine crumbs form. Transfer to large bowl.

2. Add 1 cup buttermilk and REDHOT sauce all at once. Stir together just until mixture starts to form a ball. (Dough will be dry. Do not over mix.)

3. Turn dough out onto lightly floured board. With palms of hands, gently knead 8 times. Using floured rolling pin or hands, roll dough to ¾-inch thickness. Using 2½-inch round biscuit cutter, cut out 16 biscuits, re-rolling dough as necessary.

4. Place biscuits 2 inches apart on large foil-lined baking sheet. Brush tops with remaining 2 tablespoons buttermilk; sprinkle with sesame seeds, if desired. Bake 12 to 15 minutes or until golden.   *Makes 16 biscuits*

*Or, place dry ingredients in large bowl. Cut in butter and shortening until fine crumbs form using pastry blender or 2 knives. Add buttermilk and REDHOT sauce; mix just until moistened. Continue with step 3.

Prep Time: 30 minutes
Cook Time: 12 minutes

◆ Oatmeal Apple Muffins ◆

1¼ cups uncooked quick-cooking rolled oats
1 cup milk
1 teaspoon vanilla
1¼ cups all-purpose flour
1 tablespoon baking powder
1 teaspoon ground cinnamon
½ teaspoon baking soda
½ teaspoon salt
1½ cups chopped Golden Delicious apples
½ cup chopped walnuts
¾ cup packed brown sugar
1 egg
⅓ cup butter or margarine, softened

Combine oats, milk and vanilla in mixing bowl; set aside. Combine flour, baking powder, cinnamon, baking soda and salt; toss with apples and walnuts. Beat sugar and egg in large mixing bowl; add butter and beat until creamy. Add oat mixture; stir in flour mixture just until blended. *Do not overmix.* Spoon into greased muffin tins. Bake at 400°F 20 to 22 minutes.

Makes 12 standard muffins or 6 oversized muffins

Prep Time: about 30 minutes
Bake Time: 20 to 22 minutes

Favorite recipe from **Washington Apple Commission**

◆ Norwegian Almond Muffins ◆

2 cups all-purpose flour, divided
1 package RED STAR® Active Dry Yeast or QUICK•RISE™ Yeast
¼ cup plus 1 tablespoon sugar, divided
1 teaspoon salt
1 teaspoon ground cardamom
½ cup water
¼ cup milk
¼ cup butter or margarine
¼ cup almond paste
1 egg
½ teaspoon almond extract
⅛ cup cherry preserves
¼ cup chopped almonds

Preheat oven to 350°F.

Combine 1 cup flour, yeast, ¼ cup sugar, salt and cardamom in small bowl; mix well. Heat water, milk, butter and almond paste until very warm (120° to 130°F; butter does not need to melt). Add to flour mixture. Add egg and almond extract. Beat with electric mixer at low speed until moistened. Beat 3 minutes at medium speed. By hand, gradually stir in remaining 1 cup flour to make soft batter.

Spoon batter into well-greased muffin cups. Cover; let rise in warm place 1 to 1½ hours (30 to 45 minutes for QUICK•RISE™ Yeast).

Before baking, make an indentation in top of each muffin; spoon about ½ teaspoon cherry preserves into each muffin. Combine remaining 1 tablespoon sugar and almonds; sprinkle over muffins. Bake 20 to 25 minutes or until golden brown. Cool in pans 3 minutes; remove from pans. Serve warm or cold.

Makes 12 muffins

◆ Apple Streusel Muffins ◆

¼ cup chopped pecans
2 tablespoons brown sugar
1 tablespoon flour
2 teaspoons butter or
    margarine, melted

1 package (7 ounces) apple
    cinnamon muffin mix
    plus ingredients to
    prepare mix
½ cup shredded peeled
    apple

1. Preheat oven to 425°F. Coat 18 mini-muffin cups with nonstick cooking spray.

2. Combine pecans, brown sugar, flour and butter in small bowl.

3. Prepare muffin mix according to package directions. Stir in apple. Fill each muffin cup ⅔ full. Sprinkle approximately 1 teaspoon pecan mixture on top of each muffin. Bake 12 to 15 minutes or until golden brown. Cool slightly. Serve warm. *Makes 18 mini-muffins*

Variation: For regular-size muffins, grease six 2½-inch muffin cups. Prepare topping and batter as directed. Fill muffin cups ⅔ full of batter. Sprinkle approximately 1 tablespoon pecan mixture on each muffin. Bake 18 to 20 minutes or until golden brown. *Makes 6 regular muffins*

Prep and Cook Time: 30 minutes

◆ Biscuit-Onion Wedges ◆

2½ cups biscuit mix
¾ cup milk
2 eggs, divided
1 cup finely chopped onion
⅔ cup dairy sour cream
1 teaspoon LAWRY'S®
    Seasoned Salt

¼ teaspoon LAWRY'S® Garlic
    Powder with Parsley
1½ cups (6 ounces) shredded
    cheddar cheese,
    divided
½ teaspoon hot pepper
    sauce

In medium bowl, combine biscuit mix, milk and 1 egg. In separate bowl, beat together remaining egg, onion, sour cream, Seasoned Salt and Garlic Powder with Parsley; stir in 1 cup cheese and hot pepper sauce. Stir into batter. Pour into greased 8-inch round or square baking dish. Bake on center rack in 400°F oven 20 minutes. Sprinkle top with remaining ½ cup cheese; bake 5 to 7 minutes longer or until toothpick inserted in center comes out clean and cheese is melted. Let stand 2 minutes before serving. *Makes 6 servings*

Serving Suggestion: Cut into squares or wedges. Serve warm with margarine.

Hint: Batter can also be used to make muffins or drop biscuits.

Apple Streusel Muffins

◆ Honey Sweet Potato Biscuits ◆

2 cups all-purpose flour
1 tablespoon baking
   powder
½ teaspoon salt
¼ cup vegetable shortening
¾ cup mashed cooked sweet
   potato (1 large sweet
   potato baked until
   tender, peeled and
   mashed)

⅓ cup honey
1 tablespoon grated orange
   peel
1 tablespoon grated lemon
   peel
½ cup milk (about)

Combine flour, baking powder and salt in large bowl. Cut in shortening until mixture resembles size of small peas. Add sweet potatoes, honey, orange and lemon peels; mix well. Add enough milk to make soft, but not sticky, dough. Knead 3 or 4 times on lightly floured surface. Pat dough to 1-inch thickness and cut into 2¼-inch rounds. Place on *ungreased* baking sheet.

Bake in preheated 400°F oven 15 to 18 minutes or until lightly browned. Serve warm.   *Makes 10 biscuits*

Favorite recipe from **National Honey Board**

◆ Pineapple Citrus Muffins ◆

⅓ cup honey
¼ cup butter or margarine,
   softened
1 egg
1 can (8 ounces) DOLE®
   Crushed Pineapple,
   undrained
1 tablespoon grated
   orange peel

1 cup all-purpose flour
1 cup whole wheat flour
1 cup DOLE® Chopped Dates
½ cup chopped walnuts
   (optional)
1½ teaspoons baking powder
¼ teaspoon salt
¼ teaspoon ground nutmeg

• Preheat oven to 375°F. In large bowl, beat together honey and butter 1 minute. Beat in egg, then undrained pineapple and orange peel. In medium bowl, combine remaining ingredients; stir into pineapple mixture until just blended.

• Spoon batter into 12 greased muffin cups. Bake 25 minutes or until wooden pick inserted in center comes out clean. Cool slightly in pan before turning out onto wire rack. Serve warm.   *Makes 12 muffins*

Honey Sweet Potato Biscuits

◆ Blueberry Yogurt Muffins ◆

2 cups QUAKER® Oat Bran
  hot cereal, uncooked
¼ cup firmly packed brown
  sugar
2 teaspoons baking powder
1 carton (8 ounces) plain
  low fat yogurt
2 egg whites, slightly
  beaten

¼ cup skim milk
¼ cup honey
2 tablespoons vegetable oil
1 teaspoon grated lemon
  peel
½ cup fresh or frozen
  blueberries

Heat oven to 425°F. Line 12 medium muffin cups with paper baking cups.

Combine oat bran, brown sugar and baking powder. Add combined yogurt, egg whites, skim milk, honey, oil and lemon peel, mixing just until moistened. Fold in blueberries. Fill muffin cups almost full.

Bake 18 to 20 minutes or until golden brown.   *Makes 12 muffins*

To freeze muffins: *Wrap securely in foil or place in freezer bag. Seal, label and freeze.* **To reheat frozen muffins:** *Unwrap muffins. Microwave at HIGH about 30 seconds per muffin.*

◆ Touchdown Cheese Scones ◆

2 cups all-purpose flour
2½ teaspoons baking powder
½ teaspoon baking soda
¼ teaspoon salt
2 tablespoons cold butter
  or margarine, cut in
  pieces

1 cup shredded mild
  Cheddar cheese
⅔ cup buttermilk
2 large eggs, divided
½ teaspoon TABASCO®
  brand Pepper Sauce

Preheat oven to 350°F. Sift together flour, baking powder, baking soda and salt in large bowl. Cut in butter until mixture resembles cornmeal. Stir in cheese. Blend buttermilk, 1 egg and TABASCO® Sauce together in small bowl. Make well in center of dry ingredients; add buttermilk mixture. Stir quickly and lightly with fork to form sticky dough. Turn dough out on lightly floured board. Knead gently 10 times. Divide dough in half; pat each half into circle about ½ inch thick. Cut each circle into 4 wedges. Combine remaining egg and 1 tablespoon water. Brush each wedge with egg mixture. Arrange on greased baking sheet. Bake 13 to 15 minutes or until golden.   *Makes 8 scones*

Blueberry Yogurt Muffins

◆ Orange-Currant Scones ◆

1½ cups all-purpose flour
¼ cup plus 1 teaspoon
  sugar, divided
1 teaspoon baking powder
¼ teaspoon salt
¼ teaspoon baking soda
⅓ cup currants
1 tablespoon grated fresh
  orange peel

6 tablespoons chilled
  butter or margarine,
  cut into small pieces
½ cup buttermilk, plain
  yogurt, or regular or
  nonfat sour cream

1. Preheat oven to 425°F. Combine flour, ¼ cup sugar, baking powder, salt and baking soda in large bowl. Stir in currants and orange peel.

2. Cut in butter with pastry blender or 2 knives until mixture resembles coarse crumbs. Stir in buttermilk. Stir until mixture forms soft dough that clings together. (Dough will be tacky.)

3. Lightly flour hands and shape dough into ball. Pat dough into 8-inch round on lightly greased baking sheet. Cut dough into 8 wedges with floured chef's knife.

4. Sprinkle wedges with remaining 1 teaspoon sugar. Bake 18 to 20 minutes or until lightly browned.

Makes 8 scones

◆ Oniony Corn Muffins ◆

1 package (12 ounces) corn
  muffin mix
⅔ cup milk
1 egg
1 can (7 ounces) whole
  kernel corn, drained

1⅓ cups FRENCH'S® French
  Fried Onions, slightly
  crushed

Preheat oven to 400°F. Grease 12-cup muffin pan. Prepare corn muffin mix according to package directions using milk and egg. Stir in corn and French Fried Onions. *Do not overmix.*

Fill muffin cups using ¼ cup batter for each cup. Bake 15 minutes or until toothpick inserted in center comes out clean. Cool in pan on wire rack 5 minutes. Loosen muffins from pan; remove and serve warm.

Makes 12 servings

Prep Time: 15 minutes
Bake Time: 15 minutes

Orange-Currant Scones

Sonoma Dried Tomato
◆ and Vegetable Biscuits ◆

¼ cup SONOMA® Dried Tomato Halves

2½ cups unbleached all-purpose flour

1 tablespoon sugar

2 teaspoons baking powder

2 teaspoons salt

½ teaspoon baking soda

¼ teaspoon black pepper

½ teaspoon active dry yeast

2 tablespoons warm water (110° to 115°F)

1 cup cold vegetable shortening, cut into ½-inch cubes

½ cup vegetables, cut into ¼-inch cubes (carrot, yellow squash, green bell pepper and zucchini)

2 teaspoons *each* fresh minced parsley, basil and dill *or* 1 scant teaspoon *each* dried parsley, basil and dill

1 large clove garlic, minced

¾ cup buttermilk

Preheat oven to 375°F. In small bowl, cover tomatoes with boiling water; set aside 10 minutes. In large bowl, mix flour, sugar, baking powder, salt, baking soda and pepper. In another small bowl, dissolve yeast in 2 tablespoons warm water; set aside. Cut shortening into flour mixture until crumbs resemble coarse meal. Blend yeast mixture into flour mixture to form dough. Thoroughly drain and mince tomatoes; combine with vegetables, herbs and garlic. Add half of vegetable mixture and half of buttermilk to dough; mix well and repeat with remaining vegetable mixture and buttermilk. Turn dough out onto floured surface and knead several times, adding more flour only if necessary. Pat or roll out dough to ¾ inch thickness; cut out dough with 3-inch biscuit cutter. Place biscuits, spaced 2 inches apart, on greased or parchment-lined baking sheet. Bake 20 to 24 minutes or until lightly browned and cooked through.

Makes 8 biscuits

◆ Banana Blueberry Muffins ◆

2 ripe, medium DOLE® Bananas

6 tablespoons margarine

6 tablespoons brown sugar

1 egg

1½ cups all-purpose flour

½ teaspoon baking powder

½ teaspoon baking soda

½ teaspoon salt

½ teaspoon grated lemon peel

1 cup frozen blueberries, rinsed, drained

- Purée bananas in blender (1 cup).

- Beat margarine and sugar in large bowl until light and fluffy. Mix in bananas and egg.

- Combine flour, baking powder, baking soda, salt and lemon peel in medium bowl. Blend into margarine mixture just until moistened. Fold in blueberries.

- Line 6 large muffin cups with paper liners; spray lightly with vegetable cooking spray. Spoon batter evenly into cups.

- Bake at 375°F 20 to 25 minutes.

Makes 6 muffins

Prep Time: 20 minutes
Bake Time: 25 minutes

◆ Bayou Yam Muffins ◆

1 cup all-purpose flour	**1 cup mashed yams or sweet potatoes**
1 cup yellow cornmeal	**½ cup very strong cold coffee**
¼ cup sugar	
1 tablespoon baking powder	**¼ cup butter or margarine, melted**
1¼ teaspoons ground cinnamon	**½ teaspoon TABASCO® brand Pepper Sauce**
½ teaspoon salt	
2 eggs	

Preheat oven to 425°F. Grease 12 (3×1½-inch) muffin cups. Combine flour, cornmeal, sugar, baking powder, cinnamon and salt in large bowl. Beat eggs in medium bowl; stir in yams, coffee, butter and TABASCO® Sauce. Make well in center of dry ingredients; add yam mixture and stir just to combine. Spoon batter into prepared muffin cups. Bake 20 to 25 minutes or until cake tester inserted in center of muffin comes out clean. Cool 5 minutes on wire rack. Remove from pans. Serve warm or at room temperature.   *Makes 12 muffins*

Microwave Directions: Prepare muffin batter as directed above. Spoon approximately ⅓ cup batter into each of 6 paper baking cup-lined 6-ounce custard cups or microwave-safe muffin pan cups. Cook uncovered on HIGH (100% power) 4 to 5½ minutes or until cake tester inserted in center of muffin comes out clean; turn and rearrange cups or turn muffin pan ½ turn once during cooking. Remove muffins with small spatula. Cool 5 minutes on wire rack. Remove from pans. Repeat procedure with remaining batter. Serve warm or at room temperature.

◆ Freezer Buttermilk Biscuits ◆

3 cups all-purpose flour
1 tablespoon baking
   powder
1 tablespoon sugar

1 teaspoon baking soda
½ teaspoon salt
⅔ cup shortening
1 cup buttermilk*

You can substitute soured fresh milk. To sour milk, place 1 tablespoon lemon juice plus enough milk to equal 1 cup in 2-cup measure. Stir; let stand 5 minutes before using.

Combine flour, baking powder, sugar, baking soda and salt in large bowl. Cut in shortening with pastry blender or 2 knives until mixture resembles fine crumbs. Stir buttermilk into flour mixture until mixture forms soft dough that leaves side of bowl.

Turn out dough onto well-floured surface. Knead 10 times; roll into 8-inch square. Cut dough into 16 (2-inch) squares.** Place squares on baking sheet lined with plastic wrap. Freeze about 3 hours or until firm. Remove squares and place in airtight freezer container. Freeze up to 1 month.

When ready to prepare, preheat oven to 400°F. Place frozen squares 1½ inches apart on *ungreased* baking sheets. Bake 20 to 25 minutes or until golden brown. Serve warm.
Makes 16 biscuits

**To bake immediately, preheat oven to 450°F. Place squares 1½ inches apart on ungreased baking sheets. Bake 10 to 12 minutes or until golden brown. Serve warm.*

◆ Cheese Corn Muffins ◆

½ cup yellow cornmeal
½ cup all-purpose flour
¼ cup shredded JARLSBERG
   LITE™ Cheese
2 tablespoons sugar
1 tablespoon *each:* minced
   red and green bell
   peppers

1 teaspoon baking powder
¾ teaspoon salt
½ cup plain nonfat yogurt
¼ cup (2 ounces) liquid egg
   substitute
2 tablespoons margarine,
   melted
Vegetable cooking spray

In medium bowl combine first 7 ingredients. In separate bowl, combine yogurt, egg substitute and margarine. Add dry ingredients to yogurt mixture and blend until evenly moistened. Spray muffin pan with vegetable cooking spray. Evenly divide batter to make 8 muffins. Bake at 400°F 15 to 20 minutes or until golden. Cool on wire rack 5 minutes.
Makes 8 muffins

Freezer Buttermilk Biscuits

◆ Peachy Oat Bran Muffins ◆

1½ cups oat bran
½ cup all-purpose flour
⅓ cup firmly packed brown
   sugar
2 teaspoons baking powder
1 teaspoon ground
   cinnamon
½ teaspoon salt
¾ cup lowfat milk

1 egg, beaten
¼ cup vegetable oil
1 can (15 ounces)
   DEL MONTE® LITE®
   Yellow Cling Sliced
   Peaches, drained and
   chopped
⅓ cup chopped walnuts

1. Preheat oven to 425°F. Combine oat bran, flour, brown sugar, baking powder, cinnamon and salt; mix well.

2. Combine milk, egg and oil. Add to dry ingredients; stir just enough to blend. Fold in fruit and nuts.

3. Fill greased muffin cups with batter. Sprinkle with granulated sugar, if desired.

4. Bake 20 to 25 minutes or until golden brown.

Makes 12 medium muffins

Prep Time: 10 minutes
Cook Time: 25 minutes

◆ Southwestern Sausage Drop Biscuits ◆

1 pound BOB EVANS® Zesty
   Hot Roll Sausage
3 cups all-purpose (biscuit)
   baking mix
1¼ cups (5 ounces) shredded
   sharp Cheddar cheese
1 cup seeded diced fresh or
   drained canned
   tomatoes

1 cup chopped green
   onions
1 cup milk
¼ teaspoon paprika
   Dash cayenne pepper
   Butter (optional)

Preheat oven to 350°F. Crumble and cook sausage in medium skillet until browned. Drain on paper towels. Combine remaining ingredients except butter in large bowl; mix well. Shape dough into 2-inch balls; place on *ungreased* baking sheet. Bake 12 minutes or until golden. Serve hot with butter, if desired. Refrigerate leftovers. *Makes about 2 dozen small biscuits*

Peachy Oat Bran Muffins

◆ Sun-Dried Tomato Scones ◆

2 cups buttermilk baking
    mix
¼ cup (1 ounce) grated
    Parmesan cheese
1½ teaspoons dried basil
    leaves
⅔ cup reduced-fat (2%)
    milk

½ cup chopped drained oil-
    packed sun-dried
    tomatoes
¼ cup chopped green
    onions

1. Preheat oven to 450°F. Combine baking mix, cheese and basil in medium bowl.

2. Stir in milk, tomatoes and onions. Mix just until dry ingredients are moistened. Drop by heaping teaspoonfuls onto greased baking sheet.

3. Bake 8 to 10 minutes or until light golden brown. Remove baking sheet to cooling rack; let stand 5 minutes. Remove scones and serve warm or at room temperature. *Makes 1½ dozen scones*

Prep and Cook Time: 20 minutes

◆ The Original Kellogg's® All-Bran Muffin™ ◆

1¼ cups all-purpose flour
½ cup sugar
1 tablespoon baking
    powder
¼ teaspoon salt
2 cups KELLOGG'S®
    ALL-BRAN® cereal

1¼ cups milk
1 egg
¼ cup vegetable oil
    Vegetable cooking spray

1. Stir together flour, sugar, baking powder and salt. Set aside.

2. In large mixing bowl, combine Kellogg's® All-Bran® cereal and milk. Let stand about 5 minutes or until cereal softens. Add egg and oil. Beat well. Add flour mixture, stirring only until combined. Portion batter evenly into twelve 2½-inch muffin-pan cups coated with cooking spray.

3. Bake at 400°F for 20 minutes or until lightly browned. Serve warm.

Makes 12 muffins

For muffins with reduced calories, fat and cholesterol: *Use 2 tablespoons sugar, 2 tablespoons oil, replace milk with 1¼ cups skim milk, and substitute 2 egg whites for 1 egg. Prepare and bake as directed.*

Sun-Dried Tomato Scones

◆ Pumpernickel Muffins ◆

1 cup all-purpose flour
½ cup rye flour
½ cup whole wheat flour
2 teaspoons caraway seeds
1 teaspoon baking soda
½ teaspoon salt
1 cup buttermilk

¼ cup vegetable oil
¼ cup light molasses
1 egg
1 square (1 ounce)
    unsweetened chocolate,
    melted and cooled

Preheat oven to 400°F. Grease or paper-line 12 (2½-inch) muffin cups.

Combine flours, caraway seeds, baking soda and salt in large bowl.

Combine buttermilk, oil, molasses and egg in small bowl until blended. Stir in melted chocolate. Stir into flour mixture just until moistened. Spoon evenly into prepared muffin cups.

Bake 20 to 25 minutes or until toothpick inserted in center comes out clean. Immediately remove from pan. Cool on wire rack about 10 minutes. Serve warm or cold. Store at room temperature in tightly covered container up to 2 days. *Makes 12 muffins*

◆ Nectarine Pecan Breakfast Muffins ◆

1½ cups whole wheat flour
½ cup chopped pecans
¼ cup packed brown sugar
2 teaspoons baking powder
½ teaspoon salt
½ teaspoon ground nutmeg
1½ fresh California
    nectarines, chopped
    (1 cup)

1 cup low-fat milk
1 egg, beaten
3 tablespoons vegetable oil
12 pecan halves

Preheat oven to 400°F. Grease 12 (2½-inch) muffin cups; set aside.

Combine flour, chopped pecans, sugar, baking powder, salt and nutmeg in large bowl. Combine nectarines, milk, egg and oil in medium bowl until well blended. Stir into flour mixture just until moistened. (Batter will be thick and lumpy.) Spoon evenly into prepared muffin cups. Place pecan half on top of each muffin.

Bake 20 minutes or until golden brown and toothpick inserted in center of muffins comes out clean. Remove from pan; cool on wire rack 10 minutes. Serve warm or cool completely. *Makes 12 muffins*

Favorite recipe from **California Tree Fruit Agreement**

Pumpernickel Muffins

◆ Festive Cornmeal Biscuits ◆

1¾ cups all-purpose flour
½ cup yellow cornmeal
1 tablespoon baking powder
1 tablespoon sugar
1 teaspoon salt
¼ teaspoon baking soda
3 tablespoons margarine
¾ cup buttermilk
1 egg white, beaten
Peach or strawberry preserves (optional)

1. Preheat oven to 425°F. Combine flour, cornmeal, baking powder, sugar, salt and baking soda in large bowl; mix well. Cut in margarine with pastry blender or 2 knives until mixture forms coarse crumbs. Add buttermilk; mix just until dough holds together.

2. Turn dough out onto lightly floured surface; knead 8 to 10 times. Pat dough to ½-inch thickness; cut with decorative 2-inch cookie or biscuit cutter. Spray baking sheet with nonstick cooking spray and place biscuits on sheet. Brush tops lightly with beaten egg white.

3. Bake 12 to 13 minutes or until light golden brown. Serve with preserves, if desired.

Makes 1 dozen biscuits

◆ Orange-Cream Cheese Muffins ◆

MUFFINS

1¾ cups all-purpose flour
2½ teaspoons baking powder
¼ cup granulated sugar
½ teaspoon salt
¼ cup chopped nuts
1 egg
⅓ cup orange juice
⅓ cup SMUCKER'S® Sweet Orange Marmalade
¼ cup milk
¼ cup vegetable oil

FROSTING

2 cups powdered sugar
¼ cup SMUCKER'S® Sweet Orange Marmalade
1½ ounces cream cheese, softened
1 to 2 teaspoons milk

Grease bottom only of 12 muffin cups. Combine flour, baking powder, granulated sugar and salt into bowl. Add nuts; mix well. Make well in center. Combine egg, orange juice, ⅓ cup marmalade, ¼ cup milk and oil. Add all at once to dry ingredients. Stir quickly just until dry ingredients are moistened.

Fill greased muffin cups ⅔ full. Bake at 425°F for 20 to 25 minutes. Cool.

Combine all frosting ingredients; mix well. Frost cooled muffins.

Makes 12 muffins

Festive Cornmeal Biscuits

◆ Oatmeal Honey Scones ◆

¾ **Butter Flavor* CRISCO®
Stick or ¾ cup Butter
Flavor* CRISCO® all-
vegetable shortening
plus additional for
greasing**
1 **cup firmly packed light
brown sugar**
¼ **cup honey**
1 **egg**

2 **tablespoons milk**
1½ **teaspoons vanilla**
3 **cups quick oats,
uncooked**
1 **cup all-purpose flour**
½ **teaspoon baking soda**
½ **teaspoon salt**
¼ **teaspoon ground
cinnamon**
1 **cup raisins**

*Butter Flavor Crisco® is artificially flavored.

1. Heat oven to 375°F. Grease baking sheets with shortening. Place sheets of foil on countertop for cooling scones.

2. Combine ¾ cup shortening, brown sugar, honey, egg, milk and vanilla in large bowl. Beat at medium speed of electric mixer until well blended.

3. Combine oats, flour, baking soda, salt and cinnamon. Mix into creamed mixture at low speed just until blended. Stir in raisins.

4. Pat dough into 8×5-inch rectangle, ¾ inch thick. Cut into 2-inch triangles to resemble scones. Place 2 inches apart on prepared baking sheet using pancake turner.

5. Bake one baking sheet at a time at 375°F for 10 to 12 minutes or until lightly browned. *Do not overbake.* Cool 2 minutes on baking sheet. Remove scones to foil to cool completely.   *Makes about 1½ dozen scones*

◆ Date Bran Muffins ◆

1½ **cups 100% bran cereal**
1½ **cups skim milk**
⅓ **cup margarine, melted**
1 **egg**
1 **teaspoon vanilla**
1¼ **cups all-purpose flour**
4¼ **teaspoons EQUAL® FOR
RECIPES *or* 14 packets
EQUAL® sweetener *or*
½ cup plus 4 teaspoons
EQUAL® SPOONFUL™**

1 **tablespoon baking
powder**
2 **teaspoons ground
cinnamon**
½ **teaspoon salt**
½ **cup pitted dates,
chopped**

• Combine cereal and milk in medium bowl; let stand 5 minutes. Stir in margarine, egg and vanilla. Add combined flour, Equal®, baking powder, cinnamon and salt, stirring just until mixture is blended. Stir in dates.

• Spoon batter into greased muffin pans; bake in preheated 375°F oven until muffins are browned and toothpicks inserted in centers come out clean, 20 to 25 minutes. Cool in pans on wire rack 5 minutes; remove from pans and cool on wire rack.

Makes 1 dozen muffins

◆ Dijon Pesto Zucchini Muffins ◆

2½ cups all-purpose flour
½ cup chopped walnuts
4 teaspoons baking powder
¾ teaspoon salt
2 large eggs, beaten
¾ cup milk

⅔ cup Dijon Pesto Sauce (recipe follows)
¼ cup olive oil
1 cup finely shredded zucchini

DIJON PESTO SAUCE
2 cups firmly packed washed fresh basil leaves
1 cup firmly packed washed fresh parsley
¼ cup slivered almonds
¼ cup (1 ounce) grated Parmesan cheese

3 cloves garlic, coarsely chopped
½ cup FRENCH'S® Dijon Mustard
1 tablespoon FRENCH'S® Worcestershire Sauce
⅔ cup olive oil

Preheat oven to 425°F. Combine flour, walnuts, baking powder and salt in large bowl; set aside. Whisk together eggs, milk, pesto sauce and ¼ cup oil in medium bowl until blended. Stir in zucchini. Pour egg mixture into dry ingredients. Stir just until dry ingredients are moistened. (Do not overmix.) Spoon batter into 12 greased 2½-inch muffin cups.

Bake 20 to 23 minutes or until toothpick inserted into muffin centers comes out dry. Cool completely on wire rack.

Makes 12 muffins

Dijon Pesto Sauce: *Place basil, parsley, almonds, cheese and garlic in food processor. Cover and process until finely chopped. Add mustard and Worcestershire; process until well blended. Gradually add ⅔ cup oil in steady stream, processing until thick sauce forms.*

Prep Time: 15 minutes
Cook Time: 20 minutes

◆ Broccoli & Cheddar Muffins ◆

3 cups buttermilk baking
   and pancake mix
2 eggs, lightly beaten
⅔ cup milk
1 teaspoon dried basil
   leaves

1 box (10 ounces) BIRDS
   EYE® frozen Chopped
   Broccoli, thawed and
   drained
1 cup shredded Cheddar
   cheese

• Preheat oven to 350°F. Combine baking mix, eggs, milk and basil. Mix until moistened. (Do not overmix.)

• Add broccoli and cheese; stir just to combine. Add salt and pepper to taste.

• Spray 12 muffin cups with nonstick cooking spray. Pour batter into muffin cups. Bake 25 to 30 minutes or until golden brown.

• Cool 5 minutes in pan. Loosen sides of muffins with knife; remove from pan and serve warm.   *Makes 1 dozen large muffins*

Southwestern Corn Muffins: Prepare 1 box corn muffin mix according to package directions; add ⅔ cup BIRDS EYE® frozen Corn and 1 teaspoon chili powder to batter. Mix well; bake according to package directions.

Prep Time: 5 to 10 minutes
Bake Time: 25 to 30 minutes

◆ Cranberry Oat Bran Muffins ◆

2 cups all-purpose flour
1 cup oat bran
½ cup packed brown sugar
2 teaspoons baking powder
½ teaspoon baking soda
½ teaspoon salt (optional)
½ cup MIRACLE WHIP® Light
   Reduced Calorie Salad
   Dressing

3 egg whites, slightly
   beaten
½ cup skim milk
⅓ cup orange juice
1 teaspoon grated orange
   peel
1 cup coarsely chopped
   cranberries

Preheat oven to 375°F. Line 12 medium muffin cups with paper baking cups or spray with nonstick cooking spray. Mix together dry ingredients. Add combined dressing, egg whites, milk, juice and peel; mix just until moistened. Fold in cranberries. Fill prepared muffin cups almost full.

Bake 15 to 17 minutes or until golden brown.   *Makes 12 muffins*

Broccoli & Cheddar Muffins

◆ Peach-Almond Scones ◆

2 cups all-purpose flour
¼ cup plus 1 tablespoon
  sugar, divided
2 teaspoons baking powder
½ teaspoon salt
5 tablespoons margarine or
  butter
½ cup sliced almonds,
  lightly toasted, divided

2 tablespoons milk
1 egg
1 can (16 ounces) peaches,
  drained and finely
  chopped
½ teaspoon almond extract

Preheat oven to 425°F. Combine flour, ¼ cup sugar, baking powder and salt in large bowl. Cut in margarine with pastry blender or 2 knives until mixture resembles coarse crumbs. Stir in ¼ cup almonds. Lightly beat milk and egg in small bowl. Reserve 2 tablespoons milk mixture; set aside. Stir peaches and almond extract into remaining milk mixture. Stir into flour mixture until soft dough forms.

Turn out dough onto well-floured surface. Gently knead 10 to 12 times. Roll out into 9×6-inch rectangle. Cut dough into 6 (3-inch) squares using floured knife; cut diagonally into halves, forming 12 triangles. Place 2 inches apart on *ungreased* baking sheets. Brush triangles with reserved milk mixture. Sprinkle with remaining ¼ cup almonds and 1 tablespoon sugar.

Bake 10 to 12 minutes or until golden brown. Remove from baking sheets and cool on wire racks 10 minutes. Serve warm.   *Makes 12 scones*

◆ Cinnamon Apple-Nut Muffins ◆

¾ cup finely chopped
  peeled apples
½ cup sugar, divided
1 teaspoon ground
  cinnamon
1 cup all-purpose flour
¾ cup whole wheat flour
2 teaspoons baking powder

¼ teaspoon salt
1 cup low-fat milk
2 tablespoons melted
  margarine
2 egg whites, lightly
  beaten
¼ cup chopped walnuts
Sugar for topping

Preheat oven to 400°F. In small bowl, toss apples with ¼ cup sugar and cinnamon. In large bowl, combine remaining ¼ cup sugar, flours, baking powder and salt. Mix together milk, margarine and egg whites. Stir milk mixture into dry ingredients just until moistened. Add apples and nuts. Fill lightly greased muffin cups ¾ full; sprinkle each top lightly with sugar. Bake 20 to 25 minutes.   *Makes 1 dozen muffins*

Favorite recipe from **The Sugar Association, Inc.**

Peach-Almond Scones

◆ Sweet Potato Biscuits ◆

2½ cups all-purpose flour
¼ cup packed brown sugar
1 tablespoon baking powder
¾ teaspoon salt
¾ teaspoon ground cinnamon

¼ teaspoon ground ginger
¼ teaspoon ground allspice
½ cup vegetable shortening
½ cup chopped pecans
¾ cup mashed canned sweet potatoes
½ cup milk

Preheat oven to 450°F.

Combine flour, sugar, baking powder, salt, cinnamon, ginger and allspice in medium bowl. Cut in shortening with pastry blender or 2 knives until mixture resembles coarse crumbs. Stir in pecans.

Whisk together sweet potatoes and milk in separate medium bowl until smooth.

Make well in center of dry ingredients. Add sweet potato mixture; stir until mixture forms soft dough that clings together and forms ball.

Turn out dough onto well-floured surface. Knead dough gently 10 to 12 times.

Roll or pat dough to ½-inch thickness. Cut out dough with floured 2½-inch biscuit cutter.

Place biscuits 2 inches apart on *ungreased* large baking sheet. Bake 12 to 14 minutes or until tops and bottoms are golden brown. Serve warm.

Makes about 12 biscuits

◆ Cherry Orange Poppy Seed Muffins ◆

2 cups all-purpose flour
¾ cup granulated sugar
1 tablespoon poppy seeds
1 tablespoon baking powder
¼ teaspoon salt
1 cup milk

¼ cup (½ stick) butter, melted
1 egg, slightly beaten
½ cup dried tart cherries
3 tablespoons grated orange peel

Combine flour, sugar, poppy seeds, baking powder and salt in large mixing bowl. Add milk, melted butter and egg, stirring just until dry ingredients are moistened. Gently stir in cherries and orange peel. Fill paper-lined muffin cups ¾ full.

Bake in preheated 400°F oven 18 to 22 minutes or until toothpick inserted in center comes out clean. Let cool in pan 5 minutes. Remove from pan and serve warm or let cool completely.

Makes 12 muffins

Favorite recipe from **Cherry Marketing Institute, Inc.**

Sweet Potato Biscuits

◆ Apple Butter Spice Muffins ◆

½ cup sugar
1 teaspoon ground
   cinnamon
¼ teaspoon ground nutmeg
⅛ teaspoon ground allspice
½ cup pecans or walnuts,
   chopped

2 cups all-purpose flour
2 teaspoons baking powder
¼ teaspoon salt
1 cup milk
¼ cup vegetable oil
1 egg
¼ cup apple butter

Preheat oven to 400°F. Grease or paper-line 12 (2½-inch) muffin cups.

Combine sugar, cinnamon, nutmeg and allspice in large bowl. Toss 2 tablespoons sugar mixture with pecans in small bowl; set aside.

Add flour, baking powder and salt to remaining sugar mixture. Combine milk, oil and egg in medium bowl. Stir into flour mixture just until moistened.

Spoon 1 tablespoon batter into each prepared muffin cup. Spoon 1 teaspoon apple butter into each cup. Spoon remaining batter evenly over apple butter. Sprinkle reserved pecan mixture over each muffin. Bake 20 to 25 minutes or until golden brown and toothpick inserted in center comes out clean. Immediately remove from pan; cool on wire rack 10 minutes. Serve warm or cold.   *Makes 12 muffins*

Peppered Colby Muffins
◆ with BelGioioso® Mascarpone ◆

2 cups all-purpose flour
1 tablespoon baking
   powder
2 teaspoons sugar
¾ teaspoon salt
¾ teaspoon ground black
   pepper
1 cup milk

3 tablespoons butter
1 egg
1 cup (4 ounces) grated
   Colby cheese
¾ cup (6 ounces)
   BELGIOIOSO®
   Mascarpone

Grease 10 muffin cups, or line with paper baking cups; set aside.

Preheat oven to 400°F. In large bowl, combine flour, baking powder, sugar, salt and pepper. In medium bowl, whisk together milk, butter and egg. Add egg mixture and Colby cheese to flour mixture; stir until just combined. Spoon batter into prepared muffin cups. Bake 15 to 20 minutes or until golden brown. Meanwhile, let BelGioioso Mascarpone sit at room temperature 15 minutes. Turn muffins onto wire rack to cool immediately. Let cool and serve with mascarpone.   *Makes 10 muffins*

Apple Butter Spice Muffins

COOKIES

◆ Chocolate Crackletops ◆

2 cups all-purpose flour
2 teaspoons baking powder
2 cups granulated sugar
½ cup (1 stick) butter or
   margarine
4 squares (1 ounce each)
   unsweetened baking
   chocolate, chopped

4 large eggs, lightly beaten
2 teaspoons vanilla extract
1¾ cups "M&M's"® Chocolate
   Mini Baking Bits
   Additional granulated
   sugar

Combine flour and baking powder; set aside. In 2-quart saucepan over medium heat combine 2 cups sugar, butter and chocolate, stirring until butter and chocolate are melted; remove from heat. Gradually stir in eggs and vanilla. Stir in flour mixture until well blended. Chill mixture 1 hour. Stir in "M&M's"® Chocolate Mini Baking Bits; chill mixture an additional 1 hour.

Preheat oven to 350°F. Line cookie sheets with foil. With sugar-dusted hands, roll dough into 1-inch balls; roll balls in additional granulated sugar. Place about 2 inches apart onto prepared cookie sheets. Bake 10 to 12 minutes. *Do not overbake.* Cool completely on wire racks. Store in tightly covered container.   *Makes about 5 dozen cookies*

Chocolate Crackletops

◆ Chocolate Bunny Cookies ◆

**1 package DUNCAN HINES®
Chewy Fudge Brownie
Mix (19.8 ounces)**
1 egg
¼ cup water
¼ cup vegetable oil

**1⅓ cups pecan halves
(96 halves)**
**1 container DUNCAN HINES®
Dark Chocolate Fudge
Frosting**
Vanilla milk chips

1. Preheat oven to 350°F. Grease baking sheets.

2. Combine brownie mix, egg, water and oil in large bowl. Stir with spoon until well blended, about 50 strokes. Drop by 2 level teaspoonfuls 2 inches apart on prepared baking sheets. Place 2 pecan halves, flat-side up, on each cookie for ears. Bake at 350°F 10 to 12 minutes or until set. Cool 2 minutes on baking sheets. Remove to cooling racks. Cool completely.

3. Spread Dark Chocolate Fudge frosting on one cookie. Place vanilla milk chips, upside down, on frosting for eyes and nose. Dot each eye with frosting using toothpick. Repeat for remaining cookies. Allow frosting to set before storing cookies between layers of waxed paper in airtight container.

Makes 4 dozen cookies

Tip: For variety, frost cookies with Duncan Hines® Vanilla Frosting and use semi-sweet chocolate chips for the eyes and noses.

◆ Snow-Covered Almond Crescents ◆

**1 cup (2 sticks) margarine
or butter, softened**
¾ cup powdered sugar
**½ teaspoon almond extract
or 2 teaspoons vanilla
extract**
2 cups all-purpose flour
¼ teaspoon salt (optional)

**1 cup QUAKER® Oats (quick
or old-fashioned,
uncooked)**
**½ cup finely chopped
almonds**
**Additional powdered
sugar**

Preheat oven to 325°F. Beat margarine, ¾ cup powdered sugar and almond extract until fluffy. Add flour and salt; mix until well blended. Stir in oats and almonds. Shape level measuring tablespoonfuls of dough into crescents. Place on *ungreased* cookie sheet about 2 inches apart.

Bake 14 to 17 minutes or until bottoms are light golden brown. Remove to wire rack. Sift additional powdered sugar generously over warm cookies. Cool completely. Store tightly covered.

Makes about 4 dozen cookies

Chocolate Bunny Cookies

◆ Toffee Spattered Sugar Stars ◆

1¼ cups granulated sugar
1 Butter Flavor* CRISCO®
   stick or 1 cup Butter
   Flavor* CRISCO® all-
   vegetable shortening
2 eggs
¼ cup light corn syrup or
   regular pancake syrup
1 tablespoon vanilla

3 cups plus 4 tablespoons
   all-purpose flour,
   divided
¾ teaspoon baking powder
½ teaspoon baking soda
½ teaspoon salt
1 package (6 ounces) milk
   chocolate English
   toffee chips, divided

Butter Flavor Crisco® is artificially flavored.

1. Place sugar and shortening in large bowl. Beat at medium speed of electric mixer until well blended. Add eggs, syrup and vanilla; beat until well blended and fluffy.

2. Combine 3 cups flour, baking powder, baking soda and salt. Add gradually to shortening mixture, beating at low speed until well blended.

3. Divide dough into 4 equal pieces; shape each into disk. Wrap with plastic wrap. Refrigerate 1 hour or until firm.

4. Heat oven to 375°F. Place sheets of foil on countertop for cooling cookies.

5. Sprinkle about 1 tablespoon flour on large sheet of waxed paper. Place disk of dough on floured paper; flatten slightly with hands. Turn dough over; cover with another large sheet of waxed paper. Roll dough to ¼-inch thickness. Remove top sheet of waxed paper. Sprinkle about ¼ of toffee chips over dough. Roll lightly into dough. Cut out with floured star or round cookie cutter. Place 2 inches apart on *ungreased* baking sheet. Repeat with remaining dough and toffee chips.

6. Bake one baking sheet at a time at 375°F for 5 to 7 minutes or until cookies are lightly browned around edges. *Do not overbake.* Cool 2 minutes on baking sheet. Remove cookies to foil to cool completely.

Makes about 3½ dozen cookies

*Top to bottom: Pecan Cookies (page 108)
and Toffee Spattered Sugar Stars*

◆ Banana Crescents ◆

½ cup DOLE® Chopped
   Almonds, toasted
6 tablespoons sugar,
   divided
½ cup margarine, cut into
   pieces
1½ cups plus 2 tablespoons
   all-purpose flour

⅛ teaspoon salt
1 extra-ripe, medium DOLE®
   Banana
2 to 3 ounces semisweet
   chocolate chips

• Pulverize almonds with 2 tablespoons sugar.

• Beat margarine, almonds, remaining 4 tablespoons sugar, flour and salt.

• Purée banana; add to almond mixture and mix until well blended.

• Roll tablespoonfuls of dough into logs, then shape into crescents. Place on *ungreased* cookie sheet. Bake in 375°F oven 25 minutes or until golden. Cool on wire rack.

• Melt chocolate in microwavable dish at MEDIUM (50% power) 1½ to 2 minutes, stirring once. Dip ends of cookies in chocolate. Refrigerate until chocolate is set.

Makes 2 dozen cookies

◆ Smucker's® Grandmother's Jelly Cookies ◆

1½ cups sugar
1 cup butter or margarine,
   softened
1 egg
1½ teaspoons vanilla extract

3½ cups all-purpose flour
1 teaspoon salt
¾ cup SMUCKER'S® Red
   Raspberry, Strawberry
   or Peach Preserves

In large bowl, cream together sugar and butter until light and fluffy. Add egg and vanilla; beat well. Stir in flour and salt; mix well. Stir to make smooth dough. (If batter gets too hard to handle, mix with hands.)

Refrigerate about 2 hours.

Preheat oven to 375°F. Lightly grease baking sheets. On lightly floured board, roll out half of dough to about ⅛-inch thickness. Cut with 2½-inch cookie cutter. Roll out remaining dough; cut with 2½-inch cutter with hole in middle. Place on baking sheets. Bake 8 to 10 minutes or until lightly browned. Cool about 30 minutes.

To serve, spread preserves on plain cookie; top with cookie with hole.

Makes about 3 dozen cookies

Banana Crescents

Yummy Chocolate Cookies
◆ with Orange Frosting ◆

COOKIES
- ¾ **Butter Flavor* CRISCO®
  Stick or ¾ cup Butter
  Flavor* CRISCO all-
  vegetable shortening
  plus additional for
  greasing**
- 1 **cup granulated sugar**
- 1 **egg**
- ½ **teaspoon vanilla**
- 1¾ **cups all-purpose flour**
- ½ **cup unsweetened cocoa**
- 1 **teaspoon baking soda**
- ½ **teaspoon salt**
- 1 **cup mashed ripe bananas
  (2 to 3 medium
  bananas)**
- 1 **cup raisins**
- ½ **teaspoon grated orange
  peel**
- 2 **teaspoons orange juice**

FROSTING
- 1 **package (3 ounces)
  cream cheese, softened**
- ¼ **Butter Flavor* CRISCO
  Stick or ¼ cup Butter
  Flavor* CRISCO all-
  vegetable shortening**
- 3 **cups confectioners' sugar**
- 2 **tablespoons orange juice**
- ⅛ **teaspoon grated orange
  peel (optional)
  Yellow and red food color
  (optional)**

*Butter Flavor Crisco® is artificially flavored.

1. Preheat oven to 350°F. Grease cookie sheet with shortening.

2. For Cookies, combine granulated sugar, ¾ cup shortening, egg and vanilla in large bowl. Beat at medium speed of electric mixer until well blended and creamy.

3. Combine flour, cocoa, baking soda and salt in medium bowl. Stir well. Add alternately with bananas to creamed mixture, beating at low speed until well blended. Stir in raisins, ½ teaspoon orange peel and 2 teaspoons orange juice with spoon. Drop by heaping teaspoonfuls 2 inches apart onto prepared cookie sheet.

4. Bake at 350°F for 12 minutes or until set. Cool 2 minutes on cookie sheet before removing to wire rack. Cool completely.

5. For Frosting, combine cream cheese and ¼ cup shortening in medium bowl. Beat at medium speed until well blended. Gradually add confectioners' sugar and 2 tablespoons orange juice; beat until creamy. Add ⅛ teaspoon orange peel and food color, if desired. Beat until blended. Frost cookies.

Makes about 3 dozen cookies

*Yummy Chocolate Cookies with
Orange Frosting*

◆ Pecan Cookies ◆

1¼ cups confectioners' sugar
1 Butter Flavor* CRISCO®
   Stick or 1 cup Butter
   Flavor* CRISCO® all-
   vegetable shortening
2 eggs
¼ cup light corn syrup or
   regular pancake syrup

1 tablespoon vanilla
2 cups all-purpose flour
1½ cups finely chopped
   pecans
¾ teaspoon baking powder
½ teaspoon baking soda
½ teaspoon salt
   Confectioners' sugar

Butter Flavor Crisco® is artificially flavored.

1. Heat oven to 350°F. Place sheets of foil on countertop for cooling cookies.

2. Place 1¼ cups confectioners' sugar and shortening in large bowl. Beat at medium speed of electric mixer until well blended. Add eggs, syrup and vanilla; beat until well blended and fluffy.

3. Combine flour, pecans, baking powder, baking soda and salt. Add to shortening mixture; beat at low speed until well blended.

4. Shape dough into 1-inch balls. Place 2 inches apart on *ungreased* baking sheet.

5. Bake for 15 to 18 minutes or until bottoms of cookies are light golden brown. *Do not overbake.* Cool 2 minutes on baking sheet. Roll in confectioners' sugar while warm. Remove cookies to foil to cool completely. Reroll in confectioners' sugar prior to serving.
   Makes about 4 dozen cookies

◆ Favorite Lemon Cookies ◆

2 cups all-purpose flour
½ teaspoon baking soda
¼ teaspoon salt
1 cup granulated sugar
⅓ cup butter or margarine,
   softened
1 egg

Grated peel and juice of
   1 SUNKIST® lemon
   (3 tablespoons juice)
Lemon Frosting (recipe
   follows) or decorating
   icing*

Decorating icing comes in tubes in assorted colors.

Sift together flour, baking soda and salt. In large bowl, cream together sugar and butter. Add egg, lemon peel and juice; beat well. Gradually blend in dry ingredients. Divide dough into 4 parts; cover and chill 1 hour or longer.

On lightly floured board, roll ¼ of dough at a time to ⅛-inch thickness. Cut with lightly floured cookie cutters and place on well-greased cookie sheets. Bake at 375°F 10 minutes or until lightly browned. Remove and cool on wire racks. Spread cookies with Lemon Frosting.

Makes about 4 to 5 dozen cookies

Lemon Frosting

3 cups confectioners' sugar, divided
⅓ cup butter or margarine, softened, divided

Grated peel of ½ SUNKIST® lemon
2 to 3 tablespoons fresh squeezed lemon juice

In bowl, cream together 1 cup sugar and butter. Add remaining 2 cups sugar, lemon peel and juice; mix until smooth. To prevent frosting from drying out too quickly, cover with damp cloth while frosting cookies.

Makes about 1⅓ cups

◆ Orange Marmalade Cookies ◆

COOKIES

2 cups granulated sugar
½ cup shortening
2 eggs
1 cup sour cream
½ cup SMUCKER'S® Sweet Orange Marmalade

4 cups all-purpose flour
2 teaspoons baking powder
1 teaspoon baking soda
½ teaspoon salt

ICING

3 cups powdered sugar
½ cup butter or margarine
¼ cup SMUCKER'S® Sweet Orange Marmalade

Orange juice

Combine granulated sugar, shortening and eggs; beat until well mixed. Add sour cream and ½ cup marmalade; mix well. Add remaining cookie ingredients; mix well. Chill dough.

Drop by rounded teaspoonfuls onto greased cookie sheets. Bake at 400°F for 8 to 10 minutes. Cool.

Combine all icing ingredients, adding enough orange juice for desired spreading consistency (none may be needed). Ice cooled cookies.

Makes 5 dozen cookies

◆ Watermelon Slices ◆

1 package DUNCAN HINES®
   Golden Sugar Cookie
   Mix
1 egg
¼ cup canola oil

1½ tablespoons water
12 drops red food coloring
5 drops green food coloring
   Chocolate sprinkles

1. Combine cookie mix, egg, oil and water in large bowl. Stir until thoroughly blended; reserve ⅓ cup dough.

2. For red cookie dough, combine remaining dough with red food coloring. Stir until evenly tinted. On waxed paper, shape dough into 12-inch-long roll with one side flattened. Cover; refrigerate with flat side down until firm.

3. For green cookie dough, combine reserved ⅓ cup dough with green food coloring in small bowl. Stir until evenly tinted. Place between 2 layers of waxed paper. Roll dough into 12×4-inch rectangle. Refrigerate 15 minutes. Preheat oven to 375°F.

4. To assemble, remove green dough rectangle from refrigerator. Remove top layer of waxed paper. Trim edges along both 12-inch sides. Remove red dough log from refrigerator. Place red dough log, flattened side up, along center of green dough. Mold green dough up to edge of flattened side of red dough. Remove bottom layer of waxed paper. Trim excess green dough, if necessary.

5. Cut chilled roll, flat side down, into ¼-inch-thick slices with sharp knife. Place slices 2 inches apart on *ungreased* baking sheets. Sprinkle chocolate sprinkles on red dough for seeds. Bake at 375°F for 7 minutes or until set. Cool 1 minute on baking sheets. Remove to cooling racks. Cool completely. Store between layers of waxed paper in airtight container. *Makes 3 to 4 dozen cookies*

◆ Chunky Peanut Butter Cookies ◆

½ cup chunky peanut butter
2 tablespoons reduced-
   calorie margarine
1⅓ cups packed brown sugar

2 egg whites
½ teaspoon vanilla
1⅛ cups all-purpose flour
¼ teaspoon baking soda

Preheat oven to 375°F. Spray cookie sheet with nonstick cooking spray. In large bowl, beat peanut butter and margarine with electric mixer on medium speed. Beat in sugar, egg whites and vanilla. Blend in flour and baking soda. Drop by teaspoonfuls, about 2 inches apart, onto cookie sheet. Press each cookie flat with back of fork. Bake 8 to 10 minutes. *Makes about 34 cookies*

Favorite recipe from **The Sugar Association, Inc.**

Watermelon Slices

◆ Peanut Butter Chewies ◆

1½ cups creamy peanut
   butter
1½ cups firmly packed brown
   sugar
1 Butter Flavor* CRISCO®
   Stick or 1 cup Butter
   Flavor* CRISCO® all-
   vegetable shortening
2 eggs

1 can (14 ounces)
   sweetened condensed
   milk
2 teaspoons vanilla
2 cups all-purpose flour
1 teaspoon baking soda
1 teaspoon salt
1½ cups chopped pecans

Butter Flavor Crisco® is artificially flavored.

1. Heat oven to 350°F. Place sheets of foil on countertop for cooling cookies.

2. Combine peanut butter, sugar and shortening in large bowl. Beat at medium speed of electric mixer until well blended. Beat in eggs, sweetened condensed milk and vanilla.

3. Combine flour, baking soda and salt. Mix into shortening mixture at low speed until just blended. Stir in pecans.

4. Drop rounded tablespoonfuls of dough 2 inches apart onto *ungreased* baking sheets.

5. Bake one baking sheet at a time at 350°F for 10 to 11 minutes or until lightly browned on bottom. *Do not overbake.* Cool 2 minutes on baking sheets. Remove cookies to foil to cool completely.

Makes about 4 dozen cookies

◆ Almond Raspberry Macaroons ◆

2 cups BLUE DIAMOND®
   Blanched Almond Paste
1 cup granulated sugar
6 large egg whites

Powdered sugar
Seedless raspberry jam,
   stirred until smooth

Beat almond paste and granulated sugar until mixture resembles coarse cornmeal. Beat in egg whites, a little at a time, until thoroughly combined. Place heaping teaspoonfuls onto cookie sheet lined with waxed paper or parchment paper. Coat finger with powdered sugar and make indentation in middle of each cookie. (Coat finger with powdered sugar each time.) Bake at 350°F for 15 to 20 minutes or until lightly browned. Remove from oven and fill each indentation with about ¼ teaspoon raspberry jam. Cool. If using waxed paper, carefully peel paper off cookies when cooled.

Makes about 30 cookies

Peanut Butter Chewies

◆ Peanut Butter Secrets ◆

COOKIES

1¼ cups firmly packed light brown sugar
¾ cup creamy peanut butter
½ CRISCO® Stick or ½ cup CRISCO® all-vegetable shortening
3 tablespoons milk
1 tablespoon vanilla

1 egg
1¾ cups all-purpose flour
¾ teaspoon salt
¾ teaspoon baking soda
30 to 36 chocolate covered miniature peanut butter cups, unwrapped

GLAZE

1 cup semisweet chocolate chips
2 tablespoons creamy peanut butter

1 teaspoon Butter Flavor* CRISCO® Stick or 1 teaspoon Butter Flavor* CRISCO® all-vegetable shortening

Butter Flavor Crisco® is artificially flavored.

1. Heat oven to 375°F. Place sheets of foil on countertop for cooling cookies.

2. Combine brown sugar, ¾ cup peanut butter, ½ cup shortening, milk and vanilla in large bowl. Beat at medium speed of electric mixer until well blended. Add egg. Beat just until blended.

3. Combine flour, salt and baking soda. Add to shortening mixture at low speed. Mix just until blended.

4. Form rounded tablespoonfuls around each peanut butter cup. Enclose entirely. Place 2 inches apart onto *ungreased* baking sheet. Flatten slightly in crisscross pattern with tines of fork.

5. Bake one baking sheet at a time at 375°F for 7 to 8 minutes or until set and just beginning to brown. *Do not overbake.* Cool 2 minutes on baking sheet. Remove cookies to foil to cool completely.

6. For glaze, combine chocolate chips, 2 tablespoons peanut butter and 1 teaspoon shortening in microwave-safe cup. Microwave at MEDIUM (50% power). Stir after 1 minute. Repeat until smooth (or melt on rangetop in small saucepan on very low heat). Dip cookie tops in glaze.

Makes about 3 dozen cookies

◆ Crispy Oat Drops ◆

1 cup (2 sticks) butter or margarine, softened
½ cup granulated sugar
½ cup firmly packed light brown sugar
1 large egg
2 cups all-purpose flour
½ cup quick-cooking or old-fashioned oats, uncooked

1 teaspoon cream of tartar
½ teaspoon baking soda
¼ teaspoon salt
1¾ cups "M&M's"® Semi-Sweet Chocolate Mini Baking Bits
1 cup toasted rice cereal
½ cup shredded coconut
½ cup coarsely chopped pecans

Preheat oven to 350°F. In large bowl cream butter and sugars until light and fluffy; beat in egg. In medium bowl combine flour, oats, cream of tartar, baking soda and salt; blend flour mixture into creamed mixture. Stir in "M&M's"® Semi-Sweet Chocolate Mini Baking Bits, cereal, coconut and pecans. Drop by heaping tablespoonfuls about 2 inches apart onto *ungreased* cookie sheets. Bake 10 to 13 minutes or until lightly browned. Cool completely on wire racks. Store in tightly covered container. *Makes about 4 dozen cookies*

◆ Hot 'n' Nutty Cookies ◆

¾ cup unsalted butter, softened
1 cup granulated sugar
1 cup packed brown sugar
2 cups peanut butter, smooth or crunchy
½ cup macadamia nuts, chopped (optional)

2 eggs
1 teaspoon vanilla extract
1 teaspoon TABASCO® brand Pepper Sauce
3 cups all-purpose flour
1 teaspoon salt
1 teaspoon baking soda

Preheat oven to 350°F. Lightly butter and flour cookie sheet.

Cream butter, granulated sugar and brown sugar in large bowl. Stir in peanut butter and macadamia nuts; mix until well blended. Add eggs, vanilla and TABASCO® sauce. Mix until well combined.

Mix together flour, salt and baking soda in another bowl. Add to nut mixture and stir until blended.

Spoon about 1 heaping tablespoon of batter on prepared cookie sheet. Coat tines of fork in flour and score each cookie in crisscross pattern. Bake 15 to 17 minutes or until edges begin to turn golden. Set aside to cool on racks.

Makes 2 dozen cookies

Crispy Oat Drops

◆ Peanut Butter & Jelly Cookies ◆

1 package DUNCAN HINES®
   Peanut Butter Cookie
   Mix
¾ cup quick-cooking oats
   (not instant or old-
   fashioned)

1 egg
¼ cup canola oil
½ cup grape jelly
½ cup confectioners' sugar
2 teaspoons water

1. Preheat oven to 375°F.

2. Combine cookie mix, oats, egg and oil in large bowl. Stir until thoroughly blended. Divide dough into 4 equal portions. Shape each portion into 12-inch-long log on waxed paper. Place logs on *ungreased* cookie sheets. Press back of spoon down center of each log to form indentation. Bake at 375°F for 10 to 12 minutes or until light golden brown. Press back of spoon down center of each log again. Cool 2 minutes on cookie sheets. Remove to cooling racks. Cool completely. Spoon 2 tablespoons jelly along indentation of each log.

3. Combine sugar and water in small bowl. Stir until smooth. Drizzle over each log. Allow glaze to set. Cut each log diagonally into 12 slices with large, sharp knife. Store between layers of waxed paper in airtight container.

Makes about 48 cookies

◆ Gingerbread Kids ◆

2 ripe, small DOLE® Bananas
4 cups all-purpose flour
1 teaspoon baking soda
1½ teaspoons ground ginger
1 teaspoon ground
   cinnamon

½ cup butter, softened
½ cup packed brown sugar
½ cup dark molasses
   Prepared icing and
   candies

• Purée bananas in blender. Combine flour, baking soda, ginger and cinnamon. Cream butter and sugar until light and fluffy. Beat in molasses and bananas until blended. Stir in flour mixture with wooden spoon until completely blended. (Dough will be stiff.) Cover; refrigerate 1 hour.

• Preheat oven to 375°F. Divide dough into 4 parts. Roll out each part to ⅛-inch thickness on lightly floured surface. Cut out cookies using small gingerbread people cutters. Use favorite cookie cutters for any smaller amounts of remaining dough.

• Bake on greased cookie sheets 10 to 15 minutes or until just brown around edges. Cool completely on wire racks. Decorate as desired with favorite icing and candies.

Makes 30 to 35 cookies

Peanut Butter & Jelly Cookies

◆ Cream Cheese and Jelly Cookies ◆

1 package (8 ounces)
   reduced-fat cream
   cheese, softened
¾ cup margarine, softened
2½ teaspoons EQUAL® FOR
   RECIPES *or* 8 packets
   EQUAL® sweetener *or*
   ⅓ cup EQUAL®
   SPOONFUL™

2 cups all-purpose flour
¼ teaspoon salt
¼ cup black cherry or
   seedless raspberry
   spreadable fruit

• Beat cream cheese, margarine and Equal® in medium bowl until fluffy; mix in flour and salt to form soft dough. Cover and refrigerate until dough is firm, about 3 hours.

• Roll dough on lightly floured surface into circle ⅛ inch thick; cut into rounds with 3-inch cutter. Place rounded ¼ teaspoon spreadable fruit in center of each round; fold rounds into halves and crimp edges firmly with tines of fork. Pierce tops of cookies with tip of sharp knife. Bake cookies on greased cookie sheets in preheated 350°F oven until lightly browned, about 10 minutes. Cool on wire racks. *Makes about 3 dozen cookies*

◆ Spicy Lemon Crescents ◆

1 cup (2 sticks) butter or
   margarine, softened
1½ cups powdered sugar,
   divided
½ teaspoon lemon extract
½ teaspoon grated lemon
   zest
2 cups cake flour
½ cup finely chopped
   almonds, walnuts or
   pecans

1 teaspoon ground
   cinnamon
½ teaspoon ground
   cardamom
½ teaspoon ground nutmeg
1¾ cups "M&M's"® Chocolate
   Mini Baking Bits

Preheat oven to 375°F. Lightly grease cookie sheets; set aside. In large bowl cream butter and ½ *cup sugar;* add lemon extract and zest until well blended. In medium bowl combine flour, nuts, cinnamon, cardamom and nutmeg; add to creamed mixture until well blended. Stir in "M&M's"® Chocolate Mini Baking Bits. Using 1 tablespoon of dough at a time, form into crescent shapes; place about 2 inches apart onto prepared cookie sheets. Bake 12 to 14 minutes or until edges are golden. Cool 2 minutes on cookie sheets. Gently roll warm crescents in remaining *1 cup sugar.* Cool completely on wire racks. Store in tightly covered container. *Makes about 2 dozen cookies*

◆ Fruit Burst Cookies ◆

1 cup margarine or butter,
   softened
¼ cup sugar
1 teaspoon almond extract

2 cups all-purpose flour
½ teaspoon salt
1 cup finely chopped nuts
   SMUCKER'S® Simply Fruit

Cream margarine and sugar until light and fluffy. Blend in almond extract. Combine flour and salt; add to mixture and blend well. Shape level tablespoonfuls dough into balls; roll in nuts. Place 2 inches apart on *ungreased* cookie sheets; flatten slightly. Indent centers; fill with fruit spread. Bake at 400°F for 10 to 12 minutes or just until lightly browned. Cool.

Makes 2½ dozen cookies

◆ Apple 'n Spice Pizza Cookie ◆

¾ cup (1½ sticks) butter,
   softened
¾ cup granulated sugar
½ cup firmly packed brown
   sugar
1 egg
1 teaspoon vanilla extract
1½ cups unsifted all-purpose
   flour

1½ teaspoons ground
   cinnamon
¾ teaspoon baking soda
¾ teaspoon salt
1 cup shredded apple
   (1 medium)
¾ cup uncooked oats

TOPPING

1 package (6 ounces)
   semisweet chocolate
   chips
1 cup chopped pecans

½ cup sifted confectioners'
   sugar
2 teaspoons milk

Preheat oven to 375°F. Generously grease 14-inch round pizza pan. In large electric mixer bowl, beat butter, granulated sugar and brown sugar until creamy. Beat in egg and vanilla. Add flour, cinnamon, baking soda and salt; beat until batter is smooth. Stir in apple and oats. Spread batter evenly into pizza pan. Bake 20 to 25 minutes or until golden.

Remove from oven. Sprinkle chips onto hot cookie. Let stand 5 minutes or until chips soften and look shiny. Spread with metal spatula to make frosting. Sprinkle nuts on top. Cool completely.

In small bowl, combine confectioners' sugar and milk; mix until smooth. Drizzle on top of pizza cookie. *Makes 1 (14-inch) cookie*

Favorite recipe from **The Sugar Association, Inc.**

◆ Double Chocolate Oat Cookies ◆

1 package (12 ounces)
    semi-sweet chocolate
    pieces, divided (about
    2 cups)
½ cup margarine or butter,
    softened
½ cup sugar
1 egg
¼ teaspoon vanilla
¾ cup all-purpose flour
¾ cup QUAKER® Oats (quick
    or old fashioned,
    uncooked)
1 teaspoon baking powder
¼ teaspoon baking soda
¼ teaspoon salt (optional)

Preheat oven to 375°F. Melt 1 cup chocolate pieces in small saucepan; set aside. Beat margarine and sugar until fluffy; add melted chocolate, egg and vanilla. Add combined flour, oats, baking powder, baking soda and salt; mix well. Stir in remaining chocolate pieces. Drop by rounded tablespoonfuls onto *ungreased* cookie sheet. Bake 8 to 10 minutes. Cool 1 minute on cookie sheet; remove to wire rack. *Makes about 3 dozen cookies*

◆ Brownie Turtle Cookies ◆

2 squares (1 ounce each)
    unsweetened baking
    chocolate
⅓ cup solid vegetable
    shortening
1 cup granulated sugar
½ teaspoon vanilla extract
2 large eggs
1¼ cups all-purpose flour
½ teaspoon baking powder
½ teaspoon salt
1 cup "M&M's"® Milk
    Chocolate Mini Baking
    Bits, divided
1 cup pecan halves
⅓ cup caramel ice cream
    topping
⅓ cup shredded coconut
⅓ cup finely chopped
    pecans

Preheat oven to 350°F. Lightly grease cookie sheets; set aside. Heat chocolate and shortening in 2-quart saucepan over low heat, stirring constantly until melted; remove from heat. Mix in sugar, vanilla and eggs. Blend in flour, baking powder and salt. Stir in ⅔ *cup "M&M's"® Milk Chocolate Mini Baking Bits.* For each cookie, arrange 3 pecan halves, with ends almost touching at center, on prepared cookie sheets. Drop dough by rounded teaspoonfuls onto center of each group of pecans; mound the dough slightly. Bake 8 to 10 minutes just until set. *Do not overbake.* Cool completely on wire racks. In small bowl combine ice cream topping, coconut and chopped nuts; top each cookie with about 1½ teaspoons mixture. Press remaining ⅓ *cup "M&M's"® Milk Chocolate Mini Baking Bits* into topping. *Makes about 2½ dozen cookies*

Double Chocolate Oat Cookies

◆ Jam-Up Oatmeal Cookies ◆

1½ cups firmly packed brown sugar
1 Butter Flavor* CRISCO® Stick or 1 cup Butter Flavor* CRISCO® all-vegetable shortening plus additional for greasing
2 eggs
2 teaspoons almond extract
2 cups all-purpose flour
1 teaspoon baking powder

1 teaspoon salt
½ teaspoon baking soda
2½ cups quick oats (not instant or old fashioned), uncooked
1 cup finely chopped pecans
1 jar (12 ounces) strawberry jam
Granulated sugar for sprinkling

Butter Flavor Crisco® is artificially flavored.

1. Combine brown sugar and 1 cup shortening in large bowl. Beat at medium speed of electric mixer until well blended. Beat in eggs and almond extract.

2. Combine flour, baking powder, salt and baking soda. Mix into shortening mixture at low speed until just blended. Stir in oats and chopped nuts with spoon. Cover and refrigerate at least 1 hour.

3. Heat oven to 350°F. Grease baking sheets with shortening. Place sheets of foil on countertop for cooling cookies.

4. Roll out dough, ½ at a time, to about ¼-inch thickness on floured surface. Cut out with 2½-inch round cookie cutter. Place 1 teaspoon jam in center of ½ of rounds. Top with remaining rounds. Press edges to seal. Prick centers; sprinkle with granulated sugar. Place 1 inch apart on baking sheets.

5. Bake one baking sheet at a time at 350°F for 12 to 15 minutes or until lightly browned. *Do not overbake.* Cool 2 minutes on baking sheets. Remove cookies to foil to cool completely.   *Makes about 2 dozen cookies*

Jam-Up Oatmeal Cookies

◆ Peanut Butter Stars ◆

1 package DUNCAN HINES® Peanut Butter Cookie Mix	1 package (3½ ounces each) chocolate sprinkles
1 egg	1 package (7 ounces each) milk chocolate candy stars
¼ cup vegetable oil	
1 tablespoon water	

1. Preheat oven to 375°F.

2. Combine cookie mix, contents of peanut butter packet from Mix, egg, oil and water in large bowl. Stir until thoroughly blended. Shape dough into 1-inch balls. Roll in chocolate sprinkles. Place 2 inches apart on *ungreased* baking sheets. Bake at 375°F for 8 to 10 minutes or until set. Immediately place milk chocolate candy stars on top of hot cookies. Cool 1 minute on baking sheets. Remove to cooling racks. Cool completely. Store in airtight containers.

Makes 4½ to 5 dozen cookies

Tip: For evenly baked cookies, place baking sheets in center of oven, not touching the sides.

◆ Date-Oatmeal Cookies ◆

1 cup all-purpose flour	⅔ cup packed brown sugar
1 cup DOLE® Chopped Dates or Pitted Prunes, chopped	1 medium ripe DOLE® Banana, mashed (½ cup)
¾ cup quick-cooking oats	¼ cup margarine, softened
1 teaspoon ground cinnamon	1 egg
¾ teaspoon baking powder	1 teaspoon vanilla extract
	Vegetable cooking spray

• Combine flour, dates, oats, cinnamon and baking powder in bowl; set aside.

• Beat together sugar, banana, margarine, egg and vanilla until well blended. Add flour mixture; stir until ingredients are moistened.

• Drop dough by rounded teaspoonfuls, 2 inches apart, onto baking sheets sprayed with vegetable cooking spray.

• Bake at 375°F 10 to 12 minutes or until lightly brown. Remove cookies to wire rack; cool. Store in airtight container.

Makes 32 cookies

Prep Time: 15 minutes
Bake Time: 12 minutes

Peanut Butter Stars

◆ Mini Pizza Cookies ◆

1 (20-ounce) tube
refrigerated sugar
cookie dough
2 cups (16 ounces)
prepared pink frosting
"M&M's"® Chocolate Mini
Baking Bits

Variety of additional toppings
such as shredded
coconut, granola,
raisins, nuts, small
pretzels, snack mixes,
sunflower seeds,
popped corn and mini
marshmallows

Preheat oven to 350°F. Lightly grease cookie sheets; set aside. Divide dough into 8 equal portions. On lightly floured surface, roll each portion of dough into ¼-inch-thick circle; place about 2 inches apart onto prepared cookie sheets. Bake 10 to 13 minutes or until golden brown on edges. Cool completely on wire racks. Spread top of each pizza with frosting; sprinkle with "M&M's"® Chocolate Mini Baking Bits and 2 or 3 suggested toppings.

Makes 8 cookies

◆ Orange Pecan Refrigerator Cookies ◆

2⅓ cups all-purpose flour
½ teaspoon baking soda
¼ teaspoon salt
½ cup butter or margarine,
softened
½ cup packed brown sugar
½ cup granulated sugar

1 egg, lightly beaten
Grated peel of 1 SUNKIST®
Orange
3 tablespoons fresh
squeezed orange juice
¾ cup pecan pieces

In bowl, stir together flour, baking soda and salt. In large bowl, blend together butter, brown sugar and granulated sugar. Add egg, orange peel and juice; beat well. Stir in pecans. Gradually beat in flour mixture. (Dough will be stiff.) Divide mixture in half and shape each half (on a long piece of waxed paper) into a roll about 1¼ inches in diameter and 12 inches long. Roll up tightly in waxed paper. Chill several hours or overnight.

Cut into ¼-inch slices and arrange on lightly greased cookie sheets. Bake at 350°F for 10 to 12 minutes or until lightly browned. Cool on wire racks.

Makes about 6 dozen cookies

Chocolate Filled Sandwich Cookies: *Cut each roll into ⅛-inch slices and bake as above. When cool, to make each sandwich cookie, spread about 1 teaspoon canned chocolate fudge frosting on bottom side of one cookie; cover with second cookie of same shape.* Makes about 4 dozen double cookies

Mini Pizza Cookies

◆ Chocolate Peanut Butter Cup Cookies ◆

COOKIES

- 1 cup semi-sweet chocolate chips
- 2 squares (1 ounce each) unsweetened baking chocolate
- 1 cup sugar
- ½ Butter Flavor* CRISCO® Stick or ½ cup Butter Flavor* CRISCO® all-vegetable shortening

- 2 eggs
- 1 teaspoon salt
- 1 teaspoon vanilla
- 1½ cups plus 2 tablespoons all-purpose flour
- ½ teaspoon baking soda
- ¾ cup finely chopped peanuts
- 36 miniature peanut butter cups, unwrapped

DRIZZLE

- 1 cup peanut butter chips

Butter Flavor Crisco® is artificially flavored.

1. Heat oven to 350°F. Place sheets of foil on countertop for cooling cookies.

2. For cookies, combine chocolate chips and chocolate squares in microwave-safe measuring cup or bowl. Microwave at MEDIUM (50% power). Stir after 2 minutes. Repeat until smooth (or melt on rangetop in small saucepan on very low heat). Cool slightly.

3. Combine sugar and shortening in large bowl. Beat at medium speed of electric mixer until blended and crumbly. Beat in eggs, 1 at a time, then salt and vanilla. Reduce speed to low. Add chocolate slowly. Mix until well blended. Stir in flour and baking soda with spoon until well blended. Shape dough into 1¼-inch balls. Roll in nuts. Place 2 inches apart on *ungreased* baking sheet.

4. Bake at 350°F for 8 to 10 minutes or until set. *Do not overbake.* Press peanut butter cup into center of each cookie immediately. Press cookie against cup. Cool 2 minutes on baking sheet before removing to cooling rack. Cool completely.

5. For drizzle, place peanut butter chips in heavy resealable food storage bag. Seal. Microwave at MEDIUM. Knead bag after 1 minute. Repeat until smooth (or melt by placing bag in hot water). Cut tiny tip off corner of bag. Squeeze out and drizzle over cookies. *Makes 3 dozen cookies*

Chocolate Peanut Butter Cup Cookies

◆ Lemon Cookies ◆

⅔ cup **MIRACLE WHIP® Salad Dressing**
1 **two-layer yellow cake mix**
2 **eggs**
2 **teaspoons grated lemon peel**

⅔ cup **ready-to-spread vanilla frosting**
4 **teaspoons lemon juice**

• Preheat oven to 375°F.

• Blend salad dressing, cake mix and eggs at low speed with electric mixer until moistened. Add peel. Beat on medium speed 2 minutes. (Dough will be stiff.)

• Drop rounded teaspoonfuls of dough, 2 inches apart, onto greased cookie sheet.

• Bake 9 to 11 minutes or until lightly browned. (Cookies will still appear soft.) Cool 1 minute; remove from cookie sheet. Cool completely on wire rack.

• Stir together frosting and juice until well blended. Spread on cookies.

Makes about 4 dozen cookies

◆ Oatmeal Chocolate Chip Cookies ◆

1 **can (20 ounces) DOLE® Crushed Pineapple, undrained**
1½ **cups packed brown sugar**
1 **cup margarine, softened**
1 **egg**
¼ **teaspoon almond extract**
4 **cups uncooked rolled oats**
2 **cups all-purpose flour**
1 **teaspoon baking powder**

1 **teaspoon salt**
1 **teaspoon ground cinnamon**
½ **teaspoon ground nutmeg**
2 **cups flaked coconut**
1 **package (12 ounces) semisweet chocolate chips**
¾ **cup DOLE® Slivered Almonds, toasted**

• Preheat oven to 350°F. Grease cookie sheets. Drain pineapple well, reserving ½ cup syrup.

• In large bowl, beat brown sugar and margarine until light and fluffy. Beat in egg. Beat in pineapple, reserved ½ cup liquid and almond extract.

• In small bowl, combine oats, flour, baking powder, salt, cinnamon and nutmeg. Add to margarine mixture; beat until blended. Stir in coconut, chocolate chips and almonds.

• Drop by heaping tablespoonfuls onto prepared cookie sheets. Flatten cookies slightly with back of spoon. Bake 20 to 25 minutes or until golden. Cool on wire racks.

Makes about 5 dozen cookies

◆ Kahlúa® Kisses ◆

¾ teaspoon instant coffee
    powder
⅓ cup water
1 cup plus 2 tablespoons
    sugar, divided

¼ cup KAHLÚA® Liqueur
3 egg whites, at room
    temperature
¼ teaspoon cream of tartar
    Dash salt

In heavy 2-quart saucepan, dissolve coffee powder in water. Add 1 cup sugar; stir over low heat until sugar dissolves. *Do not allow to boil.* Stir in Kahlúa®. Brush down sides of pan with pastry brush frequently dipped in cold water. Bring mixture to a boil over medium heat. *Do not stir.* Boil until candy thermometer registers 240° to 242°F, about 15 minutes, adjusting heat if necessary to prevent boiling over. Mixture will be very thick. Remove from heat (temperature will continue to rise).

Immediately beat egg whites with cream of tartar and salt until soft peaks form. Add remaining 2 tablespoons sugar; continue beating until stiff peaks form. Gradually beat hot Kahlua® syrup into egg whites, beating after each addition to thoroughly mix. Continue beating 4 to 5 minutes or until meringue is very thick, firm and cooled to lukewarm.

Line baking sheet with foil, shiny side down. Using pastry bag fitted with large star tip, pipe meringue into kisses about 1½ inches wide at base and 1½ inches high onto baking sheet. Bake on center rack of 200°F oven for 4 hours. Without opening door, turn off oven. Let kisses dry in oven 2 more hours or until crisp. Remove from oven; cool completely on baking sheet. Store in airtight container up to 1 week. *Makes 2½ dozen cookies*

◆ Chunky Butter Christmas Cookies ◆

1¼ cups butter, softened
1 cup packed brown sugar
½ cup dairy sour cream
1 egg
2 teaspoons vanilla
1½ cups all-purpose flour
1 teaspoon baking soda
1 teaspoon salt

1½ cups uncooked old
    fashioned or quick oats
1 (10-ounce) package
    white chocolate pieces
1 cup flaked coconut
1 (3½-ounce) jar
    macadamia nuts,
    coarsely chopped

Beat butter and sugar in large bowl until light and fluffy. Blend in sour cream, egg and vanilla. Add combined flour, baking soda and salt; mix well. Stir in oats, white chocolate pieces, coconut and nuts. Drop rounded teaspoonfuls of dough, 2 inches apart, onto *ungreased* cookie sheet. Bake in preheated 375°F oven 10 to 12 minutes or until edges are lightly browned. Cool 1 minute; remove to cooling rack. *Makes 5 dozen cookies*

Favorite recipe from **Wisconsin Milk Marketing Board**

◆ Marvelous Macaroons ◆

1 can (8 ounces) DOLE®
  Crushed Pineapple,
  undrained
1 can (14 ounces)
  sweetened condensed
  milk
1 package (7 ounces)
  flaked coconut

½ cup margarine, melted
½ cup DOLE® Chopped
  Almonds, toasted
1 teaspoon grated lemon
  peel
¼ teaspoon almond extract
1 cup all-purpose flour
1 teaspoon baking powder

• Preheat oven to 350°F. Drain pineapple well, pressing out excess juice with back of spoon. In large bowl, combine drained pineapple, milk, coconut, margarine, almonds, lemon peel and almond extract.

• In small bowl, combine flour and baking powder. Beat into pineapple mixture until blended. Drop heaping tablespoonfuls of dough 1 inch apart onto greased cookie sheets.

• Bake 13 to 15 minutes or until lightly browned. Garnish with whole almonds, if desired. Cool on wire racks. Store in covered container in refrigerator.

Makes about 3½ dozen cookies

◆ Peanut Butter Oatmeal Treats ◆

1¾ cups all-purpose flour
1 teaspoon baking soda
½ teaspoon salt
1 cup granulated sugar
1 cup firmly-packed light
  brown sugar
½ cup butter or margarine,
  softened
½ cup SMUCKER'S® Creamy
  Natural Peanut Butter
  or LAURA SCUDDER'S®
  Smooth Old-Fashioned
  Peanut Butter

2 eggs
¼ cup milk
1 teaspoon vanilla
2½ cups uncooked oats
1 cup semi-sweet chocolate
  chips

Combine flour, baking soda and salt; set aside. In large mixing bowl, combine sugars, butter and peanut butter. Beat until light and creamy. Beat in eggs, milk and vanilla. Stir in flour mixture, oats and chocolate chips. Drop dough by rounded teaspoonfuls about 3 inches apart onto *ungreased* cookie sheets.

Bake at 350°F for 15 minutes or until lightly browned.

Makes 3½ dozen cookies

Marvelous Macaroons

◆ Cherry Surprises ◆

1 package DUNCAN HINES®
   Golden Sugar Cookie
   Mix
36 to 42 candied cherries

½ cup semisweet chocolate
   chips
1 teaspoon shortening

1. Preheat oven to 375°F. Grease cookie sheets.

2. Prepare cookie mix following package directions for original recipe. Shape thin layer of dough around each candied cherry. Place 2 inches apart on prepared cookie sheets. Bake at 375°F for 8 minutes or until set but not browned. Cool 1 minute on cookie sheets. Remove to cooling racks. Cool completely.

3. Combine chocolate chips and shortening in small resealable plastic food storage bag. Place bag in bowl of hot water for several minutes. Dry with paper towel. Knead until blended and chocolate is smooth. Snip pinpoint hole in corner of bag. Drizzle chocolate over cooled cookies. Allow drizzle to set before storing between layers of waxed paper in airtight container.

Makes 3 to 3½ dozen cookies

◆ Milky Way® Bar Cookies ◆

3 MARS® MILKY WAY® Bars
   (2.15 ounces each),
   chopped, divided
2 tablespoons milk
½ cup butter or margarine,
   softened
⅓ cup packed light brown
   sugar

1 egg
½ teaspoon vanilla extract
1⅔ cups all-purpose flour
½ teaspoon baking soda
¼ teaspoon salt
½ cup chopped walnuts

Preheat oven to 350°F. Stir 1 Mars® Milky Way® Bar with milk in small saucepan over low heat until melted and smooth; cool. In large bowl, beat butter and brown sugar until creamy. Beat in egg, vanilla and melted Mars® Milky Way® Bar mixture. Combine flour, baking soda and salt in small bowl. Stir into chocolate mixture. Add remaining chopped Mars® Milky Way® Bars and nuts; stir gently. Drop dough by rounded teaspoonfuls onto *ungreased* cookie sheets.

Bake 12 to 15 minutes or until cookies are just firm to the touch. Cool on wire racks.

Makes about 2 dozen cookies

Cherry Surprises

◆ Butter Flavored Brickle Drizzles ◆

COOKIES

¾ Butter Flavor* CRISCO®
Stick or ¾ cup Butter
Flavor* CRISCO® all-
vegetable shortening
plus additional for
greasing
1¼ cups firmly packed light
brown sugar
⅓ cup milk
1 egg

1½ teaspoons vanilla
3 cups quick oats,
uncooked
1 cup all-purpose flour
½ teaspoon baking soda
½ teaspoon salt
¼ teaspoon ground
cinnamon
1 cup almond brickle chips

DRIZZLE

1 cup milk chocolate chips

Butter Flavor Crisco® is artificially flavored.

1. Heat oven to 375°F. Grease baking sheets with shortening. Place sheets of foil on countertop for cooling cookies.

2. For cookies, combine ¾ cup shortening, brown sugar, milk, egg and vanilla in large bowl. Beat at medium speed of electric mixer until well blended.

3. Combine oats, flour, baking soda, salt and cinnamon. Mix into creamed mixture at low speed just until blended.

4. Shape dough into 1-inch balls. Press tops into brickle chips. Place cookies, brickle side up, 2 inches apart onto prepared baking sheet.

5. Bake one baking sheet at a time at 375°F for 9 to 11 minutes or until lightly browned. *Do not overbake.* Cool 2 minutes on baking sheet. Remove cookies to foil to cool completely.

6. For drizzle, place chocolate chips in heavy resealable plastic bag. Seal. Microwave at MEDIUM (50% power). Knead bag after 1 minute. Repeat until smooth (or melt by placing in bowl of hot water). Cut tiny tip off corner of bag. Squeeze out and drizzle over cookies.   *Makes about 2½ dozen cookies*

Butter Flavored Brickle Drizzles

◆ Chocolate Chip Lollipops ◆

1 package **DUNCAN HINES®**
    Chocolate Chip Cookie
    Mix
1 **egg**

⅓ cup **canola oil**
2 tablespoons **water**
    Flat ice cream sticks
    Assorted decors

1. Preheat oven to 375°F.

2. Combine cookie mix, egg, oil and water in large bowl. Stir until thoroughly blended. Shape dough into 32 (1-inch) balls. Place balls 3 inches apart on *ungreased* baking sheets. Push ice cream stick into center of each ball. Flatten dough ball with hand to form round lollipop. Decorate by pressing decors onto dough. Bake at 375°F for 8 to 9 minutes or until light golden brown. Cool 1 minute on baking sheets. Remove to cooling racks. Cool completely. Store in airtight container.

Makes 2½ to 3 dozen cookies

Tip: For best results, use shiny baking sheets for baking cookies. Dark baking sheets cause cookie bottoms to become too brown.

◆ Jack o'Lantern Cookies ◆

1 cup **butter or margarine,**
    softened
½ cup **firmly packed light**
    brown sugar
½ cup **granulated sugar**
2 **eggs**
1 teaspoon **vanilla extract**
1⅓ cups **all-purpose flour**
1 teaspoon **baking soda**
1½ cups **uncooked rolled oats**
    (quick or old-fashioned)

1 package (6 ounces) **dried**
    fruit bits
1½ cups (6 ounces) **GJETOST**
    cheese, cut into ¼-inch
    cubes
1 cup **chopped walnuts**
2 cups **confectioners' sugar**
2 to 3 tablespoons **milk**
    Orange and green food
    coloring

Preheat oven to 375°F. In small bowl with electric mixer, cream butter and sugars until light and fluffy. Blend in eggs and vanilla. In another small bowl, combine flour and baking soda; stir into dough. Blend in oats, fruit, cheese and walnuts. Shape tablespoons of dough into balls and place 2 inches apart on *ungreased* cookie sheets. Press down lightly with glass. Bake 10 minutes or until golden. Cool on wire racks.

In medium bowl, blend confectioners' sugar with enough milk to make thick frosting. Divide in half. Color ½ with green food coloring and remainder with orange food coloring. Decorate cookies in pumpkin design.

Makes about 4½ dozen cookies

Favorite recipe from **Norseland Inc.**

Chocolate Chip Lollipops

◆ Caramel Nut Chocolate Cookies ◆

1½ cups firmly packed light
    brown sugar
⅔ CRISCO® Stick or ⅔ cup
    CRISCO® all-vegetable
    shortening
1 tablespoon water
1 teaspoon vanilla
2 eggs
1¾ cups all-purpose flour
⅓ cup unsweetened cocoa
    powder

½ teaspoon salt
¼ teaspoon baking soda
2 cups (12 ounces)
    miniature semisweet
    chocolate chips
1 cup chopped pecans
20 to 25 caramels,
    unwrapped and halved

1. Heat oven to 375°F. Place sheets of foil on countertop for cooling cookies.

2. Place brown sugar, shortening, water and vanilla in large bowl. Beat at medium speed of electric mixer until well blended. Add eggs; beat well.

3. Combine flour, cocoa, salt and baking soda. Add to shortening mixture; beat at low speed just until blended. Stir in chocolate chips.

4. Shape dough into 1¼-inch balls. Dip tops in chopped pecans. Place 2 inches apart on *ungreased* baking sheet. Press caramel half in center of each ball.

5. Bake one baking sheet at a time at 375°F for 7 to 9 minutes or until cookies are set. *Do not overbake.* Cool 2 minutes on baking sheet. Remove cookies to foil to cool completely.
Makes about 4 dozen cookies

◆ Cap'n's Cookies ◆

1 cup firmly packed brown
    sugar
½ cup (1 stick) margarine
    or butter, softened
2 eggs
1 teaspoon vanilla
1½ cups all-purpose flour

1 teaspoon baking powder
½ teaspoon salt (optional)
2 cups CAP'N CRUNCH®
    Cereal, any flavor
1 cup raisins or semi-sweet
    chocolate pieces

Preheat oven to 375°F. Lightly grease cookie sheet. Beat sugar and margarine until fluffy. Blend in eggs and vanilla. Add combined flour, baking powder and salt; mix well. Stir in cereal and raisins. Drop by rounded teaspoonfuls onto prepared cookie sheet.

Bake 10 to 12 minutes or until light golden brown. Cool 2 minutes on cookie sheet; remove to wire rack. Cool completely. Store tightly covered.
Makes about 3 dozen cookies

Caramel Nut Chocolate Cookies

◆ Honey Nut Rugelach ◆

1 cup butter or margarine, softened
3 ounces cream cheese, softened
½ cup honey, divided
2 cups all-purpose flour
1 teaspoon lemon juice

1 teaspoon ground cinnamon, divided
1 cup finely chopped walnuts
½ cup dried cherries or cranberries

Cream butter and cream cheese until fluffy. Add 3 tablespoons honey and mix well. Mix in flour until dough holds together. Form into ball, wrap and refrigerate 2 hours or longer. Divide dough into 4 equal portions. On floured surface, roll one portion of dough into 9-inch circle. Combine 2 tablespoons honey and lemon juice; mix well. Brush dough with ¼ of honey mixture; sprinkle with ¼ teaspoon cinnamon. Combine walnuts and cherries in small bowl; drizzle with remaining 3 tablespoons honey and mix well. Spread ¼ of walnut mixture onto circle of dough, stopping ½ inch from outer edge. Cut circle into 8 triangular pieces. Roll up dough starting at wide outer edge and rolling toward tip. Gently bend both ends to form crescent. Place on oiled parchment paper-lined baking sheet and refrigerate 20 minutes or longer. Repeat with remaining dough and filling. Bake at 350°F 20 to 25 minutes or until golden brown. Cool on wire racks.   *Makes 32 cookies*

Freezing Tip: Unbaked cookies can be placed in freezer-safe containers or bags and frozen until ready to bake.

Favorite recipe from **National Honey Board**

◆ Thumbprint Cookies ◆

1 cup butter or margarine
¼ cup sugar
1 teaspoon almond extract
2 cups all-purpose flour
½ teaspoon salt

1 cup finely chopped nuts, if desired
SMUCKER'S® Preserves or Jam (any flavor)

Combine butter and sugar; beat until light and fluffy. Blend in almond extract. Add flour and salt; mix well.

Shape level tablespoonfuls of dough into balls; roll in nuts. Place on *ungreased* cookie sheets; flatten slightly. Indent centers; fill with preserves or jam.

Bake at 400°F for 10 to 12 minutes or just until lightly browned.
Makes 2½ dozen cookies

◆ Oat Pecan Praline Cookies ◆

1¼ cups firmly packed brown
    sugar
1 cup (2 sticks) margarine
    or butter, softened
2 eggs
2 tablespoons molasses
1 teaspoon maple flavoring
1¼ cups all-purpose flour

1 teaspoon baking soda
2½ cups QUAKER® Oats
    (quick or old-fashioned,
    uncooked)
1 cup pecans, coarsely
    chopped
¾ cup pecan halves (about
    48 halves)

Beat together sugar and margarine until creamy. Add eggs, molasses and maple flavoring; beat well. Add combined flour and baking soda; mix well. Stir in oats and chopped nuts; mix well. Cover dough; chill at least 1 hour.

Heat oven to 350°F. Lightly grease cookie sheet. Shape dough into 1-inch balls. Place 3 inches apart on prepared cookie sheet. Flatten each ball by pressing 1 pecan half in center. Bake 10 to 12 minutes or until deep golden brown. Immediately remove to wire rack; cool completely. Store in tightly covered container.

Makes about 4 dozen cookies

◆ Chocolate Candy Cookies ◆

⅔ cup MIRACLE WHIP® Salad
    Dressing
1 two-layer devil's food
    cake mix

2 eggs
1 (8-ounce) package candy-
    coated chocolate
    candies

• Preheat oven to 375°F.

• Blend salad dressing, cake mix and eggs at low speed with electric mixer until moistened. Beat on medium speed 2 minutes. Stir in chocolate candies. (Dough will be stiff.)

• Drop by rounded teaspoonfuls, 2 inches apart, onto greased cookie sheets.

• Bake 9 to 11 minutes or until almost set. (Cookies will still appear soft.) Cool 1 minute; remove from cookie sheets.

Makes about 4½ dozen cookies

◆ Peanut Butter Spritz Sandwiches ◆

**1 package DUNCAN HINES®
Peanut Butter Cookie
Mix**
¼ cup canola oil

1 egg
**4 bars (1.55 ounces each)
milk chocolate**

1. Preheat oven to 375°F.

2. Combine cookie mix, contents of peanut butter packet from Mix, oil and egg in large bowl. Stir until thoroughly blended. Fill cookie press with dough. Press desired shapes 2 inches apart onto *ungreased* baking sheet. Bake at 375°F for 7 to 9 minutes or until set but not browned. Cool 1 minute on baking sheet.

3. Cut each milk chocolate bar into 12 sections by following division marks on bars.

4. To assemble, carefully remove one cookie from cookie sheet. Place one milk chocolate section on bottom of warm cookie; top with second cookie. Press together to make sandwich. Repeat with remaining cookies. Place sandwich cookies on wire rack until chocolate is set. Store in airtight container.

Makes 3½ to 4 dozen sandwich cookies

Tip: For best appearance, use cookie press plates that give solid shapes.

Double Chocolate Peanut Cookies
◆ Made with Snickers® Bars ◆

¾ cup margarine, softened
⅓ cup granulated sugar
**⅓ cup firmly packed light
brown sugar**
1 large egg
1 teaspoon vanilla extract
1½ cups all-purpose flour

**2 tablespoons unsweetened
cocoa powder**
¾ teaspoon baking soda
¼ teaspoon salt
**4 SNICKERS® Bars (2.07
ounces each), coarsely
chopped**

Preheat oven to 350°F.

In large mixing bowl, cream margarine and sugars. Add egg and vanilla; beat until light and fluffy. Combine flour, cocoa powder, baking soda and salt; gradually blend into creamed mixture. Stir in chopped Snickers® Bars until evenly blended. Drop by heaping tablespoonfuls about 2 inches apart onto *ungreased* cookie sheets. Bake 9 to 13 minutes. Cool 1 minute on cookie sheets; remove to wire cooling racks. Store in tightly covered container.

Makes about 3 dozen cookies

Peanut Butter Spritz Sandwiches

◆ Nutty Toppers ◆

PEANUT BUTTER LAYER
- 1¼ cups firmly packed light brown sugar
- ¾ cup creamy peanut butter
- ½ CRISCO® Stick or ½ cup CRISCO® all-vegetable shortening
- 3 tablespoons milk
- 1 tablespoon vanilla
- 1 egg
- 1¾ cups all-purpose flour
- ¾ teaspoon salt
- ¾ teaspoon baking soda

CHOCOLATE LAYER
- ½ cup dough from Peanut Butter Layer
- 1 egg
- 1 tablespoon unsweetened cocoa powder
- 48 pecans or walnut halves

1. Heat oven to 375°F. Place sheets of foil on countertop for cooling cookies.

2. For peanut butter layer, combine brown sugar, peanut butter, shortening, milk and vanilla in large bowl. Beat at medium speed of electric mixer until well blended. Add 1 egg. Beat just until blended. Combine flour, salt and baking soda. Add to shortening mixture at low speed. Mix just until blended.

3. For chocolate layer, combine ½ cup reserved dough from Peanut Butter Layer, 1 egg and cocoa. Beat at low speed until blended.

4. Form peanut butter layer dough into 1-inch balls. Place 2 inches apart on *ungreased* baking sheets. Flatten slightly with bottom of greased and sugared glass. Place leveled ½ teaspoon of chocolate layer on flattened dough. Press nut into each center. Repeat with remaining dough.

5. Bake one baking sheet at a time at 375°F for 7 to 8 minutes or until set and just beginning to brown. *Do not overbake.* Cool 2 minutes on baking sheets. Remove cookies to foil to cool completely.   *Makes about 3 dozen cookies*

◆ Almond Lace Cookies ◆

- ¼ cup butter
- ½ cup sugar
- ½ cup BLUE DIAMOND® Blanched Almond Paste
- ¼ cup all-purpose flour
- 2 tablespoons milk
- 2 teaspoons grated orange peel
- ½ teaspoon almond extract
- ¼ teaspoon salt

Cream butter and sugar. Beat in almond paste. Add remaining ingredients. Mix well. Drop rounded teaspoonfuls onto cookie sheet, 3 inches apart (cookies will spread). Bake at 350°F for 8 to 10 minutes or until edges are lightly browned. Cool 3 to 4 minutes on cookie sheet; remove and cool on wire rack.   *Makes 1½ dozen cookies*

Nutty Toppers

◆ Double Nut Chocolate Chip Cookies ◆

1 package **DUNCAN HINES®** **Moist Deluxe Yellow Cake Mix**
½ cup butter or margarine, melted
1 egg

1 cup semisweet chocolate chips
½ cup finely chopped pecans
1 cup sliced almonds, divided

1. Preheat oven to 375°F. Grease cookie sheets.

2. Combine cake mix, butter and egg in large bowl. Mix at low speed with electric mixer until just blended. Stir in chocolate chips, pecans and ¼ cup almonds. Shape rounded tablespoonfuls of dough into balls. Place remaining ¾ cup almonds in shallow bowl. Press tops of cookies in almonds. Place 1 inch apart on prepared cookie sheets.

3. Bake 9 to 11 minutes or until lightly browned. Cool 2 minutes on cookie sheets. Remove to cooling racks.   *Makes 3 to 3½ dozen cookies*

◆ Chocolate Covered Cherry Cookies ◆

1 cup sugar
½ cup butter, softened
1 egg
1½ teaspoons vanilla
1½ cups all-purpose flour
¼ cup unsweetened cocoa powder
¼ teaspoon baking powder
¼ teaspoon baking soda

¼ teaspoon salt
42 maraschino cherries, drained reserving 4 to 5 teaspoons juice
1 (6-ounce) package semi-sweet chocolate pieces
½ cup sweetened condensed milk

Beat sugar and butter in large bowl until light and fluffy. Blend in egg and vanilla. Combine flour, cocoa, baking powder, baking soda and salt in small bowl. Add to sugar mixture; mix well. Shape dough into 1-inch balls; place on *ungreased* cookie sheet. Indent centers; fill each with 1 cherry. Combine chocolate pieces and sweetened condensed milk in small saucepan; stir over low heat until smooth. Blend in enough reserved cherry juice to reach spreading consistency. Drop 1 teaspoon chocolate mixture over each cherry, spreading to cover cherry. Bake in preheated 350°F oven 12 minutes or until set.

Makes 3½ dozen cookies

Favorite recipe from **Wisconsin Milk Marketing Board**

Double Nut Chocolate Chip Cookies

◆ Chocolate Raspberry Thumbprints ◆

½ cup (1 stick) butter or
   margarine, softened
½ cup granulated sugar
½ cup firmly packed light
   brown sugar
1 large egg
1 teaspoon vanilla extract

2 cups all-purpose flour
½ teaspoon baking powder
1¾ cups "M&M's"® Chocolate
   Mini Baking Bits,
   divided
Powdered sugar
½ cup raspberry jam

In large microwave-safe bowl melt butter in microwave; add sugars and mix well. Stir in egg and vanilla. In medium bowl combine flour and baking powder; blend into butter mixture. *Stir in 1¼ cups "M&M's"® Chocolate Mini Baking Bits;* refrigerate dough 1 hour. Preheat oven to 350°F. Lightly grease cookie sheets. Roll dough into 1-inch balls and place about 2 inches apart onto prepared cookie sheets. Make an indentation in center of each ball with thumb. Bake 8 to 10 minutes. Remove from oven and reindent, if necessary; transfer to wire racks. Lightly dust warm cookies with powdered sugar; fill each indentation with ½ teaspoon raspberry jam. Sprinkle with remaining *½ cup "M&M's"® Chocolate Mini Baking Bits.* Cool completely. Dust with additional powdered sugar, if desired. Store in tightly covered container.

Makes about 4 dozen cookies

◆ Pineapple Raisin Jumbles ◆

2 cans (8 ounces each)
   DOLE® Crushed
   Pineapple, undrained
½ cup margarine, softened
½ cup sugar
1 teaspoon vanilla extract
1 cup all-purpose flour

4 teaspoons grated orange
   peel
1 cup DOLE® Blanched
   Slivered Almonds,
   toasted
1 cup DOLE® Seedless Raisins

• Preheat oven to 350°F. Drain pineapple well, pressing out excess liquid with back of spoon.

• In large bowl, beat margarine and sugar until light and fluffy. Stir in pineapple and vanilla. Beat in flour and orange peel. Stir in almonds and raisins.

• Drop heaping tablespoons of dough 2 inches apart onto greased cookie sheets.

• Bake 20 to 22 minutes or until firm. Cool on wire racks.

Makes 2 to 2½ dozen cookies

Chocolate Raspberry Thumbprints

BROWNIES & BAR COOKIES

◆ Brownie Kiss Cups ◆

1 package DUNCAN HINES®	**⅓ cup water**
Chewy Fudge Brownie	**⅓ cup canola oil**
Mix	**25 milk chocolate candy**
1 egg	**kisses, unwrapped**

1. Preheat oven to 350°F. Place 25 (2-inch) foil liners in muffin pans or on cookie sheets.

2. Combine brownie mix, egg, water and oil in large bowl. Stir with spoon until well blended, about 50 strokes. Fill each liner with 2 tablespoonfuls batter. Bake at 350°F for 17 to 20 minutes. Remove from oven. Place 1 milk chocolate candy kiss on each cupcake. Bake 1 minute longer. Cool 5 to 10 minutes in pans. Remove to cooling racks. Cool completely.   *Makes 25 brownie cups*

Brownie Kiss Cups

◆ Four-Layer Oatmeal Bars ◆

OAT LAYER

½ cup Butter Flavor*
CRISCO® all-vegetable
shortening plus
additional for greasing
1 egg
1½ cups quick oats,
uncooked

1 cup firmly packed brown
sugar
¾ cup plus 2 tablespoons
all-purpose flour
1 teaspoon cinnamon
¾ teaspoon baking soda
¼ teaspoon salt

FRUIT LAYER

1½ cups sliced, peeled fresh
peaches** (cut slices in
half crosswise)
¾ cup crushed pineapple,
undrained
¾ cup sliced, peeled Granny
Smith apple (cut slices
in half crosswise)

½ cup chopped walnuts or
pecans
¼ cup granulated sugar
2 tablespoons cornstarch
½ teaspoon ground nutmeg

CREAM CHEESE LAYER

1 (8-ounce) package cream
cheese, softened
1 egg
¼ cup granulated sugar

½ teaspoon fresh lemon
juice
½ teaspoon vanilla

Butter Flavor Crisco® is artificially flavored.
** *Diced canned peaches, well drained, can be used in place of fresh peaches.*

1. Preheat oven to 350°F. Grease 11×7-inch glass baking dish with shortening.

2. For oat layer, combine ½ cup shortening and 1 egg in large bowl. Stir with fork until blended. Add oats, brown sugar, flour, cinnamon, baking soda and salt. Stir until well blended and crumbs form. Press 1¾ cups crumbs lightly onto bottom of prepared dish. Reserve remaining crumbs. Bake 10 minutes. Cool completely.

3. For fruit layer, combine peaches, pineapple, apple, nuts, ¼ cup granulated sugar, cornstarch and nutmeg in medium saucepan. Cook and stir on medium heat until mixture comes to a boil and thickens. Cool completely. *Increase oven temperature to 375°F.*

4. For cream cheese layer, combine cream cheese, 1 egg, ¼ cup granulated sugar, lemon juice and vanilla in medium bowl. Beat at medium speed of electric mixer until well blended. Spread over cooled oat layer. Spoon cooled fruit mixture over cheese layer. Spread gently to cover cream cheese. Sprinkle reserved crumbs over fruit. Bake 30 minutes. Cool to room temperature. Refrigerate. Cut into bars about 2×1¾ inches.   *Makes about 20 bars*

Four-Layer Oatmeal Bars

◆ Devil's Fudge Brownies ◆

½ cup (1 stick) butter or
    margarine, softened
1 cup granulated sugar
2 large eggs
2 tablespoons FRANK'S®
    REDHOT® Hot Sauce
1 teaspoon vanilla extract
⅔ cup all-purpose flour

½ cup unsweetened cocoa
¼ teaspoon baking soda
1 cup chopped pecans
½ cup mini chocolate chips
    Pecan halves
    Confectioners' sugar
    Ice cream (optional)
    Fudge sauce (optional)

Beat butter, granulated sugar, eggs, REDHOT sauce and vanilla in large bowl of electric mixer on medium speed until light and fluffy. Blend in flour, cocoa and baking soda. Beat until smooth. Stir in chopped nuts and mini chips. Spread into greased deep-dish 9-inch microwave-safe pie plate. Arrange pecan halves on top.

Place pie plate on top of inverted custard cup in microwave oven. Microwave, uncovered, on HIGH 6 minutes or until toothpick inserted in center comes out clean, turning once. (Brownie may appear moist on surface. Do not overcook.) Cool completely on wire rack.

Dust top with confectioners' sugar. Cut into wedges. Serve with ice cream and fudge sauce, if desired. *Makes 8 servings*

Prep Time: 20 minutes
Cook Time: 6 minutes

◆ Creamy Cappuccino Brownies ◆

1 package (21 to 24
    ounces) brownie mix
1 tablespoon coffee
    crystals *or* 1 teaspoon
    espresso powder
2 tablespoons warm water

1 cup (8 ounces) Wisconsin
    Mascarpone cheese
3 tablespoons sugar
1 egg
    Powdered sugar

Grease bottom of 13×9-inch baking pan. Prepare brownie mix according to package directions. Pour half of batter into prepared pan. Dissolve coffee crystals in water; add Mascarpone, sugar and egg. Blend until smooth. Drop by spoonfuls over brownie batter; top with remaining brownie batter. With knife, swirl cheese mixture through brownies creating marbled effect. Bake at 375°F 30 to 35 minutes or until toothpick inserted in center comes out clean. Sprinkle with powdered sugar. *Makes 2 dozen brownies*

Favorite recipe from **Wisconsin Milk Marketing Board**

◆ Oatmeal Praline Cheese Bars ◆

COOKIE BASE

¾ cup Butter Flavor* CRISCO® all-vegetable shortening plus additional for greasing

1¼ cups firmly packed light brown sugar

1 egg

⅓ cup milk

1½ teaspoons vanilla

1½ cups uncooked quick oats

1 cup all-purpose flour

1 cup finely chopped pecans

¼ cup toasted wheat germ

½ teaspoon baking soda

½ teaspoon salt

½ teaspoon ground cinnamon

TOPPING

1 package (8 ounces) cream cheese, softened

⅓ cup firmly packed light brown sugar

2 eggs

2 tablespoons all-purpose flour

½ teaspoon vanilla

½ teaspoon salt

½ cup almond brickle chips

½ cup finely chopped pecans

Butter Flavor Crisco® is artificially flavored.

1. Heat oven to 350°F. Grease 13×9-inch baking pan with shortening.

2. For cookie base, place 1¼ cups brown sugar, ¾ cup shortening, 1 egg, milk and 1½ teaspoons vanilla in large bowl. Beat at medium speed of electric mixer until well blended.

3. Combine oats, 1 cup flour, 1 cup pecans, wheat germ, baking soda, ½ teaspoon salt and cinnamon. Add to shortening mixture; beat at low speed just until blended.

4. Spread dough onto bottom of prepared pan.

5. Bake at 350°F for 15 to 17 minutes or until surface is light golden brown and edges pull away from sides of pan. *Do not overbake.*

6. For topping, place cream cheese, ⅓ cup brown sugar, 2 eggs, 2 tablespoons flour, ½ teaspoon vanilla and ½ teaspoon salt in medium bowl. Beat at medium speed of electric mixer until smooth. Pour mixture over cookie base. Sprinkle with almond brickle chips and ½ cup pecans.

7. Bake 15 to 17 minutes longer or until topping is set. *Do not overbake.* Cool completely on cooling rack. Cut into 2×1½-inch bars. Refrigerate.

Makes about 3 dozen bars

◆ Crunchy Brownie Bars ◆

CRUNCHY LAYER

1½ cups quick-cooking oats (not instant or old fashioned)

¾ cup firmly packed light brown sugar

¾ cup all-purpose flour

¼ teaspoon baking soda

¼ teaspoon salt

¾ cup butter or margarine, melted

BROWNIE LAYER

1 package DUNCAN HINES® Fudge Brownie Mix

2 eggs

⅓ cup water

¼ cup canola oil

FROSTING

1½ squares (1½ ounces) unsweetened chocolate, chopped

3 tablespoons butter or margarine

2¼ cups confectioners' sugar (sift if lumpy)

1½ teaspoons vanilla extract

3 tablespoons hot water

1. Preheat oven to 350°F.

2. **For crunchy layer,** combine oats, brown sugar, flour, baking soda and salt in large bowl. Add melted butter; stir until blended. Press mixture onto bottom of *ungreased* 13×9×2-inch pan. Bake at 350°F for 10 minutes. (Mixture will not be completely baked.)

3. **For brownie layer,** combine brownie mix, contents of fudge packet from Mix, eggs, ⅓ cup water and oil in large bowl. Stir until thoroughly blended. Pour batter slowly over hot crunchy layer; spread evenly. Bake at 350°F for 40 to 45 minutes or until set. *Do not overbake.* Cool completely.

4. **For frosting,** place chocolate and butter in medium saucepan. Heat on low heat until melted. Add confectioners' sugar, vanilla extract and ***hot*** water. Stir until smooth. Immediately pour hot frosting on brownies; spread evenly. Let stand until frosting is set. Cut into bars.   *Makes 24 large or 32 small bars*

Tip: Always use the pan size called for in Duncan Hines® recipes. Using a different size can give the brownies a different texture.

Crunchy Brownie Bars

◆ Choco Cheesecake Squares ◆

⅓ **cup butter, softened**
⅓ **cup packed light brown**
  sugar
1 **cup plus**
    1 tablespoon
    all-purpose flour,
    divided
½ **cup chopped pecans**
  (optional)

1 **cup semisweet chocolate**
  chips
1 **package (8 ounces)**
    cream cheese, softened
¼ **cup granulated sugar**
1 **large egg**
1 **teaspoon vanilla**

Preheat oven to 350°F. Grease 8-inch square baking pan; set aside. Beat butter and brown sugar in large bowl until light and fluffy. Add 1 cup flour. Beat until well combined. Stir in nuts, if desired. (Mixture will be crumbly.) Press evenly into prepared pan. Bake 15 minutes.

Place chocolate chips in 1 cup glass measuring cup. Melt in microwave oven at HIGH 2½ to 3 minutes, stirring after 2 minutes. Beat cream cheese and granulated sugar in medium bowl until light and fluffy. Add remaining 1 tablespoon flour, egg and vanilla; beat until smooth. Gradually stir in melted chocolate, mixing well. Pour cream cheese mixture over partially baked crust. Return to oven; bake 15 minutes or until set. Remove pan to wire rack; cool completely. Cut into 2-inch squares.   *Makes about 16 squares*

◆ Chewy Red Raspberry Bars ◆

1 **cup firmly packed light**
  brown sugar
½ **cup butter or margarine,**
  at room temperature
½ **teaspoon almond extract**
1 **cup all-purpose flour**

1 **cup quick-cooking or old-**
  fashioned oats
1 **teaspoon baking powder**
½ **cup SMUCKER'S®**
  Red Raspberry
  Preserves

Combine brown sugar and butter; beat until fluffy. Beat in almond extract. Mix in flour, oats and baking powder until crumbly. Reserve ¼ cup mixture; pat remaining mixture on bottom of greased 8-inch square baking pan. Dot preserves over crumb mixture in pan; sprinkle with reserved crumb mixture.

Bake at 350°F for 30 to 40 minutes or until brown. Cool on wire rack. Cut into bars.   *Makes 12 bars*

Choco Cheesecake Squares

◆ Praline Brownies ◆

BROWNIES
1 package DUNCAN HINES®
  Chocolate Lovers' Milk
  Chocolate Chunk
  Brownie Mix

2 eggs
⅓ cup water
⅓ cup canola oil
¾ cup chopped pecans

TOPPING
¾ cup firmly packed brown
  sugar
¾ cup chopped pecans
¼ cup butter or margarine,
  melted

2 tablespoons milk
½ teaspoon vanilla extract

1. Preheat oven to 350°F. Grease 9-inch square pan.

2. For brownies, combine brownie mix, eggs, water, oil and ¾ cup pecans in large bowl. Stir with spoon until well blended, about 50 strokes. Spread in prepared pan. Bake at 350°F for 35 to 40 minutes. Remove from oven.

3. For topping, combine brown sugar, ¾ cup pecans, melted butter, milk and vanilla extract in medium bowl. Stir with spoon until well blended. Spread over hot brownies. Return to oven. Bake for 15 minutes longer or until topping is set. Cool completely in pan on wire rack. Cut into bars.

Makes about 16 brownies

◆ Banana Caramel Bars ◆

2½ cups all-purpose flour
1 cup sugar
1 teaspoon baking powder
1 cup margarine, cut up

1 large egg, beaten
2 extra-ripe, medium DOLE®
  Bananas
½ cup caramel topping

• Combine flour, sugar and baking powder in large bowl. Cut in margarine with pastry blender until mixture resembles coarse meal. Slowly stir in egg, mixing with a fork until crumbly. Pat half of mixture into 13×9-inch baking pan to form crust.

• For filling, mash bananas. Blend bananas with caramel topping. Spread evenly over crust.

• Sprinkle remaining crumb mixture over filling. Pat gently. Bake in 375°F oven 35 minutes or until golden brown. Cool pan on wire rack. Cut into bars when cooled.

Makes 24 bars

Praline Brownies

◆ Rich and Fudgy Frosted Brownies ◆

8 ounces unsweetened chocolate
1 cup butter
3 cups sugar
5 eggs
2 tablespoons light corn syrup

1 tablespoon vanilla extract
1¾ cups all-purpose flour
1 cup coarsely chopped nuts (optional)
Frosting (recipe follows)

Preheat oven to 375°F. Melt chocolate and butter in medium saucepan over low heat, stirring constantly. Set aside and let cool. Beat sugar, eggs, corn syrup and vanilla in large bowl with electric mixer on high speed 10 minutes. Blend in chocolate mixture on low speed. Add flour, beating just until blended. Stir in nuts, if desired. Spread in greased 13×9-inch pan. Bake 30 to 35 minutes. *Do not overbake.* Cool completely before frosting. *Makes 24 brownies*

Frosting

6 tablespoons butter or margarine, softened
2⅔ cups powdered sugar
⅓ cup unsweetened cocoa powder

⅓ cup milk
1 tablespoon vanilla extract

Beat butter in small bowl until creamy. Add powdered sugar and cocoa alternately with milk; beat until frosting is of spreading consistency. Stir in vanilla. Spread on cooled brownies.

Favorite recipe from **Bob Evans**®

◆ Walnut Apple Dumpling Bars ◆

6 tablespoons (¾ stick) butter or margarine
1 cup packed light brown sugar
1 cup all-purpose flour
1½ teaspoons ground cinnamon
1 teaspoon baking powder
2 eggs

1½ cups coarsely chopped walnuts
1 Granny Smith or pippin apple, coarsely grated* (about 1 cup lightly packed)
Powdered sugar

It's not necessary to peel or core apple. Use hand-held grater, turning apple as you go, until only core remains.

Preheat oven to 350°F.

Melt butter in 3-quart saucepan. Add brown sugar. Stir until sugar is melted and mixture begins to bubble; cool. In small bowl combine flour, cinnamon and baking powder; mix to blend thoroughly. Beat eggs into butter mixture in saucepan, 1 at a time, then add flour mixture. Add walnuts and apple. Turn into buttered and floured 9-inch square baking pan; smooth top. Bake 25 to 35 minutes or until toothpick inserted in center comes out clean and edges begin to pull away from sides of pan. Cool completely on rack. Cut into 3×1-inch bars. Garnish with powdered sugar. *Makes 24 bars*

Favorite recipe from **Walnut Marketing Board**

◆ Double Decker Bars ◆

**2 ripe, medium DOLE®
   Bananas, divided
1 cup granulated sugar
1 cup packed brown sugar
½ cup margarine, softened
2 eggs**

**3 tablespoons peanut
   butter
1 teaspoon vanilla extract
2 cups all-purpose flour
2 teaspoons baking powder
¼ teaspoon salt**

• Place 1 banana in blender. Process until puréed; measure ½ cup. Beat sugars and margarine in large bowl. Beat in puréed banana, eggs, peanut butter and vanilla.

• Combine flour, baking powder and salt in medium bowl. Gradually beat dry ingredients into banana mixture.

• Spread half of batter in greased 13×9-inch baking pan.

• Finely chop remaining banana; sprinkle over batter in pan. Cover with remaining batter.

• Bake 30 to 35 minutes. Cool completely. Frost with Peanut Butter Frosting. Cut into bars. *Makes about 24 bars*

Peanut Butter Frosting

**1 ripe, small DOLE® Banana
¼ cup peanut butter**

**2 tablespoons milk
2½ cups powdered sugar**

• Place banana in blender. Process until puréed; measure ¼ cup. Combine banana, peanut butter and milk. Slowly beat in powdered sugar until thick and smooth.

◆ Double Mint Brownies ◆

1 package DUNCAN HINES®
  Chocolate Lovers'
  Chewy Recipe Fudge
  Brownie Mix, Family
  Style
1 egg
⅓ cup water
⅓ cup vegetable oil
½ teaspoon peppermint
  extract

24 chocolate-covered
  peppermint patties
  (1½ inches each)
1 cup confectioners' sugar,
  divided
4 teaspoons milk, divided
  Red food coloring
  Green food coloring

1. Preheat oven to 350°F. Grease bottom of 13×9×2-inch pan. Combine brownie mix, egg, water, oil and peppermint extract in large bowl. Stir with spoon until well blended, about 50 strokes. Spread in prepared pan. Bake brownies following package directions. Place peppermint patties on warm brownies. Cool completely.

2. Combine ½ cup confectioners' sugar, 2 teaspoons milk and 1 drop red food coloring in small bowl. Stir until smooth. Place in small resealable plastic food storage bag; set aside. Repeat with remaining ½ cup confectioners' sugar, remaining 2 teaspoons milk and 1 drop green food coloring. Cut pinpoint hole in bottom corner of each bag. Drizzle pink and green glazes over brownies. Allow glazes to set before cutting into bars.   *Makes 24 brownies*

Tip: To prevent overdone edges and underdone center, wrap foil strips around outside edges of pan (do not cover bottom or top). Bake as directed.

◆ Movietime Crunch Bars ◆

6 cups CAP'N CRUNCH®
  Cereal, Regular Flavor,
  divided
1 cup salted peanuts
1 cup raisins

1 cup semisweet chocolate
  chips
1 can (14 ounces)
  sweetened condensed
  milk

Preheat oven to 350°F. Grease 13×9-inch baking pan. Crush 4 cups of cereal; spread evenly on bottom of prepared pan. Top with peanuts, raisins, chocolate chips and remaining 2 cups uncrushed cereal. Drizzle sweetened condensed milk evenly over mixture. Bake 25 to 30 minutes or until golden brown. Cool completely; cut into 2×1½-inch bars. Store tightly covered.

Makes 24 bars

Double Mint Brownies

◆ Chewy Oatmeal-Apricot-Date Bars ◆

COOKIES

¾ Butter Flavor* CRISCO®
Stick plus 4 teaspoons
or ¾ cup plus 4
teaspoons Butter
Flavor* CRISCO® all-
vegetable shortening
plus additional for
greasing
1¼ cups firmly packed brown
sugar
3 eggs
2 teaspoons vanilla
2 cups quick oats,
uncooked, divided

½ cup all-purpose flour
2 teaspoons baking powder
1 teaspoon ground
cinnamon
¼ teaspoon ground nutmeg
¼ teaspoon salt
1 cup finely grated carrots
1 cup finely minced dried
apricots
1 cup minced dates
1 cup finely chopped
walnuts
⅔ cup vanilla chips

FROSTING

2½ cups confectioners' sugar
1 (3-ounce) package cream
cheese, softened
¼ cup Butter Flavor*
CRISCO® all-vegetable
shortening

1 to 2 teaspoons milk
¾ teaspoon lemon extract
½ teaspoon vanilla
½ teaspoon finely grated
lemon peel
⅓ cup chopped walnuts

Butter Flavor Crisco® is artificially flavored.

1. Preheat oven to 350°F. Grease 13×9-inch baking pan with shortening. Flour lightly. Combine brown sugar and ¾ cup plus 4 teaspoons shortening in large bowl. Beat at medium speed of electric mixer until fluffy. Add eggs, 1 at a time, and 2 teaspoons vanilla. Beat until well blended and fluffy.

2. Process ½ cup oats in food processor or blender until finely ground. Combine ground oats with flour, baking powder, cinnamon, nutmeg and salt in medium bowl. Add oat mixture gradually to creamed mixture at low speed. Add remaining 1½ cups oats, carrots, apricots, dates, 1 cup nuts and vanilla chips. Mix until partially blended. Finish mixing with spoon. Spread in prepared pan. Bake 35 to 45 minutes or until center is set and cookie starts to pull away from sides of pan. Toothpick inserted in center should come out clean. *Do not overbake.* Cool completely.

3. For frosting, combine confectioners' sugar, cream cheese, ¼ cup shortening, milk, lemon extract, vanilla and lemon peel in medium bowl. Beat at low speed until blended. Increase speed to medium-high. Beat until fluffy. Stir in ⅓ cup nuts. Spread on baked surface. Cut into bars about 2¼×2 inches. Refrigerate.

Makes about 24 bars

Chewy Oatmeal-Apricot-Date Bars

◆ Cindy's Fudgy Brownies ◆

1 package DUNCAN HINES®
   Chewy Fudge Brownie
   Mix (21.0 ounces)
1 egg
⅓ cup water

⅓ cup vegetable oil
¾ cup semi-sweet chocolate
   chips
½ cup chopped pecans

1. Preheat oven to 350°F. Grease bottom of 13×9×2-inch pan.

2. Combine brownie mix, egg, water and oil in large bowl. Stir with spoon until well blended, about 50 strokes. Stir in chocolate chips. Spread in pan. Sprinkle with pecans. Bake at 350°F 25 to 28 minutes or until set. Cool completely. Cut into bars.   *Makes 24 brownies*

Tip: *Overbaking brownies will cause them to become dry. Follow the recommended baking times given in recipes closely.*

◆ Peanut Butter 'n Fudge Filled Bars ◆

2 cups firmly packed brown
   sugar
1 cup (2 sticks) margarine
   or butter, softened
¼ cup plus 2 tablespoons
   peanut butter, divided
2 eggs
2 cups QUAKER® Oats (quick
   or old fashioned,
   uncooked)

2 cups all-purpose flour
1 teaspoon baking soda
¼ teaspoon salt (optional)
1 (14-ounce) can sweetened
   condensed milk (not
   evaporated milk)
1 (12-ounce) package
   (2 cups) semisweet
   chocolate pieces
½ cup chopped peanuts

Heat oven to 375°F. Beat together sugar, margarine and ¼ cup peanut butter until creamy. Add eggs; beat well. Add combined oats, flour, baking soda and salt; mix well. Reserve 1 cup oat mixture for topping; set aside. Spread remaining oat mixture onto bottom of *ungreased* 13×9-inch baking pan. In medium saucepan, combine condensed milk, chocolate pieces and remaining 2 tablespoons peanut butter. Cook over low heat until chocolate is melted, stirring constantly. Remove from heat; stir in peanuts. Spread mixture evenly over crust. Drop reserved oat mixture by teaspoonfuls over chocolate mixture. Bake 30 to 35 minutes or until light golden brown. Cool completely; cut into bars. Store tightly covered.   *Makes 32 bars*

Cindy's Fudgy Brownies

◆ Ricotta Cheese Brownies ◆

BROWNIE LAYER

½ cup butter or margarine
⅓ cup unsweetened cocoa powder
1 cup sugar
2 eggs, slightly beaten

1 teaspoon vanilla
½ cup all-purpose flour
½ teaspoon baking powder
¼ teaspoon salt

CHEESE LAYER

¾ cup (6 ounces) SARGENTO® Part-Skim Ricotta Cheese
¼ cup sugar
1 egg, slightly beaten

2 tablespoons butter or margarine, softened
1 tablespoon all-purpose flour
½ teaspoon vanilla

Melt ½ cup butter in small saucepan; remove from heat. Stir in cocoa; cool. In large bowl of electric mixer, beat 1 cup sugar, 2 eggs and 1 teaspoon vanilla on medium speed until light and fluffy. In small bowl, stir together ½ cup flour, baking powder and salt. Add to egg mixture; beat until blended. Add cocoa mixture; beat until thoroughly combined. Reserve 1 cup batter; spread remaining batter into greased 8-inch square baking pan.

In small bowl of electric mixer, beat ricotta cheese, ¼ cup sugar, 1 egg, 2 tablespoons butter, 1 tablespoon flour and ½ teaspoon vanilla on medium speed until well blended. Spread over batter in pan. Drop teaspoonsful of reserved chocolate batter over ricotta mixture; spread batter with spatula to cover ricotta mixture. Bake at 350°F 40 minutes. Cool.   *Makes 16 brownies*

◆ Oatmeal Carmelita Bars ◆

¾ Butter Flavor* CRISCO® stick or ¾ cup Butter Flavor CRISCO® all-vegetable shortening, melted, plus additional for greasing
1½ cups quick oats (not instant or old fashioned), uncooked
¾ cup firmly packed brown sugar

½ cup plus 3 tablespoons all-purpose flour, divided
½ cup whole wheat flour
½ teaspoon baking soda
¼ teaspoon ground cinnamon
1⅓ cups milk chocolate chips
½ cup chopped walnuts
1 jar (12½ ounces) *or* ¾ cup caramel ice cream topping

Butter Flavor Crisco® is artificially flavored.

1. Heat oven to 350°F. Grease bottom and sides of 9×9×2-inch baking pan with shortening. Place wire rack on countertop to cool bars.

2. Combine ¾ cup shortening, oats, sugar, ½ cup all-purpose flour, whole wheat flour, baking soda and cinnamon in large bowl. Mix at low speed of electric mixer until crumbs form. Reserve ½ cup for topping. Press remaining crumbs into prepared pan.

3. Bake at 350°F for 10 minutes. Sprinkle chocolate chips and nuts over crust.

4. Combine caramel topping and remaining 3 tablespoons all-purpose flour. Stir until well blended. Drizzle over chocolate chips and nuts. Sprinkle reserved ½ cup crumbs over caramel topping.

5. Return to oven. Bake for 20 to 25 minutes or until golden brown. *Do not overbake.* Run spatula around edge of pan before cooling. Cool completely in pan on wire rack. Cut into 1½×1½-inch squares.   *Makes 3 dozen squares*

◆ Apple Lemon Bars ◆

Cookie Crust (recipe follows)
1 cup diced, peeled Washington Golden Delicious apples
⅓ cup sugar
1 egg, beaten
2 tablespoons butter or margarine, melted

2 teaspoons grated lemon peel
¾ cup all-purpose flour
¼ teaspoon ground cinnamon
¼ teaspoon baking powder
¼ teaspoon salt
Lemon Glaze (recipe follows)

Preheat oven to 350°F. Prepare Cookie Crust. Combine apples, sugar, egg, butter and lemon peel in large bowl; mix thoroughly. Combine flour, cinnamon, baking powder and salt in medium bowl; mix well. Stir flour mixture into apple mixture. Spread evenly over crust. Bake 25 minutes or until apples are tender. Cool in pan on wire rack. Brush with Lemon Glaze.

Makes 16 bars

Cookie Crust: Beat ½ cup butter or margarine, ¼ cup powdered sugar and 2 teaspoons grated lemon peel until creamy; blend in 1 cup all-purpose flour. Press onto bottom of ungreased 8-inch square baking pan. Bake at 350°F 15 to 18 minutes or until lightly browned.

Lemon Glaze: Combine ¾ cup powdered sugar and 1 tablespoon lemon juice; mix thoroughly.

Favorite recipe from **Washington Apple Commission**

◆ Blueberry Cheesecake Bars ◆

1 package DUNCAN HINES®
  Bakery Style Blueberry
  Muffin Mix
¼ cup cold butter or
  margarine
⅓ cup finely chopped
  pecans

1 (8-ounce) package cream
  cheese, softened
½ cup sugar
1 egg
3 tablespoons lemon juice
1 teaspoon grated lemon
  peel

1. Preheat oven to 350°F. Grease 9-inch square pan.

2. Rinse blueberries from Mix with cold water and drain.

3. Place muffin mix in medium bowl; cut in butter with pastry blender or 2 knives. Stir in pecans. Press onto bottom of prepared pan. Bake 15 minutes or until set.

4. Combine cream cheese and sugar in medium bowl. Beat until smooth. Add egg, lemon juice and lemon peel. Beat well. Spread over baked crust. Sprinkle with blueberries. Sprinkle topping packet from Mix over blueberries. Return to oven. Bake 35 to 40 minutes or until filling is set. Cool completely. Refrigerate until ready to serve. Cut into bars. *Makes about 16 bars*

◆ Ultimate Brownies ◆

½ cup MIRACLE WHIP®
  Salad Dressing
2 eggs, beaten
¼ cup cold water
1 (21.5-ounce) package
  fudge brownie mix

3 (7-ounce) milk chocolate
  bars, divided
Walnut halves (optional)

• Preheat oven to 350°F.

• Mix together salad dressing, eggs and water until well blended. Stir in brownie mix, mixing just until moistened.

• Coarsely chop 2 chocolate bars; stir into brownie mixture. Pour into greased 13×9-inch baking pan.

• Bake 30 to 35 minutes or until edges begin to pull away from sides of pan. Immediately top with 1 chopped chocolate bar. Let stand about 5 minutes or until melted; spread evenly over brownies. Garnish with walnut halves, if desired. Cool. Cut into squares. *Makes about 24 brownies*

Blueberry Cheesecake Bars

◆ Lemon Crème Bars ◆

CRUST
2 cups sifted all-purpose flour

¾ cup sifted confectioners' sugar

1 teaspoon grated lemon rind

½ cup unsalted butter, at room temperature

2 tablespoons cold water

LEMON FILLING
½ cup egg substitute *or* 2 large eggs

1¾ cups granulated sugar

¾ cup (3 ounces) shredded ALPINE LACE® Reduced Sodium Muenster Cheese

1½ cups sifted all-purpose flour

1 tablespoon baking powder

⅔ cup fresh lemon juice

1 teaspoon grated lemon rind

¼ cup slivered almonds (optional)

3 tablespoons sifted confectioners' sugar

Additional grated lemon rind (optional)

1. To make the Crust: Preheat the oven to 350°F and butter a 13×9×2-inch baking pan. In a medium-size bowl, mix the flour, confectioners' sugar and lemon rind, then work in the butter with your fingers until coarse crumbs form. Add the water and continue mixing until a dough forms. Press evenly onto the bottom of the baking pan and bake for 10 minutes.

2. While the crust is baking, make the Lemon Filling: In a medium-size bowl, whisk the egg substitute (or the whole eggs) until light yellow. Whisk in the granulated sugar, cheese, flour, baking powder, lemon juice and lemon rind until well blended. Pour the egg mixture over the hot crust and sprinkle with the almonds, if you wish. Return to the oven and bake 25 minutes longer or until the filling is set.

3. Cool the cookies in the pan on a wire rack for 10 minutes, then cut into 36 (2×1½-inch) bars. Cool on wire racks. Dust with the confectioners' sugar. Garnish with additional lemon rind, if you wish. Refrigerate in an airtight container.

Makes 3 dozen bars

Lemon Crème Bars

◆ Sweet Walnut Maple Bars ◆

CRUST

1 package DUNCAN HINES®
Moist Deluxe Yellow
Cake Mix, divided

⅓ cup butter or margarine,
melted

1 egg

TOPPING

1⅓ cups maple syrup (see
Tip)

3 eggs

⅓ cup firmly packed light
brown sugar

½ teaspoon maple flavoring
or vanilla extract

1 cup chopped walnuts

1. Preheat oven to 350°F. Grease 13×9×2-inch pan.

2. **For crust,** reserve ⅔ cup cake mix; set aside. Combine remaining cake mix, melted butter and egg in large bowl. Stir until thoroughly blended. (Mixture will be crumbly.) Press into pan. Bake at 350°F for 15 to 20 minutes or until light golden brown.

3. **For topping,** combine reserved cake mix, maple syrup, eggs, brown sugar and maple flavoring in large bowl. Beat at low speed with electric mixer for 3 minutes. Pour over crust. Sprinkle with walnuts. Bake at 350°F for 30 to 35 minutes or until filling is set. Cool completely. Cut into bars. Store leftover cookie bars in refrigerator.

Makes 24 bars

Tip: You may substitute your favorite maple-flavored or imitation maple syrup for the pure maple syrup, if desired.

◆ Crispy Chocolate Bars ◆

1 package (6 ounces,
1 cup) semi-sweet
chocolate chips

1 package (6 ounces, 1 cup)
butterscotch chips

½ cup peanut butter

5 cups KELLOGG'S CORN
FLAKES® cereal

Vegetable cooking spray

1. In large saucepan, combine chocolate and butterscotch chips and peanut butter. Stir over low heat until smooth. Remove from heat.

2. Add Kellogg's Corn Flakes® cereal. Stir until well coated.

3. Using buttered spatula or waxed paper, press mixture evenly into 9×9×2-inch pan coated with cooking spray. Cut into bars when cool.

Makes 16 bars

Sweet Walnut Maple Bars

◆ Chewy Coconut Bars ◆

2 eggs
7¼ teaspoons EQUAL® FOR
    RECIPES *or* 24 packets
    EQUAL® sweetener *or*
    1 cup EQUAL®
    SPOONFUL™
¼ teaspoon maple flavoring
½ cup margarine, melted
1 teaspoon vanilla

½ cup all-purpose flour
1 teaspoon baking powder
¼ teaspoon salt
1 cup unsweetened
    coconut,* finely
    chopped
½ cup chopped walnuts
    (optional)
½ cup raisins

Unsweetened coconut can be purchased in health food stores. Or, substitute sweetened coconut and decrease amount of Equal® to 5¼ teaspoons Equal® For Recipes™ or 18 packets Equal® sweetener or ¾ cup Equal® Spoonful™.

• Beat eggs, Equal® and maple flavoring in medium bowl; mix in margarine and vanilla. Combine flour, baking powder and salt in small bowl; stir into egg mixture. Mix in coconut, walnuts and raisins. Spread batter evenly in greased 8-inch square baking pan.

• Bake in preheated 350°F oven until browned and toothpick inserted in center comes out clean, about 20 minutes. Cool in pan on wire rack; cut into squares.

Makes 16 bars

◆ Spiced Date Bars ◆

1 cup packed brown sugar
½ cup margarine, softened
2 eggs
¾ cup light sour cream
2 cups all-purpose flour
1 teaspoon baking soda
1 teaspoon ground
    cinnamon

½ teaspoon ground nutmeg
1 package (8 or 10 ounces)
    DOLE ® Chopped Dates
    or Pitted Dates,
    chopped
Powdered sugar
    (optional)

• Beat brown sugar and margarine until light and fluffy. Beat in eggs, 1 at a time. Stir in sour cream.

• Combine flour, baking soda, cinnamon and nutmeg. Beat into sour cream mixture; stir in dates. Spread batter evenly into greased 13×9-inch baking pan.

• Bake at 350°F 25 to 30 minutes or until toothpick inserted in center comes out clean. Cool completely in pan on wire rack. Cut into bars. Dust with powdered sugar.

Makes 24 bars

Prep Time: 15 minutes
Bake Time: 30 minutes

◆ Marbled Peanut Butter Brownies ◆

⅔ cup all-purpose or whole-wheat flour
½ teaspoon baking powder
¼ teaspoon salt
¾ cup firmly packed brown sugar
½ cup SMUCKER'S® Creamy Natural Peanut Butter or LAURA SCUDDER'S® Smooth Old-Fashioned Peanut Butter

¼ cup butter or margarine, softened
2 eggs
1 teaspoon vanilla
3 (1-ounce) squares semisweet chocolate or ½ cup semisweet chocolate chips, melted and cooled

Combine flour, baking powder and salt; set aside.

In small bowl of electric mixer, combine brown sugar, peanut butter and butter; beat until light and creamy. Add eggs and vanilla; beat until fluffy. Stir in flour mixture just until blended. Spread in greased 8-inch square baking pan. Drizzle chocolate over batter, then swirl into batter with table knife to marbleize.

Bake in preheated 350°F oven 25 to 30 minutes or until toothpick inserted in center comes out clean. Cool in pan on rack. Cut into 24 bars.

Makes 24 bars

◆ Apricot Honey Oat Bar Cookies ◆

1½ cups uncooked old-fashioned rolled oats
½ cup finely chopped dried apricots
½ cup honey
¼ cup nonfat plain yogurt
3 tablespoons butter or margarine, melted

2 egg whites
2 tablespoons wheat germ
2 tablespoons all-purpose flour
½ teaspoon ground cinnamon
½ teaspoon vanilla
¼ teaspoon salt

Spray 8-inch square baking pan with nonstick cooking spray. Combine all ingredients in large bowl; mix well. Spread mixture evenly into prepared pan. Bake at 325°F about 25 minutes or until center is firm and edges are lightly browned. Cool and cut into 2-inch squares.

Makes 8 servings

Favorite recipe from **National Honey Board**

◆ Peanut Butter Brownie Cups ◆

BROWNIE CUPS

1 package DUNCAN HINES®
Double Fudge Brownie
Mix

2 eggs
⅓ cup water
¼ cup canola oil

TOPPING

⅓ cup sugar
⅓ cup light corn syrup

½ cup peanut butter

CHOCOLATE GLAZE

¾ cup semi-sweet chocolate
chips
3 tablespoons butter or
margarine

1 tablespoon light corn
syrup
3 tablespoons chopped
peanuts, for garnish

1. Preheat oven to 350°F. Place 24 (2-inch) foil liners on baking sheets.

2. For brownie cups, combine brownie mix, fudge packet from Mix, eggs, water and oil in large bowl. Stir with spoon until well blended, about 50 strokes. Place 2 level tablespoons batter in each foil liner. Bake 20 to 22 minutes or until firm. Cool completely.

3. For topping, combine sugar and ⅓ cup corn syrup in small heavy saucepan. Bring to a boil on medium heat. Stir in peanut butter. Drop by rounded teaspoonfuls onto each brownie cup.

4. For chocolate glaze, combine chocolate chips, butter and 1 tablespoon corn syrup in small heavy saucepan. Cook, stirring constantly, on low heat until melted. Spoon 1 rounded teaspoonful chocolate glaze onto peanut butter topping. Sprinkle with chopped peanuts. Refrigerate 15 minutes or until chocolate is firm.   *Makes 24 brownie cups*

Peanut Butter Brownie Cups

◆ Marvelous Cookie Bars ◆

½ cup (1 stick) butter or margarine, softened
1 cup firmly packed light brown sugar
2 large eggs
1⅓ cups all-purpose flour
1 cup quick-cooking or old-fashioned oats, uncooked
⅓ cup unsweetened cocoa powder

1 teaspoon baking powder
½ teaspoon salt
¼ teaspoon baking soda
½ cup chopped walnuts, divided
1 cup "M&M's"® Semi-Sweet Chocolate Mini Baking Bits, divided
½ cup cherry preserves
¼ cup shredded coconut

Preheat oven to 350°F. Lightly grease 9×9×2-inch baking pan; set aside. In large bowl cream butter and sugar until light and fluffy; beat in eggs. In medium bowl combine flour, oats, cocoa powder, baking powder, salt and baking soda; blend into creamed mixture. Stir in ¼ *cup nuts* and ¾ *cup "M&M's"® Semi-Sweet Chocolate Mini Baking Bits.* Reserve 1 cup dough; spread remaining dough into prepared pan. Combine preserves, coconut and remaining ¼ *cup nuts;* spread evenly over dough to within ½ inch of edge. Drop reserved dough by rounded teaspoonfuls over preserves mixture; sprinkle with remaining ¼ *cup "M&M's"® Semi-Sweet Chocolate Mini Baking Bits.* Bake 25 to 30 minutes or until slightly firm near edges. Cool completely. Cut into bars. Store in tightly covered container.   *Makes 16 bars*

◆ Almond Toffee Bars ◆

¾ cup butter or margarine, softened
¾ cup packed brown sugar
1½ cups all-purpose flour
½ teaspoon almond extract
½ teaspoon vanilla extract
¼ teaspoon salt

1 package (6 ounces) semi-sweet real chocolate pieces
¾ cup BLUE DIAMOND® Chopped Natural Almonds, toasted

Preheat oven to 350°F. Cream butter and sugar; blend in flour. Add extracts and salt, mixing well. Spread on bottom of *ungreased* 13×9×2-inch baking pan. Bake in 350°F oven for 15 to 20 minutes or until deep golden brown. Remove from oven and sprinkle with chocolate pieces. When chocolate has melted, spread evenly; sprinkle with almonds. Cut into bars; cool.

Makes about 40 bars

Marvelous Cookie Bars

◆ Pumpkin Jingle Bars ◆

¾ **cup MIRACLE WHIP® Salad
   Dressing**
1 **two-layer spice cake mix**
1 **(16-ounce) can pumpkin**
3 **eggs**

**Sifted confectioners'
   sugar**
Vanilla frosting
**Red and green gum
   drops, sliced**

Mix salad dressing, cake mix, pumpkin and eggs in large bowl at medium speed of electric mixer until well blended. Pour into greased 15½×10½×1-inch jelly roll pan. Bake at 350°F 18 to 20 minutes or until edges pull away from sides of pan. Cool. Sprinkle with sugar. Cut into bars. Decorate with frosting and gum drops.   *Makes about 3 dozen bars*

Prep Time: 5 minutes
Cook Time: 20 minutes

◆ Luscious Fresh Lemon Bars ◆

CRUST
   ½ **cup butter or margarine,
      softened**
   ½ **cup granulated sugar**

**Grated peel of ½
   SUNKIST® Lemon**
1¼ **cups all-purpose flour**

LEMON LAYER
   4 **eggs**
1⅔ **cups granulated sugar**
   3 **tablespoons all-purpose
      flour**
   ½ **teaspoon baking powder
      Grated peel of ½
      SUNKIST® Lemon**

**Juice of 2 SUNKIST®
   Lemons (6 tablespoons)**
1 **teaspoon vanilla extract
   Confectioners' sugar**

To make crust, in bowl blend together butter, ½ cup granulated sugar and lemon peel. Gradually stir in 1¼ cups flour to form soft crumbly dough. Press evenly onto bottom of aluminum foil-lined 13×9×2-inch baking pan. Bake at 350°F for 15 minutes. Meanwhile, to prepare lemon layer, in large bowl whisk or beat eggs well. Stir together 1⅔ cups granulated sugar, 3 tablespoons flour and baking powder. Gradually whisk sugar mixture into beaten eggs. Stir or whisk in lemon peel, lemon juice and vanilla. Pour over hot baked crust. Return to oven and bake for 20 to 25 minutes or until top and sides are lightly browned. Cool. Using foil on two sides, lift out cookie base and gently loosen foil along all sides. With long wet knife, cut into bars or squares. Sprinkle tops with confectioners' sugar.   *Makes about 3 dozen cookies*

Pumpkin Jingle Bars

◆ Black Russian Brownies ◆

1 cup butter
4 squares (1 ounce each) unsweetened chocolate
¾ teaspoon ground black pepper
4 eggs, lightly beaten
1½ cups granulated sugar
1½ teaspoons vanilla
⅓ cup KAHLÚA® Liqueur

2 tablespoons vodka
1⅓ cups all-purpose flour
½ teaspoon salt
¼ teaspoon baking powder
1 cup chopped walnuts or toasted sliced almonds
Powdered sugar (optional)

Preheat oven to 350°F. Line bottom of 13×9-inch baking pan with waxed paper. Melt butter and chocolate with pepper in small saucepan over low heat, stirring until smooth. Remove from heat; cool.

Combine eggs, granulated sugar and vanilla in large bowl; beat well. Stir in cooled chocolate mixture, Kahlúa and vodka. Combine flour, salt and baking powder; add to chocolate mixture and stir until blended. Add walnuts. Spread evenly in prepared pan.

Bake just until toothpick inserted into center comes out clean, about 25 minutes. *Do not overbake.* Cool in pan on wire rack. Cut into bars. Sprinkle with powdered sugar. *Makes about 2½ dozen brownies*

◆ Orange Pumpkin Bars ◆

BARS

1½ cups all-purpose flour
1 teaspoon baking powder
1 teaspoon pumpkin pie spice
½ teaspoon baking soda
½ teaspoon salt
1 cup solid pack canned pumpkin (not pumpkin pie filling)

¾ cup granulated sugar
⅔ cup CRISCO® Oil*
2 eggs
¼ cup firmly packed light brown sugar
2 tablespoons orange juice
½ cup chopped nuts
½ cup raisins

ICING

1½ cups confectioners' sugar
2 tablespoons orange juice
2 tablespoons butter or margarine, softened

½ teaspoon grated orange peel

*Any Crisco® Oil can be used.

1. Preheat oven to 350°F. Grease and flour 12×8-inch baking dish; set aside.

2. For bars, combine flour, baking powder, pumpkin pie spice, baking soda and salt in medium mixing bowl; set aside.

3. Combine pumpkin, granulated sugar, Crisco® Oil, eggs, brown sugar and 2 tablespoons orange juice in large mixing bowl. Beat at low speed of electric mixer until blended, scraping bowl constantly. Add flour mixture. Beat at medium speed until smooth, scraping bowl frequently. Stir in nuts and raisins. Pour into prepared pan.

4. Bake 35 minutes or until center springs back when touched lightly. Cool bars completely in pan on wire rack.

5. For icing, combine all ingredients. Beat at medium speed of electric mixer until smooth. Spread over cooled base. Cut into bars.

Makes about 24 bars

◆ Cherry Bars ◆

2 cups firmly packed brown sugar	**2 teaspoons baking soda**
¾ cup butter or margarine	**1 (21-ounce) can cherry filling and topping**
2 cups all-purpose flour	**2 tablespoons granulated sugar**
2 cups uncooked old-fashioned or quick-cooking oats	**1 tablespoon cornstarch**
	½ teaspoon almond extract

Beat brown sugar and butter in medium bowl with electric mixer at medium speed until light and fluffy. Combine flour, oats and baking soda. Add flour mixture to sugar mixture; mix on low speed until crumbly.

Spread ⅔ of oat mixture onto bottom of *ungreased* 13×9×2-inch baking pan. Press down to make crust.

Process cherry filling in food processor or blender until smooth. Pour into medium saucepan. Combine granulated sugar and cornstarch; stir into cherry filling. Cook, stirring constantly, over low heat until mixture is thick and bubbly. Stir in almond extract. Pour cherry mixture over oat layer; spread evenly. Top with remaining oat mixture.

Bake in preheated 325°F oven 45 minutes or until golden brown. Cool before cutting.

Makes 32 (2-inch) bars

Favorite recipe from **Cherry Marketing Institute, Inc.**

◆ Toffee Brownie Bars ◆

CRUST

¾ cup butter or margarine,
softened

¾ cup firmly packed brown
sugar

1 egg yolk

¾ teaspoon vanilla extract

1½ cups all-purpose flour

FILLING

1 package DUNCAN HINES®
Chewy Fudge Brownie
Mix (19.8 ounces)

1 egg

⅓ cup water

⅓ cup vegetable oil

TOPPING

1 package (12 ounces) milk
chocolate chips, melted

¾ cup finely chopped
pecans

1. Preheat oven to 350°F. Grease 15½×10½×1-inch pan.

2. For crust, combine butter, brown sugar, egg yolk and vanilla extract in large bowl. Stir in flour. Spread in pan. Bake 15 minutes or until golden.

3. For filling, prepare brownie mix following package directions. Spread over hot crust. Bake 15 minutes or until surface appears set. Cool 30 minutes.

4. For topping, spread melted chocolate on top of brownie layer; sprinkle with pecans. Cool completely. *Makes 48 bars*

Tip: Bars may be made ahead and frozen in an airtight container for several weeks.

◆ Chocolate Peanutty Crumble Bars ◆

½ cup butter or margarine

1 cup all-purpose flour

¾ cup uncooked instant
oats

⅓ cup firmly packed brown
sugar

½ teaspoon baking soda

½ teaspoon vanilla extract

4 SNICKERS® Bars (2.07
ounces each), cut into
8 slices each

Preheat oven to 350°F. Grease bottom of 8-inch square pan. Melt butter in large saucepan. Remove from heat and stir in flour, oats, brown sugar, baking soda and vanilla. Blend until crumbly. Press ⅔ of mixture into prepared pan. Arrange Snickers® Bar slices in pan, about ½ inch from edge of pan. Finely crumble remaining mixture over sliced Snickers® Bars. Bake for 25 minutes or until edges are golden brown. Cool in pan on cooling rack. Cut into bars or squares to serve. *Makes 24 bars*

Toffee Brownie Bars

◆ Marshmallow Krispie Bars ◆

1 package DUNCAN HINES®
  Fudge Brownie Mix,
  Family Size
1 package (10½ ounces)
  miniature
  marshmallows
1½ cups semi-sweet
  chocolate chips

1 cup creamy peanut
  butter
1 tablespoon butter or
  margarine
1½ cups crisp rice cereal

1. Preheat oven to 350°F. Grease bottom of 13×9-inch pan.

2. Prepare and bake brownies following package directions for basic recipe. Remove from oven. Sprinkle marshmallows on hot brownies. Return to oven. Bake for 3 minutes longer.

3. Place chocolate chips, peanut butter and butter in medium saucepan. Cook over low heat, stirring constantly, until chips are melted. Add rice cereal; mix well. Spread mixture over marshmallow layer. Refrigerate until chilled. Cut into bars.   *Makes about 2 dozen bars*

Tip: For a special presentation, cut cookies into diamond shapes.

◆ Fudgey Honey Brownies ◆

1 package (19.8 ounces)
  fudge brownie mix
⅓ cup vegetable oil
¼ cup water
2 tablespoons honey

1 egg
  Honey Whipped Cream
  (recipe follows)
  Bottled hot fudge
  topping

Combine brownie mix, oil, water, honey and egg in large bowl. Spread into greased and floured 5-cup heart-shaped baking pan*. Bake according to package directions for 8-inch square pan. Cool completely. Invert onto serving plate. Spread with Honey Whipped Cream or pipe cream through pastry tube. Drizzle with hot fudge topping.   *Makes 8 servings*

*An 8-inch square pan can be substituted.

Honey Whipped Cream: Beat 1 cup whipping cream until mixture thickens; gradually add 3 tablespoons honey and beat until soft peaks form. Fold in 1 teaspoon vanilla.   Makes about 2 cups

Favorite recipe from **National Honey Board**

Marshmallow Krispie Bars

CAKES

◆ Triple Chocolate Bundt Cake ◆

1 (18.25-ounce) box
   chocolate cake mix
1 (3.4-ounce) package
   instant chocolate
   pudding mix
4 eggs, beaten
¾ cup water
½ cup vegetable oil
½ cup sour cream

¼ cup plain yogurt
½ teaspoon vanilla extract
6 ounces (1 cup) chocolate
   chunks (sweet or
   semisweet)
6 ounces (1 cup) semisweet
   chocolate chips
½ cup sour cream
   Powdered sugar

Preheat oven to 350°F. Combine cake mix, pudding mix, eggs, water, oil, sour cream, yogurt and vanilla in large bowl; mix just until ingredients are blended. Stir in chocolate chunks and chocolate chips. Pour into greased 10-inch Bundt or tube pan. Bake 55 to 60 minutes or until cake springs back when lightly touched. Cool 1 hour in pan; remove from pan and cool completely on wire rack. Sprinkle with powdered sugar before serving.

Makes 10 to 12 servings

Favorite recipe from **Bob Evans®**

Triple Chocolate Bundt Cake

◆ Banana-Coconut Crunch Cake ◆

CAKE

1 package DUNCAN HINES®
    Moist Deluxe Banana
    Supreme Cake Mix
1 package (4-serving size)
    banana instant pudding
    and pie filling mix
1 can (16 ounces) fruit
    cocktail, in juices,
    undrained

4 eggs
¼ cup canola oil
1 cup flaked coconut
½ cup chopped pecans
½ cup firmly packed brown
    sugar

GLAZE

¾ cup granulated sugar
½ cup butter or margarine

½ cup evaporated milk
1⅓ cups flaked coconut

1. Preheat oven to 350°F. Grease and flour 13×9×2-inch pan.

2. **For cake,** combine cake mix, pudding mix, fruit cocktail with juice, eggs and oil in large bowl. Beat at medium speed with electric mixer for 4 minutes. Stir in 1 cup coconut. Pour into pan. Combine pecans and brown sugar in small bowl. Stir until well mixed. Sprinkle over batter. Bake at 350°F for 45 to 50 minutes or until toothpick inserted in center comes out clean.

3. **For glaze,** combine granulated sugar, butter and evaporated milk in medium saucepan. Bring to boil. Cook for 2 minutes, stirring occasionally. Remove from heat. Stir in 1⅓ cups coconut. Pour over warm cake. Serve warm or at room temperature. *Makes 12 to 16 servings*

Tip: *Assemble all ingredients and utensils together before beginning the recipe.*

Banana-Coconut Crunch Cake

◆ Best-Ever Short Cake ◆

2 cups all-purpose flour
2 tablespoons sugar
1 tablespoon baking
　powder
1 teaspoon salt
¾ cup shortening

1 cup milk
2 boxes (10 ounces each)
　BIRDS EYE® frozen
　Strawberries, thawed
　Whipped topping
　(optional)

• Preheat oven to 450°F. Combine flour, sugar, baking powder and salt.

• Cut shortening into flour mixture until mixture resembles coarse cornmeal.

• Blend in milk; mix well. Spread dough in 9×9-inch baking pan.

• Bake 15 minutes. Serve warm or let cool; top with strawberries before serving. Garnish with whipped topping, if desired.　　*Makes 6 to 9 servings*

Prep Time: 5 minutes
Cook Time: 15 minutes

◆ Banana Gingerbread Upside Down Cake ◆

¾ cup margarine, divided
1 cup packed brown sugar,
　divided
1 firm, large DOLE® Banana
¼ cup DOLE® Chopped Dates
1 egg
2 extra-ripe, medium DOLE®
　Bananas

¼ cup molasses
1⅔ cups all-purpose flour
1½ teaspoons ground ginger
1 teaspoon baking soda
¾ teaspoon ground allspice
½ teaspoon baking powder
½ teaspoon salt

• Melt ¼ cup margarine in 9- or 10-inch cast iron skillet. Stir in ½ cup brown sugar. Slice firm banana; arrange in single layer in brown sugar mixture. Press dates in spaces between bananas.

• Beat remaining ½ cup margarine and ½ cup brown sugar until light and fluffy. Beat in egg.

• Purée ripe bananas in blender; blend ¾ cup with molasses.

• Combine remaining ingredients in bowl; stir into beaten mixture alternately with molasses mixture until smooth. Spread batter over bananas in skillet. Bake in 350°F oven 30 minutes or until toothpick inserted in center comes out clean. Cool in pan on wire rack 10 minutes. Invert onto serving plate.
　　Makes 9 servings

Best-Ever Short Cake

◆ Arlington Apple Gingerbread Cake ◆

CAKE

4½ cups sliced, peeled Translucent, Ida Red or Jonathan apples (about 1½ pounds or 4 to 5 medium apples)

1 cup plus 1 teaspoon granulated sugar, divided

2 teaspoons ground cinnamon, divided

1 teaspoon grated lemon peel

2 teaspoons fresh lemon juice

½ cup Butter Flavor* CRISCO® Stick or ½ cup Butter Flavor* CRISCO® all-vegetable shortening

1 cup light molasses

2 eggs

3 cups all-purpose flour

2 teaspoons ground ginger

½ teaspoon ground cloves

1 cup boiling water

2 teaspoons baking soda

TOPPING (Optional)

Confectioners' sugar
Prepared lemon pie filling

Whipped cream

Butter Flavor Crisco® is artificially flavored.

1. Heat oven to 350°F.

2. For cake, arrange apple slices in bottom of *ungreased* 13×9×2-inch baking pan. Combine 1 teaspoon granulated sugar and 1 teaspoon cinnamon in small bowl. Sprinkle over apples along with lemon peel and lemon juice.

3. Combine shortening and remaining 1 cup granulated sugar in large bowl. Beat with spoon until blended. Add molasses and eggs. Beat until blended.

4. Combine flour, ginger, remaining 1 teaspoon cinnamon and cloves in medium bowl. Add to molasses mixture. Beat until blended.

5. Combine boiling water and baking soda. Stir into molasses mixture until blended. Pour over apple mixture.

6. Bake at 350°F for 50 to 60 minutes or until toothpick inserted in center comes out clean. Cool completely in pan on wire rack.

7. For topping, sprinkle top of cake with confectioners' sugar. Place spoonfuls of pie filling and whipped cream on each serving.

Makes one 13×9×2-inch cake (12 to 16 servings)

Arlington Apple Gingerbread Cake

◆ Sweet and Spicy Fruitcake ◆

3 cups chopped walnuts
2 cups chopped dried figs
1 cup chopped dried
   apricots
1 cup chocolate chips
1½ cups all-purpose flour,
   divided
¾ cup granulated sugar
4 eggs
¼ cup butter or margarine,
   softened

⅓ cup apple jelly
2 tablespoons orange-
   flavor liqueur
1 tablespoon grated
   orange peel
1 tablespoon vanilla
2 teaspoons TABASCO®
   brand Pepper Sauce
1 teaspoon baking powder

Preheat oven to 325°F. Grease two 3-cup heat-safe bowls. Line bottom and side with foil; grease foil. Combine walnuts, figs, apricots, chocolate chips and ¼ cup flour in large bowl; mix well.

Beat sugar, eggs and butter in small bowl with mixer at low speed until well blended. Add jelly, remaining 1¼ cups flour and remaining ingredients. Beat at low speed until blended. Toss mixture with dried fruit in large bowl. Spoon into prepared bowls. Cover bowls with greased foil. Bake 40 minutes; uncover and bake 40 minutes or until toothpick inserted in center comes out clean. Remove to wire racks to cool.

If desired, brush cooled fruitcakes with 1 tablespoon melted apple jelly and sprinkle each with 2 tablespoons finely chopped dried apricots. Store in cool place for up to 3 weeks.   *Makes 2 small fruitcakes*

◆ Chocolate Raspberry Cake ◆

4 (1-ounce) squares
   unsweetened chocolate
¼ cup water
½ cup butter or margarine,
   cut into small pieces
½ cup sugar
3 eggs, separated
⅓ cup unsifted all-purpose
   flour

½ cup SMUCKER'S® Red
   Raspberry Preserves or
   Apricot Preserves
Chocolate shavings (see
   Note)
Fresh raspberries

Grease and flour two 8-inch round cake pans; set aside. In medium saucepan, melt chocolate and water over low heat, stirring constantly. Add butter; stir until completely melted. Remove from heat and blend in sugar; cool.

Add egg yolks, 1 at a time, beating well after each addition. Add flour to chocolate mixture; blend well. Beat egg whites until stiff but not dry; fold into chocolate mixture. Pour into prepared cake pans.

Bake in preheated 325°F oven about 25 minutes or until toothpick inserted into center of cake comes out clean. Cool 10 minutes on wire rack; remove layers from pans. Cool completely.

Heat preserves in saucepan until melted. Spread half of preserves on 1 layer. Top with second layer; spread with remaining preserves. Garnish with chocolate shavings and raspberries.   *Makes 12 to 15 servings*

Note: For chocolate shavings, melt 1 to 2 ounces semisweet chocolate. Spread melted chocolate in thin layer on cookie sheet; refrigerate until set. Scrape with metal spatula held at 45° angle to produce shavings and curls. Chill or freeze shavings until ready to use.

Pumpkin Spice Sheet Cake
◆ with Cream Cheese Frosting ◆

- **2 cups granulated sugar**
- **1 (16-ounce) can pumpkin**
- **1 cup vegetable oil**
- **4 eggs**
- **2 cups all-purpose flour**
- **2 teaspoons baking soda**
- **1 teaspoon ground cinnamon**
- **1 teaspoon pumpkin pie spice**
- **½ teaspoon salt**
- **4 ounces Neufchâtel or other low fat cream cheese**
- **¼ cup butter or margarine, softened**
- **1 teaspoon vanilla extract**
- **1¾ cups powdered sugar, sifted**
- **1 tablespoon milk**
- **¼ cup chopped pecans (optional)**

Preheat oven to 350°F. Combine granulated sugar, pumpkin, oil and eggs in large bowl; mix well. Add flour, baking soda, cinnamon, pumpkin pie spice and salt; mix until well blended. Pour into greased 15×10×1-inch jelly roll pan. Bake 25 to 30 minutes or until toothpick inserted into center comes out clean. Set aside to cool. To prepare frosting, combine Neufchâtel cheese, butter and vanilla in large bowl; mix well. Blend in powdered sugar. Stir in milk until frosting is of spreading consistency. Frost cake and sprinkle with nuts, if desired.   *Makes 15 to 20 servings*

Favorite recipe from **Bob Evans®**

◆ Fresh Lemon Sunshine Cake ◆

1½ **cups sifted cake flour**
¼ **teaspoon salt**
6 **eggs, separated**
¼ **teaspoon cream of tartar**
1½ **cups sugar, divided**
5 **tablespoons water**

Grated peel and juice of
1 SUNKIST® Lemon
(3 tablespoons juice)
Hint o' Lemon Glaze
(recipe follows)

Sift together flour and salt. In large bowl, with electric mixer, beat egg whites and cream of tartar at high speed until soft peaks form. Gradually add ½ cup sugar, beating until medium-stiff peaks form; set aside. With same beaters, in medium bowl, beat egg yolks 2 minutes. Gradually add remaining 1 cup sugar, beating at high speed until egg yolk mixture is very thick. Beat in water and lemon juice; stir in lemon peel. Add flour mixture all at once; gently fold, then lightly stir until well-blended. Carefully fold yolk mixture into beaten egg whites. Pour batter into *ungreased* 10-inch tube pan with removable bottom. Smooth top and cut through batter with table knife to remove any large air bubbles. Bake at 325°F for 45 to 55 minutes or until cake springs back when lightly touched. Immediately invert onto neck of bottle or wire rack; cool completely upside-down. With narrow spatula or knife, loosen around tube and sides. Lift out tube and cake; loosen cake around bottom. Invert onto cake plate. Glaze top with Hint o' Lemon Glaze, allowing some to drizzle over sides.* Garnish each serving with lemon cartwheel twists, fresh berries and fresh mint leaves, if desired. *Makes 16 servings*

Or cover top of cake with thin layer of Hint o' Lemon Glaze; let dry. Cover remaining glaze with damp paper towels and plastic wrap. When top of cake is dry, drizzle or pipe remaining glaze (thinned with a few drops of lemon juice, if necessary) over top of cake in decorative pattern.

Hint o' Lemon Glaze: *In small bowl combine 1½ cups sifted confectioners' sugar and 1½ to 2 tablespoons fresh squeezed lemon juice.*

Fresh Lemon Sunshine Cake

◆ Coconut Pound Cake ◆

CAKE

1 cup Butter Flavor*
CRISCO® Stick or 1 cup
Butter Flavor* CRISCO®
all-vegetable shortening
plus additional for
greasing
2 cups sugar
5 eggs
1½ teaspoons coconut
extract

2¼ cups all-purpose flour
1½ teaspoons baking powder
½ teaspoon salt
1 cup buttermilk or sour
milk**
1 cup shredded coconut,
chopped

GLAZE

½ cup sugar
¼ cup water

1½ teaspoons coconut
extract

GARNISH (Optional)

Whipped topping or
whipped cream

Assorted fresh fruit

*Butter Flavor Crisco® is artificially flavored.
**To sour milk: Combine 1 tablespoon white vinegar plus enough milk to equal 1 cup. Stir. Wait 5 minutes before using.

1. Heat oven to 350°F. Grease 10-inch tube pan with shortening. Flour lightly. Place wire rack on countertop to cool cake.

2. For cake, combine 2 cups sugar and 1 cup shortening in large bowl. Beat at medium speed of electric mixer until blended. Add eggs, 1 at a time, beating slightly after each addition. Beat in 1½ teaspoons coconut extract.

3. Combine flour, baking powder and salt in medium bowl. Add alternately with buttermilk to creamed mixture, beating at low speed after each addition until well blended. Add coconut. Mix until blended. Spoon into pan.

4. Bake at 350°F for 50 minutes or until toothpick inserted in center comes out clean. *Do not overbake.* Remove to wire rack. Cool 5 minutes. Remove cake from pan. Place cake, top side up, on serving plate. Use toothpick to poke 12 to 15 holes in top of cake.

5. For glaze, combine ½ cup sugar, water and 1½ teaspoons coconut extract in small saucepan. Cook and stir on medium heat until mixture comes to a boil. Remove from heat. Cool 15 minutes. Spoon over cake. Cool completely.

6. For optional garnish, place spoonfuls of whipped topping and assorted fresh fruit on each serving.   *Makes one 10-inch tube cake (12 to 16 servings)*

Coconut Pound Cake

◆ Blueberry Angel Food Cake Rolls ◆

1 package DUNCAN HINES®
Angel Food Cake Mix
Confectioners' sugar
1 can (21 ounces)
blueberry pie filling

¼ cup confectioners' sugar
Mint leaves for garnish
(optional)

1. Preheat oven to 350°F. Line two 15½×10½×1-inch jelly-roll pans with aluminum foil.

2. Prepare cake following package directions. Divide into pans. Spread evenly. Cut through batter with knife or spatula to remove large air bubbles. Bake at 350°F for 15 minutes or until set. Invert cakes at once onto clean, lint-free dishtowels dusted with confectioners' sugar. Remove foil carefully. Roll up each cake with towel jelly-roll fashion, starting at short end. Cool completely.

3. Unroll cakes. Spread about 1 cup blueberry pie filling to within 1 inch of edges on each cake. Reroll and place seam-side down on serving plate. Dust with ¼ cup confectioners' sugar. Garnish with mint leaves, if desired.

Makes 2 cakes (8 servings each)

◆ Kahlúa® Black Forest Cake ◆

1 package (18.25 ounces)
chocolate fudge cake
mix with pudding
3 eggs
¾ cup water
½ cup KAHLÚA® Liqueur
⅓ cup vegetable oil

1 can (16 ounces) vanilla
or chocolate frosting
1 can (21 ounces) cherry
filling and topping
Chocolate sprinkles or
chocolate shavings for
garnish (optional)

Preheat oven to 350°F. Grease and flour 2 (9-inch) cake pans; set aside. In large mixer bowl, prepare cake mix according to package directions, using eggs, water, Kahlúa® and oil. Pour batter into prepared pans. Bake 25 to 35 minutes or until toothpick inserted in center comes out clean. Cool cake in pans 10 minutes; turn layers out onto wire racks to cool completely.

Place one cake layer bottom side up on serving plate. Spread thick layer of frosting in circle, 1½ inches around outer edge of cake. Spoon half of cherry filling into center of cake layer to frosting edge. Top with second cake layer, bottom side down. Repeat with frosting and remaining cherry filling. Spread remaining frosting around side of cake. Decorate with chocolate sprinkles or shavings, if desired.

Makes 1 (9-inch) cake

Blueberry Angel Food Cake Roll

◆ Winter Wonderland Cake ◆

1 package **DUNCAN HINES®**
Moist Deluxe Cake Mix
(any flavor)
2 containers (16 ounces
each) **DUNCAN HINES®**
Vanilla Frosting
Green food coloring

9 ice cream sugar cones
½ cup flaked coconut, finely
chopped
Marzipan
Sliced natural almonds
Nonpareil decors

1. Preheat oven to 350°F. Grease and flour 13×9×2-inch pan.

2. Prepare, bake and cool cake following package directions for basic recipe.

3. To assemble, place cake on serving plate. Frost sides and top with 1 container Vanilla Frosting. Tint remaining container of frosting with green food coloring to desired color; set aside. Break off edges of ice cream cones to form various sized trees. Frost 1 cone with green frosting. Arrange on cake; sprinkle with coconut. Repeat for remaining cones. Form marzipan into bunny shapes. Use almond slices for ears and nonpareil decors for eyes and noses. Arrange as desired. Sprinkle remaining coconut on cake.   *Makes 12 to 16 servings*

Tip: Marzipan, a cooked mixture of finely ground almonds, sugar and egg whites, is very sweet and pliable. It is available in most supermarkets packaged in cans or in plastic-wrapped logs.

◆ Country Oven Carrot Cake ◆

1 package **DUNCAN HINES®**
Moist Deluxe® Yellow
Cake Mix
3 cups grated carrots
4 eggs
1 cup finely chopped nuts

½ cup vegetable oil
2 teaspoons ground
cinnamon
1 container **DUNCAN HINES®**
Creamy Homestyle
Cream Cheese Frosting

1. Preheat oven to 350°F. Grease and flour 13×9×2-inch pan (see Tip).

2. Combine cake mix, carrots, eggs, nuts, oil and cinnamon in large bowl. Beat at low speed with electric mixer until moistened. Beat at medium speed 2 minutes. Pour into pan. Bake at 350°F 40 to 45 minutes or until toothpick inserted in center comes out clean. Cool completely. Frost cake with Cream Cheese frosting.   *Makes 12 to 16 servings*

Tip: Carrot cake can also be baked in two 8- or 9-inch round cake pans at 350°F 35 to 40 minutes or until toothpick inserted in center comes out clean. Cool cakes following package directions. Fill and frost cooled cakes. Garnish with whole pecans.

Winter Wonderland Cake

Idaho Wet Chocolate
◆ L'Orange Pound Cake ◆

3 cups granulated sugar
1½ cups (3 sticks) margarine
    or butter, softened
3 cups all-purpose flour
1 (8-ounce) container sour
    cream
1 large IDAHO® Potato,
    cooked and mashed
5 large eggs

½ cup unsweetened cocoa
    powder
½ cup orange juice
2 teaspoons orange extract
1 teaspoon baking soda
¼ teaspoon salt
    Cream Cheese Icing
    (recipe follows)
    Raspberries for garnish

CREAM CHEESE ICING

1 (3-ounce) package cream
    cheese, softened
2 tablespoons milk

2 cups confectioners' sugar
1 teaspoon vanilla extract

Preheat oven to 350°F. Grease and flour 10-inch tube pan.

In large bowl, with mixer at low speed, beat sugar with margarine just until blended. Increase speed to high; beat 3 minutes or until light and fluffy, scraping bowl often.

Reduce speed to low; add flour, sour cream, potato, eggs, cocoa, orange juice, orange extract, baking soda and salt; beat until well mixed, constantly scraping bowl. Increase speed to high; beat 2 minutes, occasionally scraping bowl. Spoon batter into prepared pan.

Bake 1 hour 30 minutes or until toothpick inserted in center of cake comes out clean.

Cool cake in pan on wire rack 15 minutes. With spatula, loosen cake from pan; remove from pan and cool completely on rack.

When cake is cool, prepare Cream Cheese Icing; spread on top of cake allowing some to drizzle down sides of cake. Garnish with raspberries.

Makes 16 servings

Cream Cheese Icing: In small bowl, with mixer at low speed, beat cream cheese and milk until smooth. Beat in confectioners' sugar and vanilla until blended and good spreading consistency, adding additional milk if necessary.

◆ Lekach Honey Cake ◆

1 cup honey
½ cup strong-brewed coffee
1 tablespoon brandy
  (optional)
2 eggs
½ cup packed brown sugar
2 tablespoons vegetable oil
2 cups all-purpose flour

1½ teaspoons baking powder
1½ teaspoons baking soda
½ teaspoon salt
½ teaspoon ground
  cinnamon
¼ teaspoon ground ginger
⅛ teaspoon ground nutmeg
⅛ teaspoon ground cloves

Combine honey, coffee and brandy, if desired, in small bowl; mix well. Beat eggs in large bowl. Add brown sugar and oil. Combine flour, baking powder, baking soda, salt and spices in medium bowl; mix well. Add flour mixture and honey mixture alternately to egg mixture. Pour batter into greased 9-inch square pan. Bake at 300°F 55 to 60 minutes or until cake springs back when lightly touched.

Makes 12 servings

Favorite recipe from **National Honey Board**

◆ Little Banana Upside Down Cakes ◆

3 tablespoons margarine,
  melted
3 tablespoons flaked
  coconut, toasted
3 tablespoons DOLE®
  Chopped Almonds,
  toasted
2 tablespoons brown sugar
1 firm, large DOLE® Banana,
  sliced

¼ cup cake flour
¼ teaspoon baking powder
  Pinch salt
1 egg
3 tablespoons granulated
  sugar
1 teaspoon rum extract

• Divide margarine, coconut, almonds, brown sugar and banana among 3 (¾-cup) soufflé dishes.

• Combine flour, baking powder and salt.

• Beat egg and granulated sugar until thick and pale. Beat in rum extract. Fold in flour mixture. Pour batter evenly into prepared dishes.

• Bake in 350°F oven 15 to 20 minutes. Invert onto serving plates.

Makes 3 servings

◆ Sock-It-To-Me Cake ◆

STREUSEL FILLING
1 package DUNCAN HINES®
   Moist Deluxe® Butter
   Recipe Golden Cake
   Mix, divided
2 tablespoons brown sugar

2 teaspoons ground
   cinnamon
1 cup finely chopped
   pecans

CAKE
4 eggs
1 cup dairy sour cream
⅓ cup vegetable oil

¼ cup water
¼ cup granulated sugar

GLAZE
1 cup confectioners' sugar

1 or 2 tablespoons milk

1. Preheat oven to 375°F. Grease and flour 10-inch tube pan.

2. For streusel filling, combine 2 tablespoons cake mix, brown sugar and cinnamon in medium bowl. Stir in pecans. Set aside.

3. For cake, combine remaining cake mix, eggs, sour cream, oil, water and granulated sugar in large bowl. Beat at medium speed with electric mixer 2 minutes. Pour two-thirds of batter into pan. Sprinkle with streusel filling. Spoon remaining batter evenly over filling. Bake at 375°F 45 to 55 minutes or until toothpick inserted in center comes out clean. Cool in pan 25 minutes. Invert onto serving plate. Cool completely.

4. For glaze, combine confectioners' sugar and milk in small bowl. Stir until smooth. Drizzle over cake.   *Makes 12 to 16 servings*

Tip: For a quick glaze, place ½ cup DUNCAN HINES® Creamy Homestyle Vanilla Frosting in small microwave-safe bowl. Microwave at HIGH (100% power) 10 seconds; add 5 to 10 seconds, if needed. Stir until smooth and thin.

Sock-It-To-Me Cake

◆ Magnificent Pound Cake ◆

CAKE
1 cup Butter Flavor*
   CRISCO® Stick or Butter
   Flavor* CRISCO® all-
   vegetable shortening
   plus additional for
   greasing
3 cups sugar

5 eggs
3⅓ cups all-purpose flour
½ teaspoon baking powder
½ teaspoon salt
1 cup milk
1 teaspoon coconut extract
1 teaspoon rum extract

GLAZE
½ cup sugar
¼ cup water

½ teaspoon pure almond
   extract

GARNISH (Optional)
Assorted fresh fruit

Butter Flavor Crisco® is artificially flavored.

1. Heat oven to 325°F. Grease 10-inch (12-cup) Bundt pan with shortening. Flour lightly.

2. For cake, combine 3 cups sugar and 1 cup shortening in large bowl. Beat at low speed of electric mixer until blended. Beat at medium speed until well blended. Add eggs, 1 at a time, beating 1 minute at low speed after each addition.

3. Combine flour, baking powder and salt in medium bowl. Add to creamed mixture alternately with milk, beginning and ending with flour mixture, beating at low speed after each addition until well blended. Add coconut extract and rum extract. Beat at medium speed 1 minute. Pour into pan.

4. Bake at 325°F for 1 hour 30 minutes to 1 hour 40 minutes or until toothpick inserted in center comes out clean. Cool 10 minutes before removing from pan. Place cake, fluted side up, on wire rack. Cool 20 minutes.

5. For glaze, combine ½ cup sugar, water and almond extract in small saucepan. Bring to a boil. Slide waxed paper under wire rack. Brush over warm cake, using all of glaze. Cool completely.

6. For optional garnish, place spoonful of assorted fresh fruit on each serving.

Makes one 10-inch Bundt cake (12 to 16 servings)

Magnificent Pound Cake

◆ Easy Cream Cake ◆

1 package DUNCAN HINES®
   Moist Deluxe® White
   Cake Mix
1⅓ cups half-and-half
1 cup flaked coconut, finely
   chopped
½ cup finely chopped
   pecans

3 egg whites
2 tablespoons vegetable oil
2 containers DUNCAN
   HINES® Cream Cheese
   Frosting

1. Preheat oven to 350°F. Grease and flour three 8-inch round pans.

2. Combine cake mix, half-and-half, coconut, pecans, egg whites and oil in large bowl. Beat at low speed with electric mixer until moistened. Beat at medium speed 2 minutes. Pour into pans. Bake at 350°F 22 to 25 minutes or until toothpick inserted in center comes out clean. Cool following package directions.

3. To assemble, place one cake layer on serving plate. Spread with ¾ cup Cream Cheese frosting. Place second cake layer on top. Spread with ¾ cup frosting. Top with third layer. Spread ¾ cup frosting on top only.

Makes 12 to 16 servings

Tip: Spread leftover frosting between graham crackers for an easy snack.

◆ Double Fudge Marble Cake ◆

1 package DUNCAN HINES®
   Moist Deluxe® Fudge
   Marble Cake Mix

1 container DUNCAN HINES®
   Milk Chocolate Frosting
¼ cup hot fudge topping

1. Preheat oven to 350°F. Grease and flour 13×9×2-inch pan.

2. Prepare, bake and cool cake following package directions for basic recipe.

3. Frost top of cooled cake with Milk Chocolate frosting. Place hot fudge topping in small microwave-safe bowl. Microwave at HIGH (100% power) 30 seconds or until thin. Drop hot fudge by spoonfuls on top of cake in 18 places. Pull tip of knife once through each hot fudge dollop to form heart shapes.

Makes 12 to 16 servings

Tip: Hot fudge topping may also be marbled in frosting by using flat blade of knife to swirl slightly.

Easy Cream Cake

◆ Sour Cream Coffeecake Cupcakes ◆

1 cup (2 sticks) butter, softened (*do not use margarine*)
2 cups plus 4 teaspoons sugar, divided
2 eggs
1 cup sour cream
1 teaspoon vanilla

2 cups all-purpose flour
1 teaspoon salt
½ teaspoon baking soda
1 cup chopped black walnuts
1 teaspoon ground cinnamon

1. Preheat oven to 350°F. Insert paper liners into 18 muffin cups.

2. Beat together butter and 2 cups sugar in large bowl. Add eggs, 1 at a time, beating well after each addition. Blend in sour cream and vanilla.

3. Combine flour, salt and baking soda in medium bowl. Add to butter mixture; mix well.

4. Stir together remaining 4 teaspoons sugar, walnuts and cinnamon in small bowl.

5. Fill prepared muffin cups ⅓ full with batter; sprinkle with ⅔ of walnut mixture. Cover with remaining batter. Sprinkle with remaining walnut mixture.

6. Bake 25 to 30 minutes or until toothpick inserted into centers comes out clean. Remove cupcakes from pan; cool on wire rack.

Makes about 1½ dozen cupcakes

Sour Cream Coffeecake Cupcakes

◆ Crisco "Americana" Cake ◆

CAKE

- ½ cup Butter Flavor* CRISCO® Stick or ½ cup Butter Flavor* CRISCO® all-vegetable shortening plus additional for greasing
- 5 eggs, separated
- ½ cup CRISCO® Stick or ½ cup CRISCO® all-vegetable shortening
- 1½ cups granulated sugar
- 2 cups sifted all-purpose flour
- 1 teaspoon baking powder
- ½ teaspoon baking soda
- ½ teaspoon salt
- 1 can (8 ounces) crushed pineapple in unsweetened juice, undrained
- 2 tablespoons dairy sour cream
- 1¼ teaspoons pure almond extract
- 1 red apple, peeled, grated (about ½ cup)
- 1 cup chopped pecans

GLAZE

- 1 cup confectioners' sugar
- 2 tablespoons milk
- 1 tablespoon fresh lemon juice

Additional chopped pecans (optional)

Butter Flavor Crisco® is artificially flavored.

1. Heat oven to 325°F. Grease 10-inch tube pan with shortening. Flour lightly.

2. For cake, beat egg whites in large bowl at high speed of electric mixer until stiff peaks form. Combine shortenings in another large bowl. Beat at medium speed of electric mixer until creamy. Add granulated sugar and egg yolks. Beat at medium speed until well blended.

3. Combine flour, baking powder, baking soda and salt in small bowl. Add to creamed mixture. Beat at low speed until mixed. Beat at medium speed until well blended. Reduce speed to low. Add pineapple with juice, sour cream and almond extract. Beat until blended. Stir in egg whites, apple and 1 cup nuts with spoon. Spoon into pan.

4. Bake at 325°F for 40 to 50 minutes or until cake springs back when touched lightly in center. Cool 5 to 7 minutes. Refrigerate 5 minutes before removing from pan. Place cake, top side up, on wire rack. Cool completely. Place cake on serving plate.

5. For glaze, combine confectioners' sugar, milk and lemon juice in small bowl. Mix with spoon. Drizzle over top of cake, letting excess glaze run down side. Sprinkle with additional nuts, if desired, before glaze hardens.

Makes one 10-inch tube cake (12 to 16 servings)

Crisco "Americana" Cake

◆ Pineapple Upside Down Cake ◆

2 cans (8 ounces each) pineapple slices in juice, undrained
¼ cup raisins
1 cup KELLOGG'S® ALL-BRAN® cereal
¾ cup whole wheat flour
½ cup all-purpose flour
1 teaspoon baking soda
1 teaspoon ground cinnamon
¼ teaspoon salt (optional)
3 tablespoons margarine, softened
¼ cup sugar
4 egg whites
1 cup (8 ounces) vanilla-flavored low-fat yogurt
1 teaspoon vanilla extract

Drain pineapple, reserving ¼ cup juice. Arrange pineapple slices in 9-inch round cake pan coated with nonstick cooking spray. Place raisins around and in centers of pineapple slices.

Stir together Kellogg's® All-Bran® cereal, whole wheat flour, all-purpose flour, baking soda, cinnamon and salt. Set aside.

In large mixing bowl, beat together margarine and sugar. Add egg whites, yogurt, vanilla and ¼ cup reserved pineapple juice, mixing until blended. Add flour mixture, stirring only until combined. Spread batter over pineapple slices and raisins.

Bake at 350°F for 35 minutes or until toothpick inserted in center comes out clean. Let stand 10 minutes. Turn cake upside down onto serving plate. Remove pan. Cool. Cut into 12 wedges. *Makes 12 servings*

◆ Almond Fudge Banana Cake ◆

3 extra-ripe, medium DOLE® Bananas
1½ cups sugar
½ cup margarine, softened
3 eggs
3 tablespoons amaretto liqueur *or* ½ to 1 teaspoon almond extract
1 teaspoon vanilla extract
1½ cups all-purpose flour
½ cup unsweetened cocoa powder
1 teaspoon baking soda
½ teaspoon salt
½ cup DOLE® Chopped Almonds, toasted, ground
Banana Chocolate Glaze (recipe follows)

• Mash bananas; set aside.

• Beat sugar and margarine until light and fluffy. Beat in eggs, liqueur and vanilla.

• Combine flour, cocoa, baking soda and salt. Stir in almonds. Add to sugar mixture alternately with bananas. Beat well.

• Pour batter into greased 10-inch Bundt pan. Bake in preheated 350°F oven 45 to 50 minutes or until toothpick inserted in center comes out almost clean and cake pulls away from side of pan. Cool 10 minutes. Remove cake from pan to wire rack to cool completely. Drizzle glaze over top and down side of cake.

Makes 16 to 20 servings

Banana Chocolate Glaze

1 extra-ripe, small DOLE® Banana, puréed

1 square (1 ounce) semisweet chocolate, melted

• With wire whisk, beat puréed banana into melted chocolate.

◆ Southern Jam Cake ◆

CAKE

1 cup granulated sugar
¾ cup butter or margarine, softened
3 eggs
1 cup (12-ounce jar) SMUCKER'S® Seedless Blackberry Jam
2½ cups all-purpose flour

1 teaspoon ground cinnamon
1 teaspoon ground cloves
1 teaspoon ground allspice
1 teaspoon ground nutmeg
1 teaspoon baking soda
¾ cup buttermilk

CARAMEL ICING (Optional)

2 tablespoons butter
½ cup firmly packed brown sugar

3 tablespoons milk
1¾ cups powdered sugar

Grease and flour tube pan. Combine granulated sugar and ¾ cup butter; beat until light and fluffy. Add eggs, 1 at a time, beating well after each addition. Fold in jam.

Combine flour, cinnamon, cloves, allspice, nutmeg and baking soda; mix well. Add to batter alternately with buttermilk, stirring just enough to blend after each addition. Spoon mixture into prepared pan.

Bake at 350°F for 50 minutes or until toothpick inserted in center comes out clean. Cool in pan for 10 minutes. Remove from pan; cool completely.

In saucepan, melt 2 tablespoons butter; stir in brown sugar. Cook, stirring constantly, until mixture boils; remove from heat. Cool 5 minutes. Stir in milk; blend in powdered sugar. Frost cake.

Makes 12 to 16 servings

◆ Fresh Berry Cobbler Cake ◆

1 pint fresh berries (blueberries, blackberries, raspberries and/or strawberries)
1 cup all-purpose flour
1¼ cups sugar, divided
1 teaspoon baking powder
¼ teaspoon salt
3 tablespoons butter or margarine
½ cup milk
1 tablespoon cornstarch
1 cup cold water
Additional berries (optional)

Preheat oven to 375°F. Place 1 pint berries in 9×9-inch baking pan; set aside. Combine flour, ½ cup sugar, baking powder and salt in large bowl. Cut in butter with pastry blender or two knives until coarse crumbs form. Stir in milk. Spoon over berries. Combine remaining ¾ cup sugar and cornstarch in small bowl. Stir in water until sugar mixture dissolves; pour over berry mixture. Bake 35 to 40 minutes or until lightly browned. Serve warm or cool completely. Garnish with additional berries, if desired.   *Makes 6 servings*

Favorite recipe from **Bob Evans®**

◆ Fudgy Peanut Butter Cake ◆

1 (18.25-ounce) box chocolate fudge cake mix
2 eggs
1½ cups plus ⅔ cup water, divided
1 (16-ounce) package chocolate fudge frosting mix
1¼ cups SMUCKER'S® Chunky Natural Peanut Butter or LAURA SCUDDER'S® Nutty Old-Fashioned Peanut Butter

Grease and flour 10-inch tube pan. In large bowl, blend cake mix, eggs and 1½ cups water until moistened; mix as directed on cake package. Pour batter into pan.

In medium bowl, combine frosting mix, peanut butter and ⅔ cup water; blend until smooth. Spoon over batter in pan.

Bake in preheated 350°F oven 35 to 45 minutes or until top springs back when touched lightly in center. Cool upright in pan 1 hour; remove from pan. Cool completely.   *Makes 12 to 15 servings*

Fresh Berry Cobbler Cake

◆ Flower Garden Cake ◆

1 package **DUNCAN HINES®**
   Moist Deluxe® Yellow or
   Devil's Food Cake Mix
1 container **DUNCAN HINES®**
   Vanilla Frosting
Green food coloring

Mini pretzels
½ **teaspoon water**
1 **cup flaked coconut**
Narrow green ribbon
Assorted candy suckers

1. Preheat oven to 350°F. Grease and flour 13×9×2-inch pan.

2. Prepare and bake cake following package directions for basic recipe. Cool in pan 15 minutes. Invert onto cooling rack. Turn right side up. Cool completely.

3. Tint Vanilla Frosting with 3 drops green food coloring. Frost sides and top of cake. Place pretzels upright along top edge to form "fence." Combine water and food coloring in small bowl. Add coconut. Toss with fork until evenly tinted. Sprinkle coconut "grass" over frosting inside pretzel "fence." Tie ribbon bows on each candy sucker stick to form leaves. Arrange assorted sucker "flowers" in "garden." *Makes 16 to 20 servings*

Tip: For a children's party, be sure to include enough candy suckers for each child.

◆ Applesauce Cake ◆

½ **cup butter or margarine,**
   softened
1 **cup honey**
1 **egg**
1 **teaspoon vanilla**
1¼ **cups all-purpose flour**
1 **cup whole wheat flour**
1 **teaspoon baking soda**
1 **teaspoon ground**
   cinnamon

½ **teaspoon salt**
½ **teaspoon ground nutmeg**
¼ **teaspoon ground cloves**
¼ **teaspoon ground allspice**
   or ginger
1 **cup chopped dates**
⅓ **cup chopped walnuts**
1 **cup unsweetened**
   applesauce

Cream butter in large bowl. Gradually beat in honey until light and fluffy. Add egg and vanilla; mix well. Combine dry ingredients in medium bowl; reserve 2 tablespoons flour mixture. Combine dates, walnuts and reserved 2 tablespoons flour mixture in small bowl; set aside. Add remaining flour mixture and applesauce alternately to creamed mixture, beginning and ending with flour mixture. Stir in date mixture. Pour batter into greased 13×9×2-inch pan. Bake at 325°F 35 minutes or until toothpick inserted near center comes out clean. *Makes 12 servings*

Favorite recipe from **National Honey Board**

Flower Garden Cake

◆ Harvest Moon Cake ◆

CAKE

1 cup granulated sugar
½ CRISCO® Stick or ½ cup CRISCO® all-vegetable shortening
2 eggs
1 cup fresh pumpkin purée or canned solid-pack pumpkin* (not pumpkin pie filling)
¼ teaspoon salt

1¾ cups cake flour
1 teaspoon baking powder
½ teaspoon baking soda
¼ teaspoon ground cinnamon
¼ teaspoon ground ginger
¼ teaspoon ground nutmeg
1 cup mini chips semi-sweet chocolate

FROSTING

⅓ cup maple syrup
¼ CRISCO® Stick or ¼ cup CRISCO® all-vegetable shortening

¼ cup sweet (unsalted) butter, softened
¼ teaspoon salt
2 cups confectioners' sugar

GARNISH (Optional)

Additional mini chips semi-sweet chocolate

Add 2 tablespoons water to pumpkin if using canned pumpkin.

1. Heat oven to 350°F. Grease 8-inch square cake pan. Flour lightly. Line bottom with waxed paper. Place wire rack on countertop for cooling cake.

2. For cake, combine granulated sugar, ½ cup shortening and eggs in large bowl. Beat at medium speed of electric mixer until creamy. Beat in pumpkin and ¼ teaspoon salt until blended.

3. Combine flour, baking powder, baking soda, cinnamon, ginger and nutmeg in small bowl. Add to pumpkin mixture gradually, beating at low speed after each addition just until mixed. Stir in 1 cup chocolate chips. Pour into pan.

4. Bake at 350°F for 35 to 55 minutes or until toothpick inserted in center comes out clean. *Do not overbake.* Cool 10 minutes before removing from pan. Invert cake on wire rack. Remove waxed paper. Turn cake top side up. Cool completely. Place cake on serving plate.

5. For frosting, combine maple syrup, ¼ cup shortening, butter and ¼ teaspoon salt in medium bowl. Beat with fork until blended. Mix in confectioners' sugar gradually, beating with spoon until creamy. Frost top and sides of cake.

6. For optional garnish, sprinkle top of cake with additional chocolate chips.

Makes one 8-inch square cake (8 to 10 servings)

Harvest Moon Cake

◆ Strawberry Celebration Cake ◆

1 package DUNCAN HINES®
Moist Deluxe®
Strawberry Supreme
Cake Mix
1 cup strawberry preserves,
heated

1 container DUNCAN HINES®
Cream Cheese Frosting
Strawberry halves, for
garnish
Mint leaves, for garnish

1. Preheat oven to 350°F. Grease and flour 10-inch Bundt or tube pan.

2. Prepare, bake and cool cake following package directions for basic recipe.

3. Split cake horizontally into three even layers. Place bottom cake layer on serving plate. Spread with ½ cup warm preserves. Repeat layering. Top with remaining cake layer. Frost cake with Cream Cheese Frosting. Garnish with strawberry halves and mint leaves. Refrigerate until ready to serve.

Makes 12 to 16 servings

Tip: For a delicious variation, substitute 1 cup seedless red raspberry jam for the strawberry preserves.

◆ Take-Along Cake ◆

1 package DUNCAN HINES®
Moist Deluxe® Swiss
Chocolate Cake Mix
1 package (12 ounces)
semi-sweet chocolate
chips
1 cup miniature
marshmallows

¼ cup butter or margarine,
melted
½ cup firmly packed brown
sugar
½ cup chopped pecans or
walnuts

1. Preheat oven to 350°F. Grease and flour 13×9×2-inch pan.

2. Prepare cake following package directions for basic recipe. Add chocolate chips and marshmallows to batter. Pour into pan. Drizzle melted butter over batter. Sprinkle with brown sugar and top with nuts. Bake at 350°F 45 to 55 minutes. Serve warm or cool completely.   *Makes 12 to 16 servings*

Tip: Chocolate should be stored in a cool, dry place. When the storage area becomes too warm, chocolate will develop "bloom," a visible gray coating. Bloom has no effect on either the flavor or the quality of the chocolate and you may still use the chocolate in baking with excellent results.

Strawberry Celebration Cake

◆ Peach & Blackberry Shortcakes ◆

¾ **cup plain low-fat yogurt**
5 **teaspoons sugar, divided**
1 **tablespoon no-sugar-
added blackberry fruit
spread**
½ **cup coarsely chopped
peeled peach**
½ **cup fresh or thawed
frozen blackberries or
raspberries**

½ **cup all-purpose flour**
¼ **teaspoon baking powder**
⅛ **teaspoon baking soda**
2 **tablespoons reduced-fat
margarine**
½ **teaspoon vanilla**

1. Place cheesecloth or coffee filter in large sieve or strainer. Spoon yogurt into sieve; place over large bowl. Refrigerate 20 minutes. Remove yogurt from sieve; discard liquid. Measure ¼ cup yogurt; blend remaining yogurt, 2 teaspoons sugar and fruit spread in small bowl. Refrigerate until ready to serve.

2. Meanwhile, combine peach, blackberries and ½ teaspoon sugar in medium bowl; set aside.

3. Preheat oven to 425°F.

4. Combine flour, baking powder, baking soda and remaining 2½ teaspoons sugar in small bowl. Cut in margarine with pastry blender until mixture resembles coarse crumbs. Combine reserved ¼ cup yogurt with vanilla. Stir into flour mixture just until dry ingredients are moistened. Shape dough into a ball.

5. Place dough on lightly floured surface. Knead dough gently 8 times. Divide dough in half. Roll out each half into 3-inch circle with lightly floured rolling pin. Place circles on *ungreased* baking sheet.

6. Bake 12 to 15 minutes or until lightly browned. Immediately remove from baking sheet. Cool shortcakes on wire rack 10 minutes or until cool enough to handle.

7. Cut shortcakes in half. Top bottom halves with fruit mixture, yogurt and remaining halves. Garnish with blackberries and mint, if desired. Serve immediately. *Makes 2 servings*

Peach & Blackberry Shortcake

◆ Gingerbread Upside-Down Cake ◆

1 can (20 ounces) DOLE® Pineapple Slices, undrained	1 egg
½ cup margarine, softened, divided	½ cup dark molasses
	1½ cups all-purpose flour
1 cup packed brown sugar, divided	1 teaspoon baking soda
	1 teaspoon ground ginger
10 maraschino cherries	½ teaspoon ground cinnamon
	½ teaspoon salt

• Preheat oven to 350°F. Drain pineapple; reserve ½ cup syrup. In 10-inch cast iron skillet, melt ¼ cup margarine. Remove from heat. Add ½ cup brown sugar and stir until blended. Arrange pineapple slices in skillet. Place 1 cherry in center of each slice.

• In large mixer bowl, beat remaining ¼ cup margarine and ½ cup brown sugar until light and fluffy. Beat in egg and molasses. In small bowl, combine flour, baking soda, ginger, cinnamon and salt.

• In small saucepan, bring reserved pineapple syrup to a boil. Add dry ingredients to creamed mixture alternately with hot syrup. Spread evenly over pineapple in skillet. Bake 30 to 40 minutes or until toothpick inserted in center comes out clean. Let stand in skillet on wire rack 5 minutes. Invert onto serving plate. *Makes 8 to 10 servings*

◆ Everyone's Favorite E-Z Lemon Cake ◆

1 package (18¼ ounces) two-layer yellow or lemon cake mix (without pudding mix preferred)	4 eggs
	1 cup water
	⅓ cup vegetable oil
1 package (3.4 ounces) *instant* lemon pudding and pie filling	Grated peel and juice of 1 SUNKIST® lemon (3 tablespoons juice)
	E-Z Lemon Glaze (recipe follows)

In large bowl, combine cake and pudding mixes, eggs, water, oil and lemon juice with electric mixer at low speed 30 seconds. Beat at medium speed 2 minutes longer. Stir in lemon peel. Pour batter into well-greased and lightly floured Bundt pan or 10-inch tube pan.

Bake at 350°F 50 to 60 minutes or until toothpick inserted in center comes out clean. Cool on wire rack 15 minutes. With narrow spatula or knife, loosen around tube and sides and invert onto cake plate. While still warm, pierce top all over with long two-prong fork or wooden skewer. Spread top with half of E-Z Lemon Glaze. Cool completely. Spoon remaining glaze over cake, allowing some to drizzle over sides.   *Makes 16 servings*

E-Z Lemon Glaze: *In small bowl, combine 1 cup confectioners' sugar, juice of ½ SUNKIST® lemon (1½ tablespoons) and ½ tablespoon water.*

◆ Cappuccino Pound Cake ◆

1 cup butter or margarine, softened
2 cups packed brown sugar
2 tablespoons instant coffee powder or crystals
1 teaspoon ground cinnamon
¼ teaspoon salt

6 eggs
1 cup sifted whole wheat flour
1 cup all-purpose flour
¼ cup milk
2 cups chopped Walnuts
Powdered sugar and additional Walnuts for garnish

In mixing bowl cream butter; add sugar, coffee powder, cinnamon and salt, beating until light and fluffy. Beat in eggs, 1 at a time, mixing well after each addition (batter may look curdled).

On low speed mix in half of flours, then milk, then remaining flour. Add chopped walnuts, mixing just until distributed. Pour into well-greased and floured 10-inch tube pan. Bake in 350°F oven 50 to 60 minutes or until toothpick inserted in center comes out clean. Cool in pan 15 minutes; loosen edges and turn out onto wire rack to cool completely. To store for several days, wrap securely in plastic wrap. Dust with powdered sugar and garnish with walnuts just before serving.   *Makes 1 (10-inch) cake*

Favorite recipe from **Walnut Marketing Board**

◆ Choca-Cola Cake ◆

CAKE

1¾ cups granulated sugar
¾ cup CRISCO® Stick or
    ¾ cup CRISCO® all-
    vegetable shortening
2 eggs
2 tablespoons unsweetened
    cocoa powder
1 tablespoon pure vanilla
    extract

¼ teaspoon salt
½ cup buttermilk or sour
    milk*
1 teaspoon baking soda
2½ cups all-purpose flour
1 cup cola soft drink (not
    sugar-free)

FROSTING

1 pound confectioners'
    sugar (3½ to 4 cups)
6 tablespoons or more cola
    soft drink (not sugar-
    free)
¼ cup unsweetened cocoa
    powder

¼ cup CRISCO® Stick or
    ¼ cup CRISCO® all-
    vegetable shortening
1 cup chopped pecans,
    divided

To sour milk: Combine 1½ teaspoons white vinegar plus enough milk to equal ½ cup. Stir. Wait 5 minutes before using.

1. Heat oven to 350°F. Line bottom of 13×9×2-inch baking pan with waxed paper.

2. For cake, combine granulated sugar and ¾ cup shortening in large bowl. Beat at medium speed of electric mixer 1 minute. Add eggs. Beat until blended. Add 2 tablespoons cocoa, vanilla and salt. Beat until blended.

3. Combine buttermilk and baking soda in small bowl. Add to creamed mixture. Beat until blended. Reduce speed to low. Add flour alternately with 1 cup cola, beginning and ending with flour, beating at low speed after each addition until well blended. Pour into pan.

4. Bake at 350°F for 30 to 35 minutes or until cake begins to pull away from sides of pan. Cool 10 minutes before removing from pan. Invert cake on wire rack. Remove waxed paper. Cool completely. Place cake on serving tray.

5. For frosting, combine confectioners' sugar, 6 tablespoons cola, ¼ cup cocoa and ¼ cup shortening in medium bowl. Beat at low, then medium speed until blended, adding more cola, if necessary, until of desired spreading consistency. Stir in ½ cup nuts. Frost top and sides of cake. Sprinkle remaining nuts over top of cake. Let stand at least 1 hour before serving.

Makes one 13×9×2-inch cake (12 to 16 servings)

Note: *Flavor of cake improves if made several hours or a day before serving.*

Choca-Cola Cake

◆ Chocolate Sprinkle Angel Food Cake ◆

**1 package DUNCAN HINES®
Angel Food Cake Mix**

**3 tablespoons chocolate
sprinkles**

1. Remove top rack from oven; move remaining rack to lowest position.
Preheat oven to 350°F.

2. Prepare batter following package directions. Fold in chocolate sprinkles.
Pour batter into *ungreased* 10-inch tube pan. Bake and cool following package
directions. *Makes 12 to 16 servings*

Tip: For a quick finish, simply dust cake with confectioners' sugar.

◆ Easy Carrot Cake ◆

**½ cup Prune Purée (recipe
follows)**
2 cups all-purpose flour
**2 teaspoons ground
cinnamon**
1½ teaspoons baking soda
½ teaspoon salt

**4 cups shredded DOLE®
Carrots**
2 cups sugar
½ cup DOLE® Pineapple Juice
2 eggs
**2 teaspoons vanilla extract
Vegetable cooking spray**

• Prepare Prune Purée; set aside.

• Combine flour, cinnamon, baking soda and salt in medium bowl; set aside.

• Beat together Prune Purée, carrots, sugar, juice, eggs and vanilla in large
bowl until blended. Add flour mixture; stir until well blended.

• Spread batter into 13×9-inch baking dish sprayed with vegetable cooking
spray.

• Bake at 375°F 30 to 35 minutes or until toothpick inserted in center comes
out clean. Cool completely in dish on wire rack. Dust with powdered sugar
and garnish with carrot curls, if desired. *Makes 12 servings*

*Prune Purée: Combine 1⅓ cups DOLE® Pitted Prunes, halved, and ½ cup hot water
in food processor or blender container. Process until prunes are finely chopped,
stopping to scrape down sides occasionally. (Purée can be refrigerated in airtight
container for up to 1 week.)*

Prep Time: 15 minutes
Bake Time: 35 minutes

Chocolate Sprinkle Angel Food Cake

◆ Honey Carrot Snacking Cake ◆

½ cup butter or margarine,
   softened
1 cup honey
2 eggs
2 cups finely grated carrots
½ cup golden raisins
⅓ cup chopped nuts
   (optional)
¼ cup orange juice
2 teaspoons vanilla

1 cup all-purpose flour
1 cup whole wheat flour
2 teaspoons baking powder
1½ teaspoons ground
   cinnamon
1 teaspoon baking soda
½ teaspoon salt
½ teaspoon ground ginger
¼ teaspoon ground nutmeg

Cream butter in large bowl. Gradually beat in honey until light and fluffy. Add eggs, 1 at a time, beating well after each addition. Combine carrots, raisins, nuts, if desired, orange juice and vanilla in medium bowl. Combine remaining ingredients in separate large bowl. Add dry ingredients to creamed mixture alternately with carrot mixture, beginning and ending with dry ingredients. Pour batter into greased 13×9×2-inch pan. Bake at 350°F 35 to 45 minutes or until toothpick inserted near center comes out clean.   *Makes 12 servings*

Favorite recipe from **National Honey Board**

◆ Chocolate Marble Angel Food Cake ◆

1 package DUNCAN HINES®
Angel Food Cake Mix

3 tablespoons chocolate
   syrup

1. Remove top rack from oven; move remaining rack to lowest position. Preheat oven to 350°F.

2. Prepare batter following package directions for basic recipe. Remove half of batter to another bowl; set aside. Add chocolate syrup to reserved batter. Fold gently until blended. Alternate large spoonfuls of white and chocolate batters in *ungreased* 10-inch tube pan. Bake and cool following package directions.
Makes 12 to 16 servings

Tip: *Serve slices drizzled with chocolate syrup for extra chocolate flavor.*

Honey Carrot Snacking Cake

◆ Berry Surprise Cupcakes ◆

1 package **DUNCAN HINES®**
  Moist Deluxe® White
  Cake Mix
1⅓ cups water
3 egg whites
2 tablespoons vegetable oil
3 sheets (0.5 ounce each)
  strawberry chewy fruit
  snacks

1 container **DUNCAN HINES®**
  Creamy Homestyle
  Vanilla Frosting
2 pouches (0.9 ounce each)
  chewy fruit snack
  shapes, for garnish
  (optional)

1. Preheat oven to 350°F. Place 24 (2½-inch) paper liners in muffin cups.

2. Combine cake mix, water, egg whites and oil in large bowl. Beat at low speed with electric mixer until moistened. Beat at medium speed 2 minutes. Fill each liner half full with batter.

3. Cut 3 fruit snack sheets into 9 equal pieces. (You will have 3 extra squares.) Place each fruit snack piece on top of batter in each cup. Pour remaining batter equally over each. Bake at 350°F 18 to 23 minutes or until toothpick inserted in center comes out clean. Cool in pans 5 minutes. Remove to cooling racks. Cool completely. Frost cupcakes with vanilla frosting. Decorate with fruit snack shapes, if desired. *Makes 12 to 16 servings*

Tip: To make a Berry Surprise Cake, prepare cake following package directions. Pour half of batter into prepared 13×9×2-inch pan. Place 4 fruit snack sheets evenly on top. Pour remaining batter over all. Bake and cool as directed on package. Frost and decorate as described above.

Berry Surprise Cupcakes

CHEESECAKES

◆ Apple Cheesecake ◆

1 cup graham cracker
   crumbs
3 tablespoons margarine,
   melted
   Sugar
1 teaspoon ground
   cinnamon, divided
2 (8-ounce) packages
   cream cheese, softened

2 eggs
½ teaspoon vanilla
4 cups peeled, thin apple
   slices (about 2½
   pounds apples)
½ cup chopped pecans

1. Preheat oven to 350°F.

2. Combine crumbs, margarine, 3 tablespoons sugar and ½ teaspoon cinnamon in small bowl; mix well. Press onto bottom and up side of 9-inch pie plate. Bake crust 10 minutes.

3. Beat together cream cheese and ½ cup sugar in large bowl until well blended. Add eggs, 1 at a time, beating well after each addition. Blend in vanilla; pour into crust.

4. Combine ⅓ cup sugar and remaining ½ teaspoon cinnamon in large bowl. Add apples; toss gently to coat. Spoon apple mixture over cream cheese mixture. Sprinkle with pecans.

5. Bake 1 hour 10 minutes or until set. Cool completely. Store in refrigerator.

Makes one 9-inch cheesecake

Apple Cheesecake

◆ Rich Chocolate Cheesecake ◆

1¼ cups graham cracker crumbs

4 tablespoons margarine, melted

1 teaspoon EQUAL® FOR RECIPES *or* 3 packets EQUAL® sweetener *or* 2 tablespoons EQUAL® SPOONFUL™

2 packages (8 ounces each) reduced-fat cream cheese, softened

1 package (8 ounces) fat-free cream cheese, softened

5½ teaspoons EQUAL® FOR RECIPES *or* 18 packets EQUAL® sweetener *or* ¾ cup EQUAL® SPOONFUL™

2 eggs

2 egg whites

2 tablespoons cornstarch

1 cup reduced-fat sour cream

⅓ cup European or Dutch-process cocoa

1 teaspoon vanilla

Fresh mint sprigs, raspberries, nonfat whipped topping and orange peel (optional)

• Mix graham cracker crumbs, margarine and 1 teaspoon Equal® For Recipes *or* 3 packets Equal® sweetener *or* 2 tablespoons Equal® Spoonful™ in bottom of 9-inch springform pan. Pat mixture evenly on bottom and ½ inch up side of pan.

• Beat cream cheese and 5½ teaspoons Equal® For Recipes *or* 18 packets Equal® sweetener *or* ¾ cup Equal® Spoonful™ in large bowl until fluffy; beat in eggs, egg whites and cornstarch. Mix in sour cream, cocoa and vanilla until well blended. Pour mixture into crust.

• Place cheesecake in roasting pan on oven rack; add 1 inch hot water to roasting pan. Bake cheesecake in preheated 300°F oven just until set in the center, 45 to 50 minutes. Remove cheesecake from roasting pan; return cheesecake to oven. Turn oven off and let cheesecake cool 3 hours in oven with door ajar. Refrigerate 8 hours or overnight. Remove side of pan; place cheesecake on serving plate. Garnish, if desired.   *Makes 16 servings*

Rich Chocolate Cheesecake

◆ Lemon Cheesecake ◆

CRUST
35 vanilla wafers
¾ cup slivered almonds, toasted
⅓ cup sugar
¼ cup butter, melted

FILLING
3 packages (8 ounces each) cream cheese, softened
¾ cup sugar
4 eggs
⅓ cup whipping cream
¼ cup lemon juice
1 tablespoon grated lemon peel
1 teaspoon vanilla

TOPPING
1 pint strawberries
2 tablespoons sugar

1. Preheat oven to 375°F. For crust, combine wafers, almonds and ⅓ cup sugar in food processor; process until fine crumbs are formed. Combine sugar mixture with melted butter in medium bowl. Press mixture evenly on bottom and 1 inch up side of 9-inch springform pan. Set aside.

2. For filling, beat cream cheese and ¾ cup sugar in large bowl on high speed of electric mixer 2 to 3 minutes or until fluffy. Add eggs, 1 at a time, beating after each addition. Add whipping cream, lemon juice, lemon peel and vanilla; beat just until blended. Pour into prepared crust. Place springform pan on baking sheet. Bake 45 to 55 minutes or until set. Cool completely on wire rack. Cover and refrigerate at least 10 hours or overnight.

3. To complete recipe, for topping, hull and slice strawberries. Combine with 2 tablespoons sugar in medium bowl. Let stand 15 minutes. Serve over cheesecake.

Makes 16 servings

Make-Ahead Time: 10 hours or overnight
Final Prep/Stand Time: 20 minutes

Lemon Cheesecake

◆ Chocolate Sour Cream Cheesecake ◆

**Chocolate Crumb Crust
(recipe follows)**

**3 packages (8 ounces each)
fat-free cream cheese,
softened**

**1 cup reduced-fat sour
cream**

2 eggs

⅔ cup sugar

**⅓ cup unsweetened cocoa
powder**

**¼ cup fat-free chocolate
syrup**

**3 tablespoons all-purpose
flour**

1. Preheat oven to 350°F. Prepare Chocolate Crumb Crust; set aside. Beat cream cheese in large bowl with electric mixer at high speed until fluffy. Beat in sour cream until smooth. Beat in eggs, 1 at a time. Mix in sugar, cocoa, chocolate syrup and flour until smooth. Pour over crust.

2. Bake 50 to 60 minutes or until set in center. Loosen cheesecake from edge of pan with knife. Cool on wire rack. Cover; refrigerate overnight.

3. Remove side of pan. Garnish cheesecake with dollops of nonfat whipped topping, chocolate shavings and chocolate curls, if desired.

Makes 12 servings

Chocolate Crumb Crust

**1¼ cups graham cracker
crumbs**

2 tablespoons sugar

**2 tablespoons unsweetened
cocoa powder**

**4 tablespoons margarine,
melted**

1. Preheat oven to 350°F. Combine graham cracker crumbs, sugar and cocoa in bottom of 9-inch springform pan; stir in margarine. Pat mixture evenly onto bottom and 1 inch up side of pan.

2. Bake 8 minutes or until lightly browned. Cool on wire rack.

Makes 1 (9-inch) crust

Chocolate Sour Cream Cheesecake

◆ Walnut Brownie Cheesecake ◆

CRUST
1¼ cups fine chocolate wafer crumbs (about 25 cookies, processed in blender or food processor)

3 tablespoons melted margarine

FILLING
4 cups (30 ounces) SARGENTO® Light Ricotta Cheese
1¼ cups packed light brown sugar
½ cup half-and-half
⅓ cup unsweetened cocoa powder

¼ cup all-purpose flour
1 teaspoon vanilla
¼ teaspoon salt
3 eggs
½ cup (2 ounces) coarsely chopped walnuts
Confectioners' sugar (optional)

Lightly grease side of 8- or 9-inch springform pan. Combine crust ingredients; mix well. Press evenly over bottom of pan. Chill while preparing filling. In bowl of electric mixer, combine ricotta cheese, brown sugar, half-and-half, cocoa, flour, vanilla and salt; beat until smooth. Add eggs, 1 at a time; beat until smooth. Stir in walnuts. Pour batter over crust. Bake at 350°F 1 hour 10 minutes or until center is just set. Turn off oven; cool in oven with door propped open 30 minutes. Remove to wire cooling rack; loosen cake from rim of pan with metal spatula. Cool completely; chill at least 4 hours. Sift confectioners' sugar over cheesecake immediately before serving, if desired.

Makes 8 servings

◆ Cheesecake Sensation ◆

¼ cup graham cracker crumbs
4 (8-ounce) packages cream cheese, softened
4 eggs
1¾ cups sugar
2 tablespoons lemon juice

2 tablespoons grated lemon peel
1 teaspoon vanilla
½ cup SMUCKER'S® Natural Apricot Syrup
½ cup SMUCKER'S® Strawberry Preserves

Butter inside of straight-side casserole or soufflé dish 8 inches wide and 3 inches deep. Do not use springform pan. Sprinkle with graham cracker crumbs and shake around bottom and sides until coated. Set aside.

Combine cream cheese, eggs, sugar, lemon juice, lemon peel and vanilla; beat at low speed and, as ingredients blend, increase speed to high, scraping bowl several times. Continue beating until thoroughly blended and smooth. Pour batter into prepared dish; shake gently to level mixture. Set dish inside slightly wider pan; add boiling water to larger pan to depth of about ½ inch. Do not let edge of cheesecake dish touch rim of larger pan.

Bake at 325°F for 1½ to 2 hours or until set. Turn off oven; let cake sit in oven 20 minutes longer. Lift cake dish out of larger pan and place on wire rack. Cool about 2 hours or until cake reaches room temperature.

Invert plate over cheesecake and carefully turn upside down so cake comes out crumb side up. Slowly spoon syrup over cake. Just before serving, spoon preserves in narrow ring around outer rim of cake.

Makes 12 to 14 servings

◆ Vanilla Cheesecake with Strawberries ◆

1 (3-ounce) package ladyfingers
2 egg whites, beaten
15 ounces part-skim ricotta cheese
1 cup nonfat plain yogurt
3 tablespoons sugar

2 tablespoons cornstarch dissolved in ¼ cup water
2 tablespoons lemon juice
1 teaspoon vanilla
Strawberry Sauce (recipe follows)

Preheat oven to 300°F. Spray 7-inch springform pan with nonstick cooking spray. Trim ½ inch from ladyfingers and with trimmed ends at bottom, use to line side of pan. In food processor, beat egg whites until soft peaks form; remove to large mixing bowl. In food processor, mix remaining ingredients, except Strawberry Sauce, and blend until smooth. Gently fold beaten egg whites into cheese mixture. Pour mixture into prepared pan and bake 1 hour 15 minutes or until cake is lightly brown and almost set in center. Cool 1 hour, then cover with foil or plastic wrap and refrigerate overnight.

Before serving, prepare Strawberry Sauce. Slice reserved berries into halves and place in circle on cake. Pour sauce over individual slices.

Makes 8 servings

Strawberry Sauce

4 cups fresh *or* 20 ounces frozen strawberries

1 tablespoon sugar

Reserve 5 whole berries for garnish. Purée remaining berries in food processor or blender; add sugar. Pour into serving boat, cover, and chill until ready to serve.

Favorite recipe from **The Sugar Association, Inc.**

Creamy Cheesecake
◆ with Raspberry Sauce ◆

1¼ cups graham cracker crumbs
¾ cup *plus* 2 tablespoons sugar, divided
4 tablespoons margarine, melted
2 tablespoons cornstarch
1 envelope unflavored gelatin
1 cup fat-free (skim) milk

1 egg, beaten
2 packages (8 ounces each) fat-free cream cheese, softened
½ cup reduced-fat sour cream
1 teaspoon vanilla
Raspberry Sauce (recipe follows)
1 cup fresh raspberries

1. Preheat oven to 350°F. Combine graham cracker crumbs and 2 tablespoons sugar in bottom of 9-inch springform pan; mix in melted margarine. Reserve 2 tablespoons crumb mixture; pat remaining mixture evenly on bottom and 1 inch up side of pan. Bake 5 to 8 minutes or until lightly browned. Cool on wire rack.

2. Combine cornstarch and gelatin in small saucepan; stir in milk. Bring mixture to a boil, over medium heat, stirring constantly; boil about 1 minute or until thickened, stirring constantly. Using wire whisk, stir about ½ of cornstarch mixture into beaten egg; whisk egg mixture back into remaining cornstarch mixture in saucepan. Reduce heat to low. Cook and stir 2 minutes. Remove from heat; cool completely.

3. Beat cream cheese in large bowl with electric mixer until fluffy. Add sour cream and remaining ¾ cup sugar; beat until smooth. Add cornstarch mixture and vanilla; beat until combined. Pour into crust; sprinkle with reserved 2 tablespoons crumb mixture. Refrigerate several hours or until firm.

4. Prepare Raspberry Sauce. Carefully loosen side of pan with metal spatula or knife; remove side. Place cheesecake on serving plate; top with fresh raspberries. Serve with Raspberry Sauce.   *Makes 12 servings*

Raspberry Sauce: Combine 1 package (12 ounces) frozen thawed raspberries and ½ cup sugar in food processor or blender; process until smooth. Strain and discard seeds. Refrigerate sauce until ready to serve.   Makes about 2 cups sauce

Creamy Cheesecake with Raspberry Sauce

◆ Creamy Banana Cheesecake ◆

20 **vanilla sandwich cream cookies**
¼ **cup margarine or butter, melted**
3 **packages (8 ounces each) cream cheese, softened**
⅔ **cup sugar**
2 **tablespoons cornstarch**
3 **eggs**
¾ **cup mashed bananas (about 2)**

½ **cup whipping cream**
2 **teaspoons vanilla**
¼ **fresh peeled pineapple, cut in chunks *or* 1 can (20 ounces) pineapple chunks, drained**
1 **pint strawberries, cut into halves**
2 **tablespoons hot fudge ice cream topping**
Mint leaves (optional)

Preheat oven to 350°F. Place cookies in food processor or blender; process with on/off pulses until finely crushed. Add margarine; process with pulses until blended. Press crumb mixture onto bottom of 10-inch springform pan; refrigerate.

Beat cream cheese in large bowl with electric mixer at medium speed until creamy. Add sugar and cornstarch; beat until blended. Add eggs, 1 at a time, beating well after each addition. Beat in bananas, whipping cream and vanilla.

Pour cream cheese mixture into prepared crust. Place pan on cookie sheet and bake 15 minutes. *Reduce oven temperature to 200°F.* Continue baking 75 minutes or until center is almost set. Loosen edge of cheesecake; cool completely on wire rack before removing rim of pan.

Refrigerate cheesecake, uncovered, 6 hours or overnight. Place pineapple and strawberries over top of cake. Allow cheesecake to stand at room temperature 15 minutes before serving. For fudge drizzle, place topping in small resealable plastic freezer bag; seal bag. Microwave at HIGH 20 seconds. Cut off tiny corner of bag; drizzle over fruit. Garnish with mint leaves, if desired.

Makes 8 servings

Creamy Banana Cheesecake

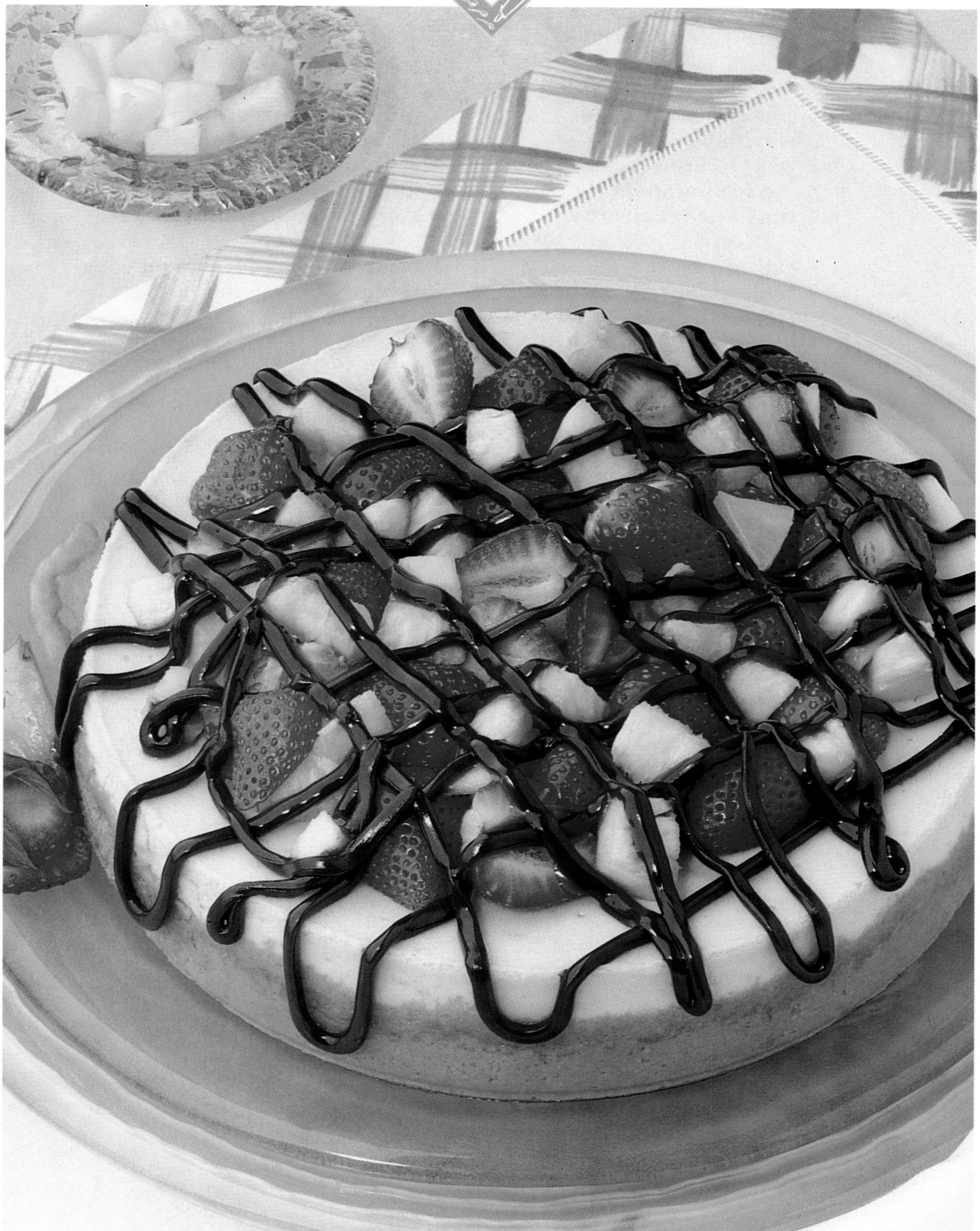

◆ Pumpkin Cheesecake ◆

⅓ cup graham cracker crumbs

1 can (16 ounces) solid pack pumpkin

2 cups low-fat ricotta cheese

1 cup sugar

3 tablespoons all-purpose flour

1 tablespoon nonfat dry milk powder

1 tablespoon ground cinnamon

1 teaspoon ground allspice

1 egg white

¾ cup canned evaporated skimmed milk

1 tablespoon vegetable oil

1 tablespoon vanilla

1. Preheat oven to 400°F. Spray 9-inch springform pan with nonstick cooking spray. Add graham cracker crumbs; shake to coat pan evenly. Set aside.

2. Combine pumpkin and ricotta cheese in food processor or blender; process until smooth. Add sugar, flour, milk powder, cinnamon, allspice, egg white, evaporated skimmed milk, oil and vanilla; process until smooth.

3. Pour mixture into prepared pan. Bake 15 minutes. *Reduce oven temperature to 275°F;* bake 1 hour 15 minutes. Turn off oven; leave cheesecake in oven with door closed 1 hour. Remove from oven; cool completely on wire rack. Remove springform pan side. Cover cheesecake with plastic wrap; refrigerate at least 4 hours or up to 2 days. Garnish with fresh fruit, if desired.

Makes 16 servings

Pumpkin Cheesecake

◆ Orange Chiffon Cheesecake ◆

2 cups graham cracker crumbs

8 tablespoons light margarine, melted

1 teaspoon EQUAL® FOR RECIPES *or* 3 packets EQUAL® sweetener *or* 2 tablespoons EQUAL® SPOONFUL™

1 cup orange juice

1 envelope (¼ ounce) unflavored gelatin

12 ounces reduced-fat cream cheese, softened

1 cup part-skim ricotta cheese

3½ teaspoons EQUAL® FOR RECIPES *or* 12 packets EQUAL® sweetener *or* ½ cup EQUAL® SPOONFUL™

2 cups light whipped topping

2 medium oranges, peeled, seeded and chopped

Orange sections (optional)

• Spray 9-inch springform pan with nonstick cooking spray. Mix graham cracker crumbs, margarine and 1 teaspoon Equal® For Recipes *or* 3 packets Equal® sweetener *or* 2 tablespoons Equal® Spoonful™. Pat mixture evenly on bottom and halfway up side of pan. Bake in preheated 350°F oven 8 to 10 minutes or until set. Cool.

• Pour orange juice into small saucepan. Sprinkle gelatin over orange juice and let soften 1 minute. Heat, stirring constantly, until gelatin dissolves, about 3 minutes. Blend cream cheese and ricotta cheese in large bowl until smooth; stir in 3½ teaspoons Equal® For Recipes *or* 12 packets Equal® sweetener *or* ½ cup Equal® Spoonful™. Add gelatin mixture to cheese mixture; blend until smooth. Fold whipped topping into cheese mixture. Stir in chopped oranges. Spoon into prepared crust and spread evenly.

• Chill 6 hours or overnight. Remove side of pan; place cheesecake on serving plate. Garnish with orange sections, if desired.   *Makes 16 servings*

◆ Creamy Chocolate Marble Cheesecake ◆

**Cinnamon Graham Crust
(recipe follows)
3 packages (8 ounces each)
cream cheese, softened
¾ cup sugar
3 eggs**

**1 cup dairy sour cream
1 teaspoon vanilla extract
1 square (1 ounce)
unsweetened chocolate,
melted***

*For plain cheesecake, omit melted chocolate. Proceed as directed.

Preheat oven to 450°F. Prepare Cinnamon Graham Crust.

Beat cream cheese in large bowl with electric mixer on medium speed until fluffy. Beat in sugar on medium speed until light and fluffy. Beat in eggs, 1 at a time, on low speed until well blended. Stir in sour cream and vanilla on low speed. Blend melted chocolate into 1 cup batter. Spoon plain and chocolate batters alternately over crust. Cut through batters several times with a knife for marble effect.

Bake 10 minutes. *Reduce oven temperature to 250°F.* Bake 30 minutes more or until center is just set. Remove pan to wire rack. Carefully loosen edge of cake with narrow knife. Cool completely on wire rack. Refrigerate several hours or overnight.

To serve, place on plate. Carefully remove side of pan.

Makes one 9-inch cheesecake

Cinnamon Graham Crust

**1 cup graham cracker
crumbs
3 tablespoons sugar
½ teaspoon ground
cinnamon**

**3 tablespoons butter or
margarine, melted**

Preheat oven to 350°F. Combine crumbs, sugar and cinnamon in small bowl. Stir in melted butter until blended. Press onto bottom of 9-inch springform pan. Bake 10 minutes. Cool on wire rack while preparing filling.

◆ Marble Cheesecake ◆

CRUMB CRUST

- 12 cinnamon graham crackers (5×2½-inch)
- ¼ cup sugar
- ¼ teaspoon ground cinnamon
- 6 tablespoons unsalted butter, at room temperature
- 2 tablespoons cold water

MARBLE CHEESE FILLING

- ¾ cup 2% low fat milk
- 4 cups (1 pound) shredded ALPINE LACE® Reduced Sodium Muenster Cheese
- ¾ cup sugar
- 2 tablespoons all-purpose flour
- 1 cup egg substitute *or* 4 large eggs, slightly beaten
- ⅓ cup mini semi-sweet chocolate chips, melted
- 1 teaspoon vanilla extract

SOUR CREAM TOPPING

- 2 cups fat free sour cream
- 2 tablespoons sugar
- 1 teaspoon vanilla extract
- ½ pint fresh raspberries

1. To make the Crumb Crust: Preheat the oven to 350°F. Spray a 10-inch springform pan with nonstick cooking spray. In a food processor, place the graham crackers, the ¼ cup sugar and the cinnamon; process for 1 minute or until finely ground. Add the butter and water; process 30 seconds more or until moistened. Press onto the bottom and 1½ inches up the side of the pan.

2. To make the Marble Cheese Filling: In a small saucepan, bring the milk to a boil over medium-high heat. In a food processor, process the cheese, the ¾ cup sugar, and the flour for 1 minute or until coarsely ground. With the motor running, add the hot milk through the feed tube, then the egg substitute (or the 4 whole eggs). Process 1 minute or until smooth and pour into a large bowl. Measure out ½ cup of the batter, stir in the melted chips and vanilla. Set aside. Pour the white batter into the crust. Randomly spoon the chocolate batter on top. Gently cut through the batter to make chocolate swirls. Bake on the middle rack of the oven for 35 minutes. Transfer cake in pan to a rack to cool for 5 minutes.

3. While cake bakes, make the Sour Cream Topping: In a small bowl, stir together sour cream, the 2 tablespoons sugar and the vanilla. Carefully spread topping evenly on top of cake.

4. Return cake to the oven and bake 10 minutes more or until topping is set. Cool cake in pan. Chill for 1 hour, garnish with the raspberries and chill 1 hour more or overnight. If you wish, decorate with fresh mint leaves before serving.

Makes 24 servings

Marble Cheesecake

◆ White Chocolate Cheesecake ◆

12 squares (1 ounce each) white baking chocolate, divided
1½ cups all-purpose flour
½ cup granulated sugar
½ cup butter
½ cup finely chopped toasted almonds or macadamia nuts
4 eggs, divided
⅓ cup whipping cream
1 tablespoon vanilla
3 packages (8 ounces) cream cheese, softened
1 can (14 ounces) sweetened condensed milk
Additional grated white baking chocolate and toasted sliced almonds for garnish
Strawberries and powdered sugar for garnish

1. Preheat oven to 325°F.

2. Grate 4 chocolate squares; set aside.

3. Stir together flour and granulated sugar in medium bowl; cut in butter until mixture resembles coarse crumbs. Add almonds, grated chocolate and 1 beaten egg; mix until well blended.

4. Press flour mixture onto bottom and 1 inch up side of 9-inch springform pan. Refrigerate.

5. Meanwhile, chop remaining 8 chocolate squares. Place in top of double boiler. Add whipping cream. Cook, stirring constantly, over simmering water until chocolate is melted. Stir in vanilla; keep warm.

6. Beat together cream cheese and milk in medium bowl until well blended. Add remaining 3 eggs, 1 at a time, beating well after each addition. Stir in chocolate mixture. Pour into crust.

7. Bake 1 hour 20 minutes or until set. Loosen cake from rim of pan; cool before removing rim of pan. Refrigerate.

8. Garnish, if desired. Sprinkle with powdered sugar.

Makes one 9-inch cheesecake

White Chocolate Cheesecake

◆ Decadent Turtle Cheesecake ◆

2 cups crushed chocolate cookies or vanilla wafers (about 8 ounces cookies)
¼ cup (½ stick) butter, melted
2½ packages (8 ounces each) cream cheese, softened
1 cup sugar
1½ tablespoons all-purpose flour
1½ teaspoons vanilla
¼ teaspoon salt
3 eggs
2 tablespoons whipping cream
Caramel and Chocolate Toppings (recipes follow)
¾ cup chopped toasted pecans

Preheat oven to 450°F. For crust, combine cookie crumbs and butter; press onto bottom of 9-inch springform pan.

For filling, beat cream cheese in large bowl with electric mixer until creamy. Beat in sugar, flour, vanilla and salt; mix well. Add eggs, 1 at a time, beating well after each addition. Blend in cream. Pour over crust.

Bake 10 minutes; *reduce oven temperature to 200°F.* Continue baking 35 to 40 minutes or until set. Loosen cake from rim of pan; cool completely before removing rim of pan. Meanwhile, prepare Caramel and Chocolate Toppings.

Drizzle cake with toppings. Refrigerate. Sprinkle with pecans before serving.

Makes one 9-inch cheesecake

Caramel Topping: Combine ½ (14-ounce) bag caramels and ¼ cup whipping cream in small saucepan; stir over low heat until smooth.

Chocolate Topping: Combine 4 squares (1 ounce each) semisweet chocolate or 4 ounces semisweet chocolate chips, 1 teaspoon butter and 2 tablespoons whipping cream in small saucepan; stir over low heat until smooth.

Decadent Turtle Cheesecake

◆ Cherry Cream Cheese Brunch Cake ◆

CAKE

¾ Butter Flavor* CRISCO®
Stick or ¾ cup Butter
Flavor* CRISCO® all-
vegetable shortening
plus additional for
greasing

2½ cups cake flour

¾ cup sugar

1 cup (8 ounces) dairy sour
cream

1 egg

1 teaspoon pure almond
extract

1 teaspoon pure vanilla
extract

½ teaspoon baking powder

½ teaspoon baking soda

¼ teaspoon salt

FILLING

2 packages (3 ounces each)
cream cheese, softened

½ cup sugar

3 tablespoons cake flour

2 tablespoons Butter
Flavor* CRISCO® Stick or
2 tablespoons Butter
Flavor* CRISCO® all-
vegetable shortening

½ teaspoon pure vanilla
extract

1 egg

¾ cup canned cherry pie
filling

⅛ teaspoon pure almond
extract

TOPPING

Reserved 1 cup crumb
mixture

½ cup sliced almonds

Additional sliced
almonds, toasted**

Butter Flavor Crisco® is artificially flavored.

**To toast nuts, spread on baking sheet. Bake at 350°F for 5 to 10 minutes or until golden brown, stirring occasionally.*

1. Heat oven to 350°F. Grease 9-inch springform pan*** with shortening. Flour lightly.

2. For cake, combine 2½ cups flour and ¾ cup sugar in large bowl. Add ¾ cup shortening. Beat at low speed of electric mixer until coarse crumbs form. Reserve 1 cup crumbs for topping.

3. Add sour cream, egg, 1 teaspoon almond extract, 1 teaspoon vanilla, baking powder, baking soda and salt to remaining crumb mixture in bowl. Beat at medium speed until well blended. Spread batter in bottom and 2 inches up side of pan.

(continued on page 274)

Cherry Cream Cheese Brunch Cake

(Cherry Cream Cheese Brunch Cake, continued from page 272)

4. For filling, combine cream cheese, ½ cup sugar, 3 tablespoons flour, 2 tablespoons shortening and ½ teaspoon vanilla in medium bowl. Beat until blended. Add egg. Beat just until blended. Pour over batter. Combine pie filling and ⅛ teaspoon almond extract in small bowl. Spread over cream cheese mixture.

5. For topping, combine reserved 1 cup crumbs and ½ cup almonds. Sprinkle over filling.

6. Bake at 350°F for 1 hour 5 minutes or until filling is set in center, crust is deep golden brown and toothpick inserted in center comes out fairly dry except for pie filling. Cover edge of cake with foil, if necessary, to prevent overbrowning. Sprinkle additional nuts around edge and over top of cake. Cool 15 to 20 minutes. Loosen cake from side of pan with knife or metal spatula. Remove side of pan. Cool completely. Remove bottom of pan using thin metal spatula or pancake turner. Place cake on serving plate. Serve immediately or refrigerate until serving time. Refrigerate leftovers.

Makes one 9-inch cake (12 servings)

***Bake cake in 9-inch heart-shaped springform pan, if desired.*

◆ Chocolate Chip Cheesecake ◆

CRUST

1 cup oats (quick or old fashioned, uncooked)	⅓ cup Butter Flavor* CRISCO® all-vegetable shortening, melted
⅓ cup finely chopped almonds	
⅓ cup firmly packed brown sugar	

FILLING

3 (8-ounce) packages cream cheese, softened	⅓ cup milk or strong coffee
1 cup granulated sugar	1 cup mini semi-sweet chocolate pieces, divided
1½ teaspoons vanilla	2 teaspoons all-purpose flour
3 eggs	

Butter Flavor Crisco® is artificially flavored.

Heat oven to 350°F. For crust, combine all ingredients; mix well. Press onto bottom and 1-inch up sides of 9-inch springform pan or bottom only of 13×9-inch baking pan. Bake 10 to 15 minutes or until golden brown. Cool completely.

For filling, beat cream cheese, granulated sugar and vanilla at medium speed of electric mixer until fluffy. Add eggs, 1 at a time, beating well after each. Gradually mix in milk. Reserve 1 tablespoon chocolate pieces; combine remainder with flour. Stir floured chocolate pieces into cream cheese mixture; pour onto crust. Sprinkle with reserved chocolate pieces. Bake 50 to 60 minutes (45 minutes for 13×9-inch pan) or until almost set. Cool completely; loosen side with knife and remove rim. Chill. Store covered in refrigerator.

Makes 16 servings

◆ Traditional Ricotta Cheesecake ◆

CRUST

1 cup finely crushed graham crackers
¼ cup sugar

¼ cup melted margarine

FILLING

2 cups (15 ounces) SARGENTO® Light Ricotta Cheese
½ cup sugar
½ cup half-and-half
2 tablespoons all-purpose flour

1 tablespoon fresh lemon juice
1 teaspoon finely grated lemon peel
¼ teaspoon salt
2 eggs

TOPPING

1 cup light sour cream
2 tablespoons sugar

1 teaspoon vanilla

Combine graham crackers, ¼ cup sugar and margarine; mix well. Press evenly over bottom and 1½ inches up side of 8- or 9-inch springform pan. Chill while preparing filling.

In bowl of electric mixer, combine ricotta cheese, ½ cup sugar, half-and-half, flour, lemon juice, lemon peel and salt; blend until smooth. Add eggs, 1 at a time; blend until smooth. Pour into crust. Bake at 350°F 50 minutes or until center is just set. Remove from oven.

Beat sour cream with 2 tablespoons sugar and vanilla. Gently spoon onto warm cheesecake; spread evenly over surface. Return to oven 10 minutes. Turn off oven; cool in oven with door propped open 30 minutes. Remove to wire cooling rack; cool completely. Chill at least 3 hours. *Makes 8 servings*

◆ Chocolate-Berry Cheesecake ◆

1 cup chocolate wafer crumbs

1 container (12 ounces) fat-free cream cheese

1 package (8 ounces) reduced-fat cream cheese

²/₃ cup sugar

½ cup cholesterol-free egg substitute

3 tablespoons fat-free (skim) milk

1¼ teaspoons vanilla

1 cup mini semisweet chocolate chips

2 tablespoons raspberry all-fruit spread

2 tablespoons water

2½ cups fresh strawberries, stems removed, halved

1. Preheat oven to 350°F. Spray bottom of 9-inch springform pan with nonstick cooking spray.

2. Press chocolate wafer crumbs firmly onto side or bottom of prepared pan. Bake 10 minutes. Remove from oven; cool. *Reduce oven temperature to 325°F.*

3. Combine cheeses in large bowl with electric mixer. Beat at medium speed until well blended. Beat in sugar until well blended. Beat in egg substitute, milk and vanilla until well blended. Stir in chocolate chips with spoon. Pour batter into pan.

4. Bake 40 minutes or until center is set. Remove from oven; cool 10 minutes in pan on wire rack. Carefully loosen cheesecake from edge of pan. Cool completely.

5. Remove side of pan from cake. Blend fruit spread and water in medium bowl until smooth. Add strawberries; toss to coat. Arrange strawberries on top of cake. Refrigerate 1 hour before serving. Garnish with fresh mint, if desired.

Makes 16 servings

Chocolate-Berry Cheesecake

◆ Orange Cappuccino Cheesecake ◆

1½ cups finely chopped nuts
1 cup plus
    2 tablespoons sugar,
    divided
3 tablespoons butter,
    melted
4 (8-ounce) packages
    cream cheese, softened
3 tablespoons all-purpose
    flour
4 eggs

1 cup sour cream
1 tablespoon instant coffee
    powder
¼ teaspoon ground
    cinnamon
¼ cup orange juice
1 teaspoon grated orange
    peel
Cinnamon sugar,
    whipped cream and
    orange zest for garnish

1. Preheat oven to 325°F.

2. Combine nuts, 2 tablespoons sugar and butter in medium bowl; mix well. Press onto bottom of 9-inch springform pan.

3. Bake 10 minutes. Remove from oven. *Increase oven temperature to 450°F.*

4. Beat together cream cheese, remaining 1 cup sugar and flour in large bowl until well blended. Add eggs, 1 at a time, beating well after each addition. Blend in sour cream.

5. Add coffee powder and cinnamon to orange juice; stir until coffee is dissolved. Gradually add juice mixture with orange peel to cream cheese mixture, mixing until well blended. Pour over crust. Bake 10 minutes.

6. *Reduce oven temperature to 250°F.* Continue baking cheesecake 1 hour.

7. Loosen cake from rim of pan; cool 10 minutes. Sprinkle with cinnamon sugar. Lightly score top of cheesecake with sharp knife. Cool completely before removing rim of pan.

8. Spoon desired amount of whipped cream into pastry tube; pipe around edge of cheesecake. Sprinkle with orange zest, if desired.

Makes one 9-inch cheesecake

Orange Cappuccino Cheesecake

◆ Mixed Berry Cheesecake ◆

CRUST

1½ cups fruit-juice-sweetened breakfast cereal flakes*

15 dietetic butter-flavored cookies*

1 tablespoon vegetable oil

CHEESECAKE

2 packages (8 ounces each) fat-free cream cheese, softened

2 cartons (8 ounces each) nonfat raspberry yogurt

1 package (8 ounces) Neufchâtel cream cheese, softened

½ cup all-fruit seedless blackberry preserves

½ cup all-fruit blueberry preserves

6 packages artificial sweetener *or* equivalent of ¼ cup sugar

1 tablespoon vanilla

¼ cup water

1 package (0.3 ounce) sugar-free strawberry-flavored gelatin

TOPPING

3 cups fresh or frozen unsweetened mixed berries, thawed

Available in the health food section of supermarkets.

1. Preheat oven to 400°F. Spray 10-inch springform pan with nonstick cooking spray.

2. To prepare crust, combine cereal, cookies and oil in food processor; process with on/off pulses until finely crushed. Press firmly onto bottom and ½ inch up side of pan. Bake 5 to 8 minutes or until crust is golden brown.

3. To prepare cheesecake, combine cream cheese, yogurt, Neufchâtel cheese, preserves, artificial sweetener and vanilla in large bowl. Beat with electric mixer at high speed until smooth.

4. Combine water and gelatin in small microwavable bowl; microwave at HIGH for 30 seconds to 1 minute or until water is boiling and gelatin is dissolved. Cool slightly. Add to cheese mixture; beat an additional 2 to 3 minutes or until well blended. Pour into springform pan; cover and refrigerate at least 24 hours. Top cheesecake with berries before serving.

Makes 12 servings

Mixed Berry Cheesecake

PIES & TARTS

◆ Strawberry Rhubarb Pie ◆

**Pastry for double-crust
  9-inch pie**
**4 cups sliced (1-inch pieces)
  fresh rhubarb**
**3 cups (1 pint) fresh
  strawberries, sliced**
1½ cups granulated sugar

½ cup cornstarch
**2 tablespoons quick-
  cooking tapioca**
**1 tablespoon grated lemon
  peel**
¼ teaspoon ground allspice
1 egg, lightly beaten

Preheat oven to 425°F. Roll out half of pastry; place in 9-inch pie plate. Trim pastry; flute edges, sealing to edge of pie plate. Set aside. Place rhubarb and strawberries in large bowl. In medium bowl, combine sugar, cornstarch, tapioca, lemon peel and allspice; mix well. Sprinkle sugar mixture over fruit; toss to coat well. Fill pie shell evenly with fruit. (Do not mound in center.) Roll out remaining pastry to 10-inch circle. Cut into ½-inch-wide strips. Form into lattice design over fruit. Brush egg over pastry. Bake 50 minutes or until filling is bubbly and thick. Cool on wire rack. Serve warm or at room temperature.

Makes 8 servings

Strawberry Rhubarb Pie

◆ Chocolate Chip Pecan Pie ◆

CRUST
1 unbaked 9-inch Classic CRISCO® Single Crust (page 290)

FILLING
4 eggs
1 cup sugar
1 cup light corn syrup
3 tablespoons butter or margarine, melted
1 teaspoon vanilla
¼ teaspoon salt

2 cups pecan halves
½ cup semi-sweet chocolate chips
1 tablespoon plus 1½ teaspoons bourbon (optional)

1. Heat oven to 375°F. Place cooling rack on countertop for cooling pie.

2. For filling, beat eggs in large bowl at low speed of electric mixer until blended. Stir in sugar, corn syrup, butter, vanilla and salt with spoon until blended. Stir in nuts, chocolate chips and bourbon. Pour into unbaked pie crust.

3. Bake at 375°F for 55 to 60 minutes or until set. *Do not overbake.* Cover edge of pie with foil, if necessary, to prevent overbrowning. Remove pie to cooling rack to cool completely. Cool to room temperature before serving. Refrigerate leftover pie.

Makes 1 (9-inch) pie

◆ Apple Crumb Pie ◆

⅔ cup plus 6 tablespoons sugar, divided
¾ cup plus 2 tablespoons all-purpose flour, divided
¾ teaspoon ground cinnamon

7 cups peeled, sliced MacIntosh or other tart apples
1 (9-inch) unbaked deep-dish pie shell
6 tablespoons butter

Preheat oven to 400°F. Combine ⅔ cup sugar, 2 tablespoons flour and cinnamon in large bowl; stir in apples. Pour into pie shell. Combine remaining 6 tablespoons sugar and ¾ cup flour in small bowl; cut in butter until crumbly. Sprinkle crumb topping over apple mixture. Bake 45 to 50 minutes or until crumbs are lightly browned.

Makes about 8 servings

Favorite recipe from **Bob Evans®**

Chocolate Chip Pecan Pie

◆ Fresh Lemon Meringue Pie ◆

1½ cups sugar
¼ cup plus 2 tablespoons
    cornstarch
¼ teaspoon salt
½ cup cold water
½ cup fresh squeezed lemon
    juice
3 egg yolks, well beaten
1½ cups boiling water

2 tablespoons butter or
    margarine
Grated peel of ½
    SUNKIST® lemon
2 to 3 drops yellow food
    coloring (optional)
1 (9-inch) baked pie crust
Three-Egg Meringue
    (recipe follows)

In 2- to 3-quart saucepan, thoroughly combine sugar, cornstarch and salt. Gradually whisk in cold water and lemon juice. Stir in egg yolks. Add boiling water and butter. Bring to a boil over medium-high heat, stirring constantly with rubber spatula. Reduce heat to medium and boil 1 minute. Remove from heat and stir in lemon peel and food coloring. Pour into baked pie crust. Let stand, allowing thin film to form while preparing Three-Egg Meringue. Top with Three-Egg Meringue, sealing well at edges. Bake at 350°F 12 to 15 minutes. Cool 2½ to 3 hours before serving. Refrigerate leftovers.

Makes 6 to 8 servings

Three-Egg Meringue: *In bowl, with electric mixer, beat 3 egg whites with ¼ teaspoon cream of tartar until foamy. Gradually add 6 tablespoons sugar and beat until stiff peaks form.*

◆ Peanut Chocolate Surprise Pie ◆

1 cup granulated sugar
½ cup (1 stick) butter,
    melted
2 eggs
½ cup all-purpose flour
½ cup chopped peanuts
½ cup chopped walnuts
½ cup semisweet chocolate
    chips

¼ cup bourbon
1 teaspoon vanilla
1 (9-inch) unbaked deep-
    dish pie shell
Whipped cream for
    garnish
Chocolate shavings for
    garnish

Preheat oven to 350°F. Cream sugar and butter in large bowl. Add eggs and beat until well mixed. Gradually add flour; stir in nuts, chocolate chips, bourbon and vanilla. Spread mixture evenly in unbaked pie shell. Bake 40 minutes. Cool pie on wire rack. Garnish, if desired.   *Makes one 9-inch pie*

Fresh Lemon Meringue Pie

◆ Early American Pumpkin Pie ◆

1½ cups cooked pumpkin,
   canned or fresh
1 cup whole or 2% milk
1 cup sugar
2 eggs, beaten
1 tablespoon butter or
   margarine, melted
½ teaspoon ground
   cinnamon

¼ teaspoon salt
¼ teaspoon ground ginger
¼ teaspoon ground nutmeg
1 (9-inch) unbaked pie shell
Sweetened whipped
   cream or whipped
   topping (optional)
Fresh currants (optional)

Preheat oven to 425°F. Combine all ingredients except pie shell, cream and currants in large bowl; blend well. Pour into pie shell. Bake 45 to 50 minutes or until knife inserted into filling comes out clean. Cool completely. Serve with whipped cream and garnish with currants, if desired. Refrigerate leftovers.

Makes 6 to 8 servings

Favorite recipe from **Bob Evans®**

◆ Maple Pumpkin Pie ◆

1⅓ cups all-purpose flour
⅓ cup plus 1 tablespoon
   sugar, divided
¾ teaspoon salt, divided
2 tablespoons vegetable
   shortening
2 tablespoons margarine
4 to 5 tablespoons ice water

1 can (15 ounces) solid-
   pack pumpkin
1 cup evaporated skim milk
2 egg whites
⅓ cup maple syrup
1 teaspoon ground
   cinnamon
½ teaspoon ground ginger

1. Combine flour, 1 tablespoon sugar and ¼ teaspoon salt in medium bowl. Cut in shortening and margarine with pastry blender or 2 knives until mixture forms coarse crumbs. Mix in ice water, 1 tablespoon at a time, until mixture comes together and forms a soft dough. Wrap in plastic wrap. Refrigerate 30 minutes.

2. Preheat oven to 425°F. Roll out pastry on floured surface to ⅛-inch thickness. Cut into 12-inch circle. Ease pastry into 9-inch pie plate; turn edges under and flute edge.

3. Combine pumpkin, remaining ⅓ cup sugar, milk, egg whites, syrup, cinnamon, ginger and remaining ½ teaspoon salt in large bowl; mix well. Pour into unbaked pie shell. Bake 15 minutes; *reduce oven temperature to 350°F.* Continue baking 45 to 50 minutes or until center is set. Transfer to wire cooling rack; let stand at least 30 minutes before serving. *Makes 8 servings*

Early American Pumpkin Pie

◆ Classic Crisco® Crust ◆

8-, 9- OR 10-INCH SINGLE CRUST
1⅓ cups all-purpose flour
½ teaspoon salt
½ CRISCO® Stick or ½ cup
    CRISCO® Shortening

3 tablespoons cold water

8- OR 9-INCH DOUBLE CRUST
2 cups all-purpose flour
1 teaspoon salt
¾ CRISCO® Stick or ¾ cup
    CRISCO® Shortening

5 tablespoons cold water

10-INCH DOUBLE CRUST
2⅔ cups all-purpose flour
1 teaspoon salt
1 CRISCO® Stick or 1 cup
    CRISCO® Shortening

7 to 8 tablespoons cold
    water

1. Spoon flour into measuring cup and level. Combine flour and salt in medium bowl.

2. Cut in shortening using pastry blender (or 2 knives) until all flour is blended to form pea-size chunks.

3. Sprinkle with water, 1 tablespoon at a time. Toss lightly with fork until dough forms a ball.

For Single Crust Pies

1. Press dough between hands to form 5- to 6-inch "pancake." Flour rolling surface and rolling pin lightly. Roll dough into circle.

2. Trim 1 inch larger than upside-down pie plate. Loosen dough carefully.

3. Fold dough into quarters. Unfold and press into pie plate. Fold edge under. Flute.

For Baked Pie Crusts

1. For recipes using baked pie crust, heat oven to 425°F. Prick bottom and side thoroughly with fork (50 times) to prevent shrinkage.

2. Bake at 425°F for 10 to 15 minutes or until lightly browned.

For Unbaked Pie Crusts

1. For recipes using unbaked pie crust, follow baking directions given in each recipe.

For Double Crust Pies

1. Divide dough in half. Roll each half separately. Transfer bottom crust to pie plate. Trim edge even with pie plate.

2. Add desired filling to unbaked pie crust. Moisten pastry edge with water. Lift top crust onto filled pie. Trim ½ inch beyond edge of pie plate. Fold top edge under bottom crust. Flute. Cut slits in top crust to allow steam to escape. Bake according to specific recipe directions.

◆ Georgia Peach Pie ◆

CRUST

> **1 unbaked 10-inch Classic CRISCO® Double Crust (page 290)**

FILLING

> **1 can (29 ounces) yellow cling peaches in heavy syrup, undrained**
> **3 tablespoons reserved peach syrup**
> **3 tablespoons cornstarch**

> **1 cup sugar, divided**
> **3 eggs**
> **⅓ cup buttermilk**
> **½ cup butter or margarine, melted**
> **1 teaspoon vanilla**

GLAZE

> **2 tablespoons butter or margarine, melted**

> **Additional sugar**

1. Preheat oven to 400°F.

2. For filling, drain peaches, reserving 3 tablespoons syrup; set aside. Cut peaches into small pieces; place in large bowl. Combine cornstarch and 3 tablespoons sugar in medium bowl. Add 3 tablespoons reserved peach syrup; mix well. Add remaining sugar, eggs and buttermilk; mix well. Stir in ½ cup melted butter and vanilla. Pour over peaches; stir until peaches are coated. Pour filling into unbaked pie crust. Moisten pastry edge with water.

3. Cover pie with top crust. Fold top edge under bottom crust; flute with fingers or fork. Cut slits or designs in top crust to allow steam to escape.

4. For glaze, brush top crust with 2 tablespoons melted butter. Sprinkle with additional sugar.

5. Bake at 400°F for 45 minutes or until filling in center is bubbly and crust is golden brown. Cool to room temperature before serving.

Makes 1 (10-inch) pie

◆ Best Ever Apple Pie ◆

2⅓ cups all-purpose flour, divided
¾ cup plus 1 tablespoon sugar, divided
½ teaspoon baking powder
½ teaspoon salt
¾ cup plus 3 tablespoons cold unsalted butter, cut into small pieces, divided

4 to 5 tablespoons ice water
1 egg, separated
7 medium apples such as Jonathan, Macintosh or Granny Smith, peeled, cored and sliced
1 tablespoon lemon juice
1¼ teaspoons ground cinnamon
1 tablespoon sour cream

1. Combine 2 cups flour, 1 tablespoon sugar, baking powder and salt in large bowl until well blended. Cut in ¾ cup butter using pastry blender or 2 knives until mixture resembles coarse crumbs.

2. Add water, 1 tablespoon at a time, to flour mixture. Toss with fork until mixture holds together. Form dough into 2 (6-inch) discs. Wrap discs in plastic wrap; refrigerate 30 minutes or until firm.

3. Working with 1 disc at a time, unwrap dough and place on lightly floured surface. Roll out dough in short strokes, starting in middle of disc and rolling out towards edge with lightly floured rolling pin. Rotate dough ¼ turn to the right. Sprinkle more flour under dough and on rolling pin as necessary to prevent sticking. Roll out dough into 12-inch circle, ⅛ inch thick. Ease dough into 9-inch glass pie plate. *Do not stretch dough.* Trim dough leaving ½-inch overhang; brush with egg white. Set aside.

4. Preheat oven to 450°F. Place apple slices in large bowl; sprinkle with lemon juice. Combine remaining ⅓ cup flour, ¾ cup sugar and cinnamon in small bowl until well blended. Add to apple mixture; toss to coat apples evenly. Spoon filling into prepared pie crust; place remaining 3 tablespoons butter on top of filling.

5. Moisten edge of dough with water. Roll out remaining disc as described in Step 3. Place onto filled pie. Trim dough leaving ½-inch overhang; flute edge. Cut 4 small slits in top of dough to allow steam to escape.

6. Combine egg yolk and sour cream in small bowl until well blended. Cover; refrigerate until ready to use.

7. Bake 10 minutes; *reduce oven temperature to 375°F.* Bake 35 minutes. Brush egg yolk mixture evenly on pie crust with pastry brush. Bake 20 to 25 minutes or until crust is deep golden brown.

8. Cool pie completely in pie plate on wire rack. Store loosely covered at room temperature 1 day or refrigerate up to 4 days.   *Makes 1 (9-inch) pie*

Best Ever Apple Pie

◆ Walnut Maple Pie ◆

1 (9-inch) unbaked deep-dish pie shell
2 egg whites
1 egg
1 cup maple-flavored syrup
½ cup firmly packed light brown sugar
2 tablespoons all-purpose flour

1 tablespoon butter, melted
1½ teaspoons vanilla extract
½ cup chopped walnuts
½ cup walnut halves for garnish (optional)
Non-dairy whipped topping or whipped cream (optional)

Preheat oven to 400°F. Bake pie shell 8 to 10 minutes or until light brown. Cool crust 5 minutes. *Reduce oven temperature to 350°F.* Meanwhile, beat egg whites and egg in large bowl with rotary beater or fork just until mixed. Whisk in syrup, brown sugar, flour, butter and vanilla until smooth. Stir in chopped walnuts. Pour filling into baked crust; garnish with walnut halves, if desired. Cover edge of crust with foil to prevent burning. Bake 40 to 45 minutes or until knife inserted into center comes out clean. Cool 2 hours on wire rack. Top with dollops of whipped topping, if desired. Store in refrigerator.

Makes 8 servings

Favorite recipe from **Bob Evans®**

◆ Honey Pumpkin Pie ◆

1 can (16 ounces) solid pack pumpkin
1 cup evaporated low-fat milk
¾ cup honey
3 eggs, slightly beaten
2 tablespoons all-purpose flour

1 teaspoon ground cinnamon
½ teaspoon ground ginger
½ teaspoon rum extract
Pastry for single 9-inch pie crust

Combine all ingredients except pastry in large bowl; beat until well blended. Pour into pastry-lined 9-inch pie plate. Bake at 400°F 45 minutes or until knife inserted near center comes out clean.

Makes 8 servings

Favorite recipe from **National Honey Board**

Walnut Maple Pie

◆ Strawberry Cream Pie ◆

1 cup plus 1½ teaspoons all-purpose flour, divided
¼ cup plus 1 teaspoon sugar, divided
¼ teaspoon salt
¼ cup cold margarine, cut into pieces
¾ teaspoon white or cider vinegar
3 tablespoons ice water, divided

6 ounces nonfat cream cheese
2 ounces Neufchâtel cheese
¼ cup vanilla nonfat yogurt
2 egg whites
½ teaspoon vanilla
1½ cups fresh strawberries, cut in half lengthwise
¼ cup strawberry jelly

1. Combine 1 cup flour, 1 teaspoon sugar and salt in medium bowl. Cut in margarine using 2 knives or pastry blender until small crumbs form. Add vinegar and 2 tablespoons ice water; stir until moist but slightly firm. If necessary, add remaining 1 tablespoon ice water. Gather dough into a ball.

2. Preheat oven to 450°F. Roll out dough into 12-inch circle on lightly floured surface. Place dough in 9-inch glass pie dish. Bake 10 to 12 minutes or until lightly browned. Cool on wire rack. *Reduce oven temperature to 325°F.*

3. Combine cream cheese, Neufchâtel, remaining ¼ cup sugar and 1½ teaspoons flour in large bowl. Beat with electric mixer until creamy. Beat in yogurt, egg whites and vanilla; mix well. Pour cheese mixture into cooled pie crust. Bake 25 minutes or until set. Cool on wire rack.

4. Place strawberries on top of cooled pie. Melt jelly over low heat in small saucepan. Carefully brush glaze over strawberries, allowing glaze to run onto cheese mixture. Refrigerate 3 hours or overnight.   *Makes 8 servings*

◆ Old-Fashioned Caramel Pie ◆

3 large eggs
1 cup (12-ounce jar) SMUCKER'S® Caramel Topping
1 cup quick-cooking or old-fashioned oats

½ cup sugar
½ cup milk
¼ cup butter, melted
1 teaspoon vanilla
⅛ teaspoon salt
1 (9-inch) pie shell, baked

In large bowl, beat eggs. Add remaining ingredients, except pie shell; blend well. Pour into baked pie shell.

Bake at 350°F for 1 hour or until set.   *Makes 6 to 8 servings*

Strawberry Cream Pie

◆ Easy Fruit Tarts ◆

12 wonton skins
  Vegetable cooking spray
2 tablespoons apple jelly or
  apricot fruit spread
1½ cups sliced or cut-up fruit
  such as DOLE® Bananas,
  Strawberries,
  Raspberries or Red or
  Green Seedless Grapes

1 cup nonfat or low fat
  yogurt, any flavor

• Press wonton skins into 12 muffin cups sprayed with vegetable cooking spray, allowing corners to stand over edges of muffin cups.

• Bake at 375°F 5 minutes or until lightly browned. Carefully remove wonton cups to wire rack; cool.

• Cook and stir jelly in small saucepan over low heat until jelly melts.

• Brush bottoms of cooled wonton cups with melted jelly. Place two fruit slices in each cup; spoon rounded tablespoon of yogurt on top of fruit. Garnish with fruit slice and mint leaves. Serve immediately.   *Makes 12 servings*

Prep Time: 20 minutes
Bake Time: 5 minutes

◆ Peanut Crumb Apple Pie ◆

1 cup all-purpose flour
½ cup SMUCKER'S® Creamy
  Natural Peanut Butter
  or LAURA SCUDDER'S®
  Smooth Old-Fashioned
  Peanut Butter
½ cup firmly packed light
  brown sugar

¼ cup butter or margarine,
  softened
¼ teaspoon salt
1 can (30-ounce) apple pie
  filling
1 (9-inch) unbaked pie shell

Blend flour, peanut butter, brown sugar, butter and salt until mixture is crumbly. Spoon apple pie filling into unbaked crust; sprinkle peanut butter mixture over pie filling.

Bake at 400°F for 30 to 35 minutes or until filling is hot and pastry is browned.
Makes 6 to 8 servings

Easy Fruit Tarts

◆ Coconut Custard Pie ◆

Reduced-Fat Pie Pastry (recipe follows) or favorite pastry for 9-inch pie
4 eggs
¼ teaspoon salt
2 cups skim milk

½ cup flaked coconut
5½ teaspoons EQUAL® FOR RECIPES or 18 packets EQUAL® sweetener or ¾ cup EQUAL® SPOONFUL™
2 teaspoons coconut extract

• Roll pastry on floured surface into circle 1 inch larger than inverted 9-inch pie pan. Ease into pan; trim and flute edge.

• Beat eggs and salt in large bowl until thick and lemon-colored, about 5 minutes. Mix in milk, coconut, Equal® and coconut extract. Pour mixture into pastry shell.

• Bake pie in preheated 425°F oven 15 minutes. *Reduce temperature to 350°F* and bake until sharp knife inserted halfway between center and edge of pie comes out clean, 20 to 25 minutes. Cool on wire rack. Serve at room temperature, or refrigerate and serve chilled. *Makes 8 servings*

Reduced-Fat Pie Pastry

1¼ cups all-purpose flour
1 teaspoon EQUAL® FOR RECIPES or 3 packets EQUAL® sweetener or 2 tablespoons EQUAL® SPOONFUL™

¼ teaspoon salt
4 tablespoons cold margarine, cut into pieces
5 to 5½ tablespoons ice water

• Combine flour, Equal® and salt in medium bowl; cut in margarine with pastry blender until mixture resembles coarse crumbs. Mix in water, 1 tablespoon at a time, stirring lightly with fork after each addition until dough is formed. Wrap and refrigerate until ready to use.

• For prebaked crust, roll pastry on lightly floured surface into circle 1 inch larger than inverted 9-inch pie pan. Ease pastry into pan; trim and flute edge. Pierce bottom and side of pastry with fork. Bake in preheated 425°F oven until pastry is browned, 10 to 15 minutes. Cool on wire rack.
Makes pastry for 9-inch pie (8 servings)

Tip: Double recipe for double crust or lattice pies.

Classic Pumpkin Pie with Candied
◆ Pecan Topping ◆

CRUST
1 (9-inch) Classic CRISCO®
Single Crust (page 290)

FILLING
1 can (16 ounces) solid-pack pumpkin (not pumpkin pie filling)
1 can (12 ounces or 1½ cups) evaporated milk
2 eggs, lightly beaten
½ cup granulated sugar
¼ cup firmly packed light brown sugar
1 teaspoon ground cinnamon
½ teaspoon salt
½ teaspoon ground ginger
¼ teaspoon ground nutmeg
⅛ teaspoon ground cloves

TOPPING
¼ cup granulated sugar
¼ cup water
1 cup pecan pieces
2 tablespoons butter or margarine

1. Roll and press crust into 9-inch glass pie plate. *Do not bake.* Heat oven to 350°F.

2. For filling, combine pumpkin, evaporated milk, eggs, ½ cup granulated sugar, brown sugar, cinnamon, salt, ginger, nutmeg and cloves in large bowl. Mix well. Pour into unbaked pie crust.

3. Bake at 350°F for 1 hour 10 minutes or until knife inserted in center comes out clean. *Do not overbake.* Cool completely.

4. Grease baking sheet lightly with shortening.

5. For topping, combine ¼ cup granulated sugar and water in small saucepan. Cook and stir on medium heat until sugar dissolves. Increase heat. Bring to a boil. Boil 7 to 8 minutes or until mixture becomes light golden brown, stirring frequently. Stir in nuts and butter. Stir briskly. Spread quickly in thin layer on baking sheet. Cool completely. Break into pieces. Sprinkle around edge of pie. (You might not use all of topping. Cover and store any extra for later use.) Refrigerate leftover pie.   *Makes 1 (9-inch) pie (8 servings)*

◆ Country Pecan Pie ◆

Pie pastry for single
   9-inch pie crust
1¼ cups dark corn syrup
4 eggs
½ cup packed light brown
   sugar

¼ cup butter or margarine,
   melted
2 teaspoons all-purpose
   flour
1½ teaspoons vanilla extract
1½ cups pecan halves

Preheat oven to 350°F. Roll pastry on lightly floured surface to form 13-inch circle. Fit into 9-inch pie plate. Trim edges; flute. Set aside.

Combine corn syrup, eggs, brown sugar and melted butter in large bowl; beat with electric mixer on medium speed until well blended. Stir in flour and vanilla until blended. Pour into unbaked pie crust. Arrange pecans on top.

Bake 40 to 45 minutes or until center of filling is puffed and golden brown. Cool completely on wire rack. Garnish as desired.   *Makes one 9-inch pie*

◆ Little Piece of Heaven ◆

3 egg whites
1 cup sugar
½ teaspoon baking powder
½ teaspoon vanilla extract
1 cup pecans (whole or
   chopped)
¾ cup crushed buttery-
   flavored crackers

1 (1.3-ounce) packet dry
   packaged whipped
   topping mix
¾ cup drained crushed
   pineapple
3 ounces cream cheese,
   softened

Preheat oven to 350°F. Beat egg whites in large bowl until medium stiff peaks form. Slowly add sugar, baking powder and vanilla until blended. Fold in pecans and crackers. Spread crumb mixture on bottom of greased 13×9×2-inch pan; bake 20 to 25 minutes or until golden. While crust is baking, prepare whipped topping according to package directions, using ½ cup cold milk and ½ teaspoon vanilla to make 2 cups topping. Stir in pineapple and cream cheese; mix well. Spread over crust and refrigerate. Serve cold.

Makes 10 to 12 servings

Serving Suggestion: *Serve with small scoops of vanilla ice cream.*

Favorite recipe from **Bob Evans®**

Country Pecan Pie

◆ The Best Cherry Pie ◆

**Reduced-Fat Pie Pastry
(recipe follows)**
**2 bags (12 ounces each)
frozen no-sugar-added
cherries, thawed, well
drained**
**¾ cup plus 2 teaspoons
sugar, divided**

**1 tablespoon plus 1½
teaspoons cornstarch**
**1 tablespoon plus 1½
teaspoons quick-
cooking tapioca**
1 teaspoon skim milk

1. Preheat oven to 425°F.

2. Roll ⅔ of pie pastry on lightly floured surface to 9½-inch circle. Gently press pastry into 8-inch pie pan.

3. Combine cherries, ¾ cup sugar, cornstarch and tapioca in large bowl. Spoon cherry mixture into pastry. Roll remaining pastry into circle large enough to fit top of pie; trim off any excess pastry. Cover pie with crust. Press edges of top and bottom crust together; trim and flute. Cut steam vents in top of pie; brush with milk and sprinkle with remaining 2 teaspoons sugar.

4. Bake 10 minutes. *Reduce heat to 375°F;* bake 45 to 50 minutes or until pie is bubbly and crust is golden. (Cover edge of crust with aluminum foil, if necessary, to prevent burning.) Cool on wire rack; serve warm.

Makes 8 servings

Reduced-Fat Pie Pastry

2 cups all-purpose flour
2 tablespoons sugar
½ teaspoon baking powder
¼ teaspoon salt

**7 tablespoons cold
shortening**
**6 to 8 tablespoons ice
water, divided**

1. Combine flour, sugar, baking powder and salt in medium bowl. Cut in shortening with pastry blender or 2 knives until mixture resembles coarse crumbs. Mix in water, 1 tablespoon at a time, until stiff dough is formed.

2. Cover dough with plastic wrap; refrigerate 30 minutes.

Makes 1 (8-inch) double crust

Tip: When rolling out pastry for crust, repair any tears by moistening the edges with water and using small pieces of the trimmings to patch the tears.

The Best Cherry Pie

◆ Creamy Lemon Pie ◆

1 (9-inch) unbaked deep-dish pie shell
3 egg whites
2 eggs
1 cup firmly packed light brown sugar
⅓ cup milk
¼ cup granulated sugar
3 tablespoons lemon juice
1 tablespoon all-purpose flour

1 tablespoon cornmeal
1 tablespoon butter, melted
1 tablespoon grated lemon peel
2 teaspoons vanilla extract
Non-dairy whipped topping
Candied or fresh lemon slices for garnish (optional)

Preheat oven to 400°F. Bake pie shell 8 to 10 minutes or until light brown. Cool crust 5 minutes. *Reduce oven temperature to 350°F.* Meanwhile, beat egg whites and eggs in large bowl with rotary beater or fork just until mixed. Whisk in brown sugar, milk, granulated sugar, lemon juice, flour, cornmeal, butter, lemon peel and vanilla; mix well. Pour filling into baked crust. Bake 40 to 45 minutes or until knife inserted into center comes out clean. (If edge of crust browns too quickly, cover with foil). Cool 2 hours on wire rack. Decorate pie with whipped topping. Garnish with candied or fresh lemon slices, if desired. Store in refrigerator. *Makes 8 servings*

Favorite recipe from **Bob Evans®**

Creamy Lemon Pie

◆ Nectarine Pecan Tart ◆

PECAN CRUST
- 1 cup wafer crumbs
- ½ cup pecan pieces
- 2 tablespoons sugar
- 3 tablespoons unsalted butter, melted

CREAM CHEESE FILLING
- 1 package (8 ounces) plus
- 1 package (3 ounces) cream cheese, softened
- 3 tablespoons sugar
- 2 tablespoons orange juice
- ½ teaspoon vanilla

FRUIT TOPPING
- 2 ripe nectarines
- 4 tablespoons apricot jelly

1. For crust, preheat oven to 350°F. Place wafer crumbs, pecans and 2 tablespoons sugar in food processor; process until coarse crumbs form. Transfer to small bowl; stir in butter. Press crumb mixture onto bottom and partially up side of 8-inch springform pan.

2. Bake 15 minutes or until lightly brown. Cool completely on wire rack.

3. For filling, beat cream cheese, 3 tablespoons sugar, juice and vanilla in medium bowl with electric mixer at low speed until blended. Increase speed to high, beat 2 minutes or until fluffy.

4. Pour filling into cooled crust, spreading mixture out evenly to sides. Cover; refrigerate 3 hours or until set.

5. For topping, 30 minutes before serving, halve and slice nectarines. Arrange nectarines over cream cheese.

6. To complete recipe, melt jelly in small saucepan, whisking constantly, over low heat. Cool 1 minute. Drizzle jelly over nectarines. Refrigerate, uncovered, 20 minutes or until set. *Makes 6 servings*

Nectarine Pecan Tart

◆ Pumpkin Pie Crunch ◆

1 can (16 ounces) solid
   pack pumpkin
1 can (12 ounces)
   evaporated milk
1½ cups sugar
3 eggs
4 teaspoons pumpkin pie
   spice

½ teaspoon salt
1 package DUNCAN HINES®
   Moist Deluxe® Yellow
   Cake Mix
1 cup chopped pecans
1 cup butter or margarine,
   melted
Whipped topping

1. Preheat oven to 350°F. Grease bottom of 13×9×2-inch pan.

2. Combine pumpkin, evaporated milk, sugar, eggs, pumpkin pie spice and salt in large bowl. Pour into pan. Sprinkle dry cake mix evenly over pumpkin mixture. Top with pecans. Drizzle with melted butter. Bake at 350°F 50 to 55 minutes or until golden. Cool completely. Serve with whipped topping. Refrigerate leftovers. *Makes 16 to 20 servings*

Tip: For a richer flavor, try using Duncan Hines® Moist Deluxe® Butter Recipe Golden Cake Mix.

◆ Country Peach Tart ◆

Reduced-Fat Pie Pastry
   (page 300) or favorite
   pastry for 9-inch pie
1 tablespoon all-purpose
   flour
2½ teaspoons EQUAL® FOR
   RECIPES *or* 8 packets
   EQUAL® sweetener *or*
   ⅓ cup EQUAL®
   SPOONFUL™

4 cups sliced, pitted, peeled
   fresh peaches (about
   4 medium) or frozen
   peaches, thawed
Ground nutmeg

• Roll pastry on floured surface into 12-inch circle; transfer to *ungreased* cookie sheet. Combine flour and Equal®; sprinkle over peaches. Toss to coat. Arrange peaches over pastry, leaving 2-inch border around edge. Sprinkle lightly with nutmeg. Bring pastry edge toward center, overlapping as necessary. Bake tart in preheated 425°F oven until crust is browned and fruit is tender, 25 to 30 minutes. *Makes 8 servings*

Pumpkin Pie Crunch

◆ Cherry Brunch Pie ◆

½ pound bulk pork sausage
1 (16-ounce) can tart
    cherries, drained and
    coarsely chopped
1 cup shredded sharp
    Cheddar cheese (about
    4 ounces)
1 cup buttermilk baking
    mix

1 teaspoon dried basil
    leaves
½ teaspoon salt, or to taste
⅛ teaspoon ground black
    pepper, or to taste
1½ cups milk
4 eggs, slightly beaten

Cook sausage in large skillet until brown, breaking into small pieces as it cooks; drain off fat. Remove from heat. Add cherries; mix well. Spoon sausage mixture into 10-inch deep-dish pie plate. Top with cheese.

Combine baking mix, basil, salt and pepper in medium mixing bowl; mix well. Add milk and eggs; beat until smooth. Pour over cheese.

Bake in preheated 400°F oven 35 to 40 minutes or until knife inserted in center comes out clean. Let cool 5 minutes. Cut into wedges. Serve immediately.

Makes 6 servings

Note: If desired, 1½ cups frozen unsweetened tart cherries can be substituted for canned cherries. Partly thaw cherries, then coarsely chop them before adding to sausage.

Favorite recipe from **Cherry Marketing Institute, Inc.**

◆ Mini Pecan Tarts ◆

TART SHELLS
2 cups all-purpose flour
1 teaspoon granulated
    sugar
Pinch of salt

1½ sticks cold butter or
    margarine, cut into
    pieces
⅓ cup ice water

FILLING
1 cup powdered sugar
½ cup butter or margarine
⅓ cup dark corn syrup

1 cup chopped pecans
36 pecan halves

For tart shells, combine flour, granulated sugar and salt in large bowl. Using pastry blender or 2 knives, cut 1½ sticks butter into dry ingredients until mixture resembles crumbly corn meal. Add water, 1 tablespoon at a time, kneading mixture until dough forms a ball. Wrap dough in plastic wrap, flatten and refrigerate at least 30 minutes.

Preheat oven to 375°F. Grease mini-muffin pans. Roll out dough on lightly floured surface to ⅛-inch thickness. Cut out 3-inch circles using cookie cutter; press into prepared mini-muffin cups and bake about 8 minutes or until very lightly browned. Remove from oven. *Reduce oven temperature to 350°F.*

For filling, combine powdered sugar, ½ cup butter and corn syrup in 2-quart saucepan. Cook over medium heat, stirring occasionally, until mixture comes to a full boil, 4 to 5 minutes. Remove from heat; stir in chopped pecans. Spoon into warm baked shells. Top each with pecan half. Bake 5 minutes. Cool completely; remove from pans. *Makes 3 dozen tarts*

◆ New York Apple Maple Cream Pie ◆

CRUST
**1 unbaked 9-inch Classic
     CRISCO® Double Crust
     (page 290)**

FILLING
**6 cups sliced, peeled
     baking apples* (about
     2 pounds or 6 medium)
1 cup sugar**

**3 tablespoons cornstarch
½ teaspoon salt
¾ cup pure maple syrup**
½ cup whipping cream**

GLAZE
Milk   **Sugar**

*Golden Delicious, Granny Smith and Jonathan apples are suitable for pie baking.
**Substitute maple-flavored pancake and waffle syrup, if desired.

1. Heat oven to 400°F.

2. For crust, prepare. Roll and press bottom crust into 9-inch pie plate. *Do not bake.* Reserve dough scraps for decoration, if desired; roll out and cut into desired shapes using cookie cutter. Arrange on baking sheet; set aside.

3. For filling, place apples, 1 cup sugar, cornstarch and salt in large bowl. Toss to coat. Combine maple syrup and whipping cream in small bowl. Pour over apple mixture. Mix gently. Spoon into unbaked pie crust. Moisten pastry edge with water.

4. Roll out top crust. Lift onto filled pie. Trim ½ inch beyond edge of pie plate. Fold top edge under bottom crust; flute. Decorate with pastry cutouts, if desired. Cut slits into top crust to allow steam to escape.

5. For glaze, brush with milk. Sprinkle with sugar.

6. Bake at 400°F for 50 to 60 minutes or until filling in center is bubbly and crust is golden brown. Refrigerate leftover pie. *Makes 1 (9-inch) pie*

◆ Country Apple Rhubarb Pie ◆

CRUST

9-inch Classic CRISCO®
Double Crust (page 290)

FILLING

9 cups sliced, peeled
Granny Smith apples
(about 3 pounds or 6
large apples)

1½ cups chopped (about
½ inch) fresh rhubarb,
peeled if tough

¾ cup granulated sugar

½ cup firmly packed light
brown sugar

2 tablespoons all-purpose
flour

1 tablespoon cornstarch

1 teaspoon ground
cinnamon

¼ teaspoon freshly grated
nutmeg

GLAZE

1 egg, beaten

1 tablespoon water

1 tablespoon granulated
sugar

1 teaspoon ground pecans
or walnuts

⅛ teaspoon ground
cinnamon

1. For crust, prepare. Roll and press bottom crust into 9- or 9½-inch deep-dish pie plate. *Do not bake.* Heat oven to 425°F.

2. For filling, combine apples and rhubarb in large bowl. Combine ¾ cup granulated sugar, brown sugar, flour, cornstarch, 1 teaspoon cinnamon and nutmeg in medium bowl. Sprinkle over fruit. Toss to coat. Spoon into unbaked pie crust. Moisten pastry edge with water. Cover pie with lattice top, cutting strips 1 inch wide. Flute edge high.

3. For glaze, combine egg and water in small bowl. Brush over crust. Combine remaining glaze ingredients in small bowl. Sprinkle over crust.

4. Bake at 425°F for 20 minutes. *Reduce oven temperature to 350°F.* Bake 30 to 40 minutes or until filling in center is bubbly and crust is golden brown. Place sheet of foil or baking sheet under pie if it starts to bubble over. Cool to room temperature.   *Makes one 9- or 9½-inch deep-dish pie (8 servings)*

Country Apple Rhubarb Pie

◆ Three-Berry Tart ◆

2 cups all-purpose flour
5 tablespoons unsalted
   butter
¼ cup ground almonds
⅓ plus ½ cup sifted
   confectioners' sugar
5 tablespoons ice water
1 tablespoon cornstarch
⅓ cup 2% low fat milk
1 cup (4 ounces) shredded
   ALPINE LACE® Reduced
   Sodium Muenster
   Cheese

1½ cups low fat sour cream
1 cup vanilla nonfat yogurt
1 tablespoon vanilla extract
1 teaspoon grated lemon
   rind
2 cups strawberries, hulled
   and halved
1½ cups fresh raspberries
1½ cups fresh blueberries
1 cup peeled kiwi slices
½ cup red currant jelly

1. To make the almond crust: Preheat the oven to 400°F. In a medium-size bowl, mix the flour, butter, almonds and the ⅓ cup of confectioners' sugar with your fingers until coarse crumbs form. Add enough water to form a dough. Press onto the bottom and up the side of a 12-inch tart pan with a removable bottom. Prick the dough at ½-inch intervals with the tines of a fork and bake for 15 minutes or until golden brown.

2. Meanwhile, to make the cheese filling: In a small saucepan, dissolve the cornstarch in the milk. Stir in the cheese and cook over medium heat until the mixture is slightly thickened and smooth. Cool for 15 minutes.

3. In a medium-size bowl, with an electric mixer set on medium-high, beat the sour cream, yogurt, the ½ cup of confectioners' sugar, the vanilla and lemon rind for 1 minute. With the mixer running, slowly add the cheese mixture and beat until the filling is almost smooth. Pour into the tart shell and refrigerate for 30 minutes or until filling is thickened and cold.

4. To make the fresh fruit topping: Arrange the berries decoratively on top of the filling. In a small saucepan, melt the jelly over low heat, then carefully brush over the berries. Refrigerate for at least 1 hour before serving.

Makes 16 servings

Three-Berry Tart

◆ Berry Meringue Pie ◆

CRUST
> **8-inch Classic CRISCO®**
> **Single Crust (page 290)**

FILLING
> 2 cups frozen unsweetened
>   raspberries
> 1 cup frozen unsweetened
>   blackberries
> 1 cup sugar

> ⅓ cup clear jel instant
>   starch*
> ⅛ teaspoon salt
> 1 tablespoon butter or
>   margarine

MERINGUE
> 3 egg whites
> ¼ teaspoon cream of tartar
> 5 tablespoons sugar

> ½ teaspoon pure vanilla
>   extract

Substitute ¼ cup cornstarch for ⅓ cup clear jel instant starch in filling, if clear jel is unavailable. Combine with 1 cup sugar and salt in medium saucepan. Stir in juice mixture. Cook and stir on medium heat until mixture comes to a boil and is thickened. Remove from heat. Stir in butter.

1. For crust, prepare and bake. Cool while preparing filling. *Reduce oven temperature to 350°F.*

2. For filling, combine raspberries and blackberries in large microwave-safe bowl. Microwave at HIGH 3 minutes or until softened, stirring once. Press through fine strainer into medium bowl, reserving juice. Add enough hot water to juice to measure 2 cups liquid.

3. Combine 1 cup sugar, clear jel and salt in medium bowl. Mix well. Stir in juice mixture. Mix well with rotary beater or wire whisk. Stir in butter. Pour into cooled baked pie crust.

4. For meringue, combine egg whites and cream of tartar in medium bowl. Beat at medium speed of electric mixer until frothy. Add 5 tablespoons sugar, 1 tablespoon at a time, beating at high speed until stiff peaks form. Beat in vanilla. Spread over filling.

5. Bake at 350°F for 15 to 20 minutes or until light brown. Cool to room temperature before serving. Refrigerate leftovers.

Makes one 8-inch pie (8 servings)

Note: Use other combinations of fruit (such as blueberries and raspberries or blueberries and blackberries) to make juice if raspberries or blackberries are unavailable.

Berry Meringue Pie

◆ Very Cherry Pie ◆

4 cups frozen unsweetened
  tart cherries
1 cup dried tart cherries
1 cup sugar
2 tablespoons quick-
  cooking tapioca

½ teaspoon almond extract
  Pastry for 2-crust, 9-inch
  pie
¼ teaspoon ground nutmeg
1 tablespoon butter

Combine frozen cherries, dried cherries, sugar, tapioca and almond extract in large mixing bowl; mix well. (It is not necessary to thaw cherries before using.) Let cherry mixture stand 15 minutes.

Line 9-inch pie plate with pastry; fill with cherry mixture. Sprinkle with nutmeg. Dot with butter. Adjust top crust, cutting slits for steam to escape.

Bake in preheated 375°F oven about 1 hour or until crust is golden brown and filling is bubbly. If necessary, cover edge of crust with aluminum foil to prevent overbrowning.
Makes 8 servings

Note: Two (16-ounce) cans unsweetened tart cherries, well drained, can be substituted for frozen tart cherries. Dried cherries are available at gourmet and specialty food stores and at selected supermarkets.

Favorite recipe from **Cherry Marketing Institute, Inc.**

◆ Caramel-Pecan Pie ◆

3 eggs
⅔ cup sugar
1 cup (12-ounce jar)
  SMUCKER'S® Caramel
  Topping

¼ cup butter or margarine,
  melted
1½ cups pecan halves
1 (9-inch) unbaked pie shell

In mixing bowl, beat eggs slightly with fork. Add sugar, stirring until dissolved. Stir in topping and butter; mix well. Stir in pecan halves. Pour filling into pie shell.

Bake at 350°F for 45 minutes or until knife inserted near center comes out clean. Cool thoroughly on rack before serving. Cover and store in refrigerator.
Makes 6 to 8 servings

Very Cherry Pie

◆ Blackbottom Pecan Pie ◆

CRUST

8-inch Classic CRISCO®
Double Crust (page 290)

FILLING

3 tablespoons butter or
margarine
½ ounce (½ square)
unsweetened baking
chocolate
½ cup granulated sugar,
divided
½ cup finely chopped
pecans
¼ cup all-purpose flour
4 eggs, well beaten, divided
1¼ teaspoons pure vanilla
extract, divided
1 tablespoon cornstarch

¾ cup light corn syrup
¼ cup firmly packed light
brown sugar
2 tablespoons Butter
Flavor* CRISCO® Stick or
2 tablespoons Butter
Flavor* CRISCO® all-
vegetable shortening,
melted
1 tablespoon bourbon
½ teaspoon salt
1 cup coarsely chopped
pecans

GARNISH

2 tablespoons semi-sweet
chocolate chips
½ teaspoon CRISCO® Stick or
½ teaspoon CRISCO® all-
vegetable shortening

8 pecan halves

TOPPING

½ cup whipping cream
1½ teaspoons confectioners'
sugar

¼ teaspoon pure vanilla
extract

Butter Flavor Crisco® is artificially flavored.

1. For crust, prepare. Roll and press bottom crust into 8-inch pie plate. *Do not bake.* Heat oven to 350°F. Moisten pastry edge with water.

2. Roll remaining dough same as bottom. Cut into ¼-inch-wide strips. Braid 2 strips together. Place braided strip around edge. Press lightly. Repeat with remaining strips.

(continued on page 324)

Blackbottom Pecan Pie

(Blackbottom Pecan Pie, continued from page 322)

3. For filling, combine butter and chocolate in small saucepan. Stir on low heat until melted. Remove from heat. Add ¼ cup granulated sugar. Stir well. Stir in finely chopped nuts, flour, 2 tablespoons beaten egg and ¼ teaspoon vanilla. Spread in bottom of unbaked pie crust. Prick side of crust above filling about 25 times.

4. Bake at 350°F for 7 minutes or until filling is shiny. *Do not overbake.*

5. Combine remaining ¼ cup granulated sugar and cornstarch in medium bowl. Stir in remaining beaten eggs, corn syrup, brown sugar, melted shortening, bourbon, remaining 1 teaspoon vanilla and salt. Stir in coarsely chopped nuts. Spoon over bottom layer.

6. Bake at 350°F for 20 minutes. *Do not overbake.* Cover edge of pie with foil, if necessary, to prevent overbrowning. Bake an additional 20 minutes or until filling is set and crust is light golden brown. Cool to room temperature before serving.

7. For garnish, combine chocolate chips and shortening in small saucepan. Stir on low heat until melted and smooth. Dip flat part of each pecan half in melted chocolate. Place nuts, chocolate sides up, on waxed paper until chocolate is firm.

8. For topping, combine whipping cream, confectioners' sugar and ¼ teaspoon vanilla in medium bowl. Beat at high speed of electric mixer until stiff peaks form. Place 8 dollops on top of pie. Garnish each with chocolate-coated pecan half, rounded side up. Refrigerate leftovers.

Makes one 8-inch pie (8 servings)

◆ Celia's Flat Fruit Pie ◆

2 packages (8 ounces each) mixed dried fruit (pitted prunes, pears, apples, apricots and peaches)	**½ teaspoon ground cinnamon**
3 cups water	**¼ teaspoon ground cloves**
½ cup sugar	**1 teaspoon lemon juice**
	Flaky Pastry (recipe follows)

Combine fruit, water, sugar, cinnamon and cloves in 3-quart pan. Cook, stirring occasionally, over medium heat until sugar is dissolved. Cover; reduce heat and simmer 45 minutes or until fruit is tender. Pour fruit and liquid into blender or food processor container fitted with metal blade; process to make coarse purée. (Purée should measure 3 cups. If purée measures more, return to pan and cook, stirring frequently, to reduce to 3 cups.)

Stir in lemon juice. Let cool. While fruit is cooling, prepare Flaky Pastry.

Preheat oven to 400°F. Roll one pastry ball on lightly floured board to 13-inch circle about ⅛ inch thick. Fold pastry into quarters. Place in 12-inch pizza pan; unfold. Trim edge of pastry to leave ½-inch overhang. Spread fruit purée in even layer over pastry. Roll out second ball to 13-inch circle; place over filling. Cut slits or design in center. Fold edge of top crust under edge of bottom crust; flute edge. Bake 35 to 40 minutes or until pastry is golden brown. Place pie on rack. Let cool 1 hour before cutting into thin wedges.

Makes 12 servings

Flaky Pastry

3⅓ cups all-purpose flour
¾ teaspoon salt
1 cup shortening or lard

6 to 8 tablespoons cold
water

Combine flour and salt in medium bowl. With fingers, pastry blender or 2 knives, rub or cut shortening into flour mixture until it resembles fine crumbs. Gradually add water; stir with fork until mixture forms dough. Shape into 2 balls. Wrap in plastic wrap; refrigerate 30 minutes.

◆ Old-Fashioned Custard Pie ◆

3 eggs
½ cup sugar
¼ teaspoon salt
2¼ cups milk

1 teaspoon vanilla extract
1 (9-inch) unbaked pie shell
Ground nutmeg

Preheat oven to 425°F. Beat eggs lightly in medium bowl; blend in sugar and salt. Stir in milk and vanilla; mix well. Pour into pie shell; sprinkle with nutmeg. Bake 10 minutes. *Reduce oven temperature to 350°F;* bake 25 to 30 minutes more or until crust is browned and filling is set. Cool on wire rack up to 1 hour before refrigerating. *Makes 6 to 8 servings*

Favorite recipe from **Bob Evans**®

◆ Chocolate Pie ◆

1¼ cups sugar
½ cup reduced-fat biscuit mix
3 tablespoons unsweetened cocoa powder, sifted

2 tablespoons margarine, melted
1 whole egg
3 egg whites
1½ teaspoons vanilla

1. Preheat oven to 350°F. Spray 9-inch pie pan with nonstick cooking spray. Set aside.

2. Combine sugar, biscuit mix and cocoa in large bowl; mix well. Add margarine, egg, egg whites and vanilla; mix well. Pour mixture into prepared pan.

3. Bake 40 minutes or until knife inserted in center comes out clean. Garnish with powdered sugar, if desired.
Makes 8 servings

Tip: Cocoa powder is sold plain for baking, or mixed with other ingredients such as milk powder and sugar, commonly known as hot chocolate mix. Cocoa mixes should not be substituted for cocoa powder in recipes.

◆ Ginger Cream Banana Pie ◆

1½ cups gingersnap cookie crumbs
¼ cup margarine, softened
1 package (5.9 ounces) instant vanilla pudding (6 servings)
2¼ cups milk

1 tablespoon crystallized ginger
1 tablespoon grated orange peel
4 firm, medium DOLE® Bananas

• Combine gingersnap crumbs and margarine in bowl. Press on bottom and up side of 9-inch pie plate. Bake at 350°F 5 minutes. Cool.

• Combine pudding, milk, ginger and orange peel until well blended. Slice 2 bananas into bottom of pie shell. Cover with one-half filling. Slice remaining bananas over filling. Top with remaining filling. Press plastic wrap on surface. Refrigerate 3 hours. Garnish with additional banana slices, orange curls and edible flowers, if desired.
Makes 8 servings

Prep Time: 25 minutes
Chill Time: 3 hours

Chocolate Pie

◆ Luscious Cranberry and Blueberry Pie ◆

CRUST
- 1 unbaked 9-inch Classic CRISCO® Double Crust (page 290)
- ½ teaspoon ground mace

FILLING
- 1 can (16 ounces) whole berry cranberry sauce
- ⅓ cup packed brown sugar
- ¼ cup granulated sugar
- 2 tablespoons all-purpose flour
- 2 tablespoons cornstarch
- 2 tablespoons orange juice
- ½ teaspoon dried grated orange peel
- ⅛ teaspoon salt
- 2 cups fresh or frozen blueberries
- 2 tablespoons butter or margarine

GLAZE
- 1 egg, beaten

1. For crust, prepare, adding mace to flour mixture. Roll and press bottom crust into 9-inch pie plate. *Do not bake.* Reserve dough scraps for decorations, if desired. Heat oven to 425°F.

2. For filling, combine cranberry sauce, brown sugar, granulated sugar, flour, cornstarch, orange juice, orange peel and salt in large bowl. Stir in blueberries. Spoon into unbaked pie crust; dot with butter. Moisten pastry edge with water.

3. Roll out top crust; lift crust onto filled pie. Trim ½ inch beyond edge of pie plate. Fold top edge under bottom crust; flute. Cut blossom-shaped holes in top crust to allow steam to escape.

4. Cut flowers or other shapes from reserved dough. Place on top of pie.

5. For glaze, brush with egg.

6. Bake at 425°F for 40 minutes or until filling in center is bubbly and crust is golden brown. Cover edge with foil during last 10 minutes to prevent overbrowning. Cool to room temperature before serving.

Makes 1 (9-inch) pie

Luscious Cranberry and Blueberry Pie

BAKED DESSERTS

◆ Strawberry Streusel Squares ◆

1 package (about 18 ounces) yellow cake mix, divided
3 tablespoons uncooked old-fashioned oats
1 tablespoon margarine
1½ cups sliced strawberries
¾ cup plus 2 tablespoons water, divided
¾ cup diced strawberries
3 egg whites
⅓ cup unsweetened applesauce
½ teaspoon ground cinnamon
⅛ teaspoon ground nutmeg

1. Preheat oven to 350°F. Spray 13×9-inch baking pan with nonstick cooking spray; lightly flour.

2. Combine ½ cup cake mix and oats in small bowl. Cut in margarine until mixture resembles coarse crumbs; set aside.

3. Place 1½ cups sliced strawberries and 2 tablespoons water in blender or food processor. Process until smooth. Transfer to small bowl and stir in ¾ cup diced strawberries. Set aside.

4. Place remaining cake mix in large bowl. Add ¾ cup water, egg whites, applesauce, cinnamon and nutmeg. Blend 30 seconds at low speed or just until moistened. Beat at medium speed 2 minutes. Pour batter into prepared pan.

5. Spoon strawberry mixture evenly over batter, spreading lightly. Sprinkle evenly with oat mixture. Bake 31 to 34 minutes or until toothpick inserted into center comes out clean. Cool completely in pan on wire rack.

Makes 12 servings

Strawberry Streusel Squares

◆ Apple Cobbler ◆

¼ cup plus 2 tablespoons sugar, divided
½ teaspoon plus ⅛ teaspoon ground cinnamon, divided
1 package (7½ ounces) refrigerated biscuit dough
2 tablespoons melted butter or margarine
1½ tablespoons instant tapioca

½ teaspoon grated nutmeg
½ teaspoon grated fresh lemon peel
5 cups sliced, peeled Cortland or Jonathan apples (about 3 large apples)
1 tablespoon lemon juice
½ teaspoon vanilla

1. Preheat oven to 400°F. Stir together 2 tablespoons sugar and ⅛ teaspoon cinnamon in small bowl. Separate biscuits. Dip one side of each biscuit in melted butter then in cinnamon-sugar mixture. Cover and refrigerate remaining butter up to 1 day. Cover and store remaining cinnamon-sugar mixture at room temperature up to 1 day. Place biscuits, in single layer, sugar side up, in greased 1½- to 2-quart shallow casserole. Bake 10 to 13 minutes or until golden brown. Lift biscuits from casserole trying not to separate; place on wire rack to cool. Wrap biscuits in plastic wrap and store at room temperature up to 1 day. Reserve casserole for apples.

2. Combine remaining ¼ cup sugar, remaining ½ teaspoon cinnamon, tapioca, nutmeg and lemon peel in large bowl; stir until blended. Add apples; sprinkle with lemon juice and vanilla. Stir until apples are evenly coated. Spoon into reserved casserole; press gently with back of spoon to even layer. Cover and refrigerate up to 1 day.

3. To complete recipe, bake in preheated 400°F oven 25 minutes or until apples are tender and bubbly. Arrange biscuits over top. Brush with reserved butter and sprinkle with reserved cinnamon-sugar mixture. Return to oven and bake 5 minutes or until biscuits are warm. *Makes 6 servings*

Make-Ahead Time: up to 1 day in refrigerator
Final Cook Time: 30 minutes

Apple Cobbler

◆ Granola Crisp Topping with Fruit ◆

⅓ cup uncooked old-fashioned rolled oats

3 tablespoons chopped walnuts

¼ cup honey

1 egg white

¼ teaspoon vanilla

¼ teaspoon ground cinnamon

Dash salt

2 cups nonfat plain or vanilla yogurt

2 cups mixed berries

Combine oats and walnuts in medium bowl. Mix together honey, egg white, vanilla, cinnamon and salt in small bowl until well blended. Add honey mixture to oats; stir until well blended. Line 17×11-inch baking sheet with foil; spray with nonstick cooking spray. Spread oat mixture in even layer on prepared baking sheet. Bake at 325°F 15 to 17 minutes or until golden brown, tossing mixture 3 to 4 times during baking. Remove from oven. Cool completely until crisp and crunchy. Serve over yogurt and berries.   *Makes 4 servings*

Favorite recipe from **National Honey Board**

◆ Fresh Nectarine-Pineapple Cobbler ◆

1 DOLE® Fresh Pineapple

3 cups sliced ripe DOLE® Fresh Nectarines or Peaches

½ cup sugar

2 tablespoons all-purpose flour

½ teaspoon ground cinnamon

1 cup buttermilk baking mix

½ cup low fat milk

• Twist crown off pineapple. Cut pineapple in half. Refrigerate one half for another use. Cut remaining pineapple half in half. Remove fruit from shell; core fruit. Cut fruit into cubes.

• Combine pineapple, nectarines, sugar, flour and cinnamon in 8×8-inch glass baking dish; spread fruit evenly in dish.

• Stir together baking mix and milk in small bowl until just combined. Pour over fruit.

• Bake at 400°F 40 to 45 minutes or until fruit is tender and crust is browned.
Makes 8 servings

Prep Time: 20 minutes
Bake Time: 45 minutes

Granola Crisp Topping with Fruit

◆ Pears en Croûte (Baked Pears in Pastry) ◆

2 teaspoons granulated
  sugar
¼ teaspoon ground
  cinnamon
1 egg white, slightly beaten
  Cold water
¼ cup golden raisins
¼ cup chopped walnuts
2 tablespoons brown sugar
1 package DUNCAN HINES®
  Cinnamon Muffin Mix

8 small ripe pears
1 cup all-purpose flour
½ cup shortening plus
  additional for greasing
Cinnamon sticks or
  vanilla beans, for
  garnish
Caramel flavor topping,
  at room temperature
  or warmed

1. Preheat oven to 375°F. Grease 13×9×2-inch pan.

2. Combine granulated sugar and cinnamon in small bowl; set aside. Combine beaten egg white and 1 teaspoon water in small bowl; set aside.

3. Combine raisins, walnuts, brown sugar, and contents of crumb topping packet from Mix in medium bowl; set aside.

4. Core and peel pears; set aside.

5. Combine muffin mix and flour in medium bowl. Cut in ½ cup shortening with pastry blender or 2 knives until flour is blended to form pea-size chunks. Sprinkle 5 tablespoons cold water, 1 tablespoon at a time, over flour mixture. Toss lightly with fork until dough forms ball. Divide in half. Wrap one-half with plastic wrap; reserve. Roll remaining dough on well-floured surface to form 13-inch square. Cut square equally into four 6½-inch squares. Repeat using reserved dough ball.

6. To assemble, fill pear centers with 1½ tablespoons raisin mixture. Cover each pear with square of pastry. Mold with palm of hand to shape, folding corners under pear bottom. Place ¾ inch apart in prepared pan. Brush with egg white mixture. Sprinkle ¼ teaspoon cinnamon-sugar mixture over each pear.

7. Bake at 375°F for 33 to 35 minutes or until golden brown and pears are tender. Cool in pan for 5 minutes. Remove to serving dish. Insert cinnamon stick or piece of vanilla bean on top of pear to form stem. Drizzle caramel topping over pear, as desired. Serve warm or at room temperature. Refrigerate leftovers.

Makes 8 servings

Note: *To ripen pears, place in brown paper bag and store at room temperature for 24 to 48 hours.*

Tip: *Reroll leftover pastry. Cut into small leaf shapes. Place on baking sheet. Bake at 375°F for 8 to 10 minutes. Use as garnish.*

Pear en Croûte (Baked Pear in Pastry)

◆ Spiced Apricot Pastries ◆

1 cup (12-ounce jar) SMUCKER'S® Apricot or Peach Preserves
½ cup finely chopped walnuts
¾ teaspoon pumpkin pie spice
½ teaspoon grated orange peel
1 cup butter or margarine, softened

1 (8-ounce) package cream cheese, softened
2 tablespoons sugar
½ teaspoon vanilla
2 cups all-purpose flour
1 egg
1 tablespoon water
Sifted powdered sugar

Combine preserves, walnuts, pumpkin pie spice and orange peel; mix well.

Beat butter, cream cheese, sugar and vanilla at medium speed until creamy. Add flour; beat at low speed until well blended.

Divide dough into thirds. On lightly floured surface, roll out each portion of dough to ⅛-inch thickness. Cut with 3-inch round cookie cutter.

Spoon ½ teaspoon preserves mixture in center of each round. Combine egg and water; brush on edges. Fold opposite sides to center, slightly overlapping edges; pinch to seal. Place on lightly greased baking sheets.

Bake at 375°F for 10 to 14 minutes or until light golden brown. Transfer to wire racks to cool. Sprinkle with powdered sugar.   *Makes 5 dozen pastries*

◆ Fresh & Fruity Cobbler ◆

Biscuit Topping (recipe follows)
¼ cup water
5 teaspoons sugar, divided
1 teaspoon cornstarch

½ cup fresh or thawed frozen blueberries
½ cup peeled nectarine slices
½ cup strawberry halves

1. Preheat oven to 350°F. Prepare Biscuit Topping.

2. Blend ¼ cup water, 3 teaspoons sugar and cornstarch in small saucepan. Cook over medium heat 5 minutes or until mixture thickens, stirring constantly. Remove saucepan from heat; let stand 5 minutes.

3. Add blueberries, nectarine and strawberries to sugar mixture; toss to coat. Spoon fruit mixture into 2-cup casserole; sprinkle with remaining 2 teaspoons sugar. Drop tablespoonfuls topping around edge of casserole.

4. Bake 20 minutes or until topping is browned. Serve immediately.
Makes 2 servings

Biscuit Topping

⅓ cup all-purpose flour
1 tablespoon sugar
¼ teaspoon baking powder
⅛ teaspoon baking soda
1 tablespoon plus
    1 teaspoon margarine

3 tablespoons nonfat sour
    cream
2 teaspoons cholesterol-
    free egg substitute
¼ teaspoon vanilla

Combine flour, sugar, baking powder and baking soda in medium bowl. Cut in margarine with pastry blender until mixture resembles coarse crumbs. Blend sour cream, egg substitute and vanilla in small bowl. Stir into flour mixture just until dry ingredients are moistened.

◆ Stuffed Baked Apples ◆

6 small baking apples
    (Rome, Golden
    Delicious, Winesap,
    Imperial)
½ cup rolled oats
⅓ cup crushed graham
    crackers
4 tablespoons brown sugar,
    divided

1 tablespoon sliced almonds
1 tablespoon soft
    margarine
1 teaspoon lemon juice
¼ teaspoon ground
    cinnamon
1 cup warm water
1 tablespoon granulated
    sugar

Preheat oven to 350°F. Wash apples (do not peel). Core each to ½ inch above bottom of apple. Use knife or potato peeler to hollow out inside of each apple. Leave 1-inch shell around edges. Save cut-out apple and chop into small pieces.

In large bowl mix ⅔ cup chopped apple with oats, graham crackers, 3½ tablespoons brown sugar, sliced almonds, margarine, lemon juice and cinnamon.

Place apples in 8-inch baking pan. Fill apples with oat mixture. Sprinkle tops of apples with remaining ½ tablespoon brown sugar.

Combine water with granulated sugar and pour in baking pan around (not over) apples. Bake apples 30 to 40 minutes or until tender but not mushy.

Makes 6 apples

Favorite recipe from **The Sugar Association, Inc.**

◆ Cherry Cobbler ◆

1 cup all-purpose flour
¾ cup sugar, divided
2 tablespoons instant
    nonfat dry milk
    powder
2 teaspoons baking powder
¼ teaspoon baking soda
¼ teaspoon salt
2 tablespoons vegetable oil

7 tablespoons buttermilk
½ cup water
2 tablespoons cornstarch
1 package (16 ounces)
    frozen unsweetened
    cherries, thawed and
    drained
½ teaspoon vanilla
    Frozen yogurt (optional)

1. Preheat oven to 400°F. Combine flour, ¼ cup sugar, milk powder, baking powder, baking soda and salt in medium bowl. Stir in oil until mixture becomes crumbly. Add buttermilk; stir until moistened. Set aside.

2. Combine water, cornstarch and remaining ½ cup sugar in medium saucepan. Stir until cornstarch is dissolved. Cook over medium heat, stirring constantly until thickened. Add cherries and vanilla; stir until cherries are completely coated. Pour into 8-inch square baking pan; spoon biscuit mixture over cherries.

3. Bake 25 minutes or until topping is golden brown. Serve warm with frozen yogurt, if desired.

Makes 8 servings

◆ Two-Step Apple Nut Dessert ◆

1½ cups sugar
2 eggs
2 cups peeled, cored, sliced
    apples
1 cup all-purpose flour
¾ cup coarsely chopped
    pecans

2 teaspoons baking
    powder
    Whipped cream, vanilla
    yogurt or ice cream

Preheat oven to 325°F. Beat sugar and eggs in large bowl until well blended. Stir in remaining ingredients except whipped cream. Pour into greased 11×7-inch baking dish. Bake 40 to 50 minutes or until top is lightly browned and crisp. Top with whipped cream, vanilla yogurt or ice cream.

Makes 6 to 8 servings

Favorite recipe from **Bob Evans®**

Cherry Cobbler

◆ Fresh Plum Cobbler ◆

½ cup water
5½ teaspoons EQUAL® FOR
    RECIPES *or* 18 packets
    EQUAL® sweetener *or*
    ¾ cup EQUAL®
    SPOONFUL™
1½ tablespoons cornstarch
1 teaspoon lemon juice
4 cups sliced pitted plums
¼ teaspoon ground nutmeg
¼ teaspoon ground allspice,
    divided

1 cup all-purpose flour
1½ teaspoons baking powder
1¾ teaspoons EQUAL® FOR
    RECIPES *or* 6 packets
    EQUAL® sweetener *or*
    ¼ cup EQUAL®
    SPOONFUL™
½ teaspoon salt
3 tablespoons cold
    margarine, cut into
    pieces
½ cup skim milk

• Combine water, 5½ teaspoons Equal® For Recipes *or* 18 packets Equal® sweetener *or* ¾ cup Equal® Spoonful™, cornstarch and lemon juice in large saucepan; add plums and heat to boiling. Boil, stirring constantly, until thickened, about 1 minute. Stir in nutmeg and ⅛ teaspoon allspice. Pour mixture into *ungreased* 1½-quart casserole.

• Combine flour, baking powder, 1¾ teaspoons Equal® For Recipes *or* 6 packets Equal® sweetener *or* ¼ cup Equal® Spoonful™, salt and remaining ⅛ teaspoon allspice in medium bowl; cut in margarine with pastry blender until mixture resembles coarse crumbs. Stir in milk, forming dough. Spoon dough into 6 mounds on fruit.

• Bake cobbler, uncovered, in preheated 400°F oven until topping is golden brown, about 25 minutes. Serve warm.   *Makes 6 servings*

Fresh Plum Cobbler

◆ Cinnamon-Spice Apple Crisp ◆

1½ pounds tart baking apples
2 tablespoons granulated sugar
1 tablespoon lemon juice
⅔ cup packed light brown sugar
½ cup all-purpose flour
⅓ cup quick-cooking oats

½ teaspoon ground cinnamon
¼ teaspoon ground nutmeg
¼ teaspoon ground ginger
¼ teaspoon ground mace
5 tablespoons cold margarine, cut into pieces

1. Preheat oven to 375°F.

2. Mix apples, granulated sugar and lemon juice in large bowl; arrange in *ungreased* 1½-quart glass casserole.

3. Combine brown sugar, flour, oats, cinnamon, nutmeg, ginger and mace in medium bowl. Cut in margarine with pastry blender or 2 knives until mixture resembles coarse crumbs. Sprinkle brown sugar mixture over apples.

4. Bake, uncovered, about 30 minutes or until apples are tender and topping is golden. Serve warm with frozen yogurt, if desired. Sprinkle with additional ground cinnamon, if desired.   *Makes 6 servings*

◆ Honey Noodle Kugel ◆

8 ounces medium noodles
¼ cup butter or margarine, melted
4 eggs, lightly beaten
½ cup honey
½ cup raisins

4 apples, coarsely grated
1 teaspoon salt
1 teaspoon ground cinnamon
Crisp Topping (recipe follows)

Cook noodles according to package directions. Drain and place in large bowl. Add butter; mix well. Cool 10 minutes. Add eggs, honey, raisins, apples, salt and cinnamon; mix well. Place noodle mixture in greased 9-inch square baking pan. Top with Crisp Topping and cover with foil. Bake at 350°F 50 minutes. Uncover and bake 10 to 15 minutes more or until browned on top.

Makes 8 servings

Crisp Topping: Combine ⅓ cup bread crumbs and 1 teaspoon ground cinnamon; mix well. Drizzle ¼ cup honey over mixture and stir until crumbs are coated.

Makes ⅓ cup

Favorite recipe from **National Honey Board**

Cinnamon-Spice Apple Crisp

◆ Linzer Torte ◆

½ cup whole almonds, toasted

1½ cups all-purpose flour

1 teaspoon ground cinnamon

¼ teaspoon salt

¾ cup granulated sugar

½ cup butter or margarine, softened

½ teaspoon grated lemon peel

1 egg

¾ cup raspberry or apricot jam

Sifted powdered sugar

Process almonds in food processor until ground, but not pasty. Preheat oven to 375°F. Combine flour, almonds, cinnamon and salt in medium bowl; set aside. Beat granulated sugar, butter and lemon peel in large bowl with electric mixer at medium speed about 5 minutes or until light and fluffy, scraping down side of bowl once. Beat in egg until well blended. Beat in flour mixture at low speed until well blended.

Spoon ⅔ of dough onto bottom of 10-inch tart pan with removable bottom. Pat dough evenly over bottom and up side of pan. Spread jam over bottom of dough. Roll remaining ⅓ of dough on lightly floured surface into 10×5-inch rectangle. Cut dough into ten ½-inch-wide strips using pizza wheel or sharp knife.

Arrange 4 or 5 strips of dough lengthwise across jam. Arrange another 4 or 5 strips of dough crosswise across top. Trim and press ends of dough strips into edge of crust. Bake 25 to 35 minutes or until crust is golden brown. Cool completely in pan on wire rack. Remove torte from pan. Sprinkle with powdered sugar. Cut into wedges. Store, tightly covered, at room temperature 1 to 2 days.

Makes 12 servings

Linzer Torte

◆ Best-Ever Baked Rice Pudding ◆

3 eggs
⅓ cup sugar
¼ teaspoon salt
2 cups milk
2 cups *cooked* rice

½ cup golden raisins
Grated peel of 1 SUNKIST®
   lemon
Warm Lemon Sauce
   (recipe follows)

In bowl, beat eggs slightly with sugar and salt. Stir in milk, rice, raisins and lemon peel. Pour into well-buttered 1-quart casserole. Bake, uncovered, at 325°F 50 to 60 minutes or until set. Serve with Warm Lemon Sauce. Refrigerate leftovers.   *Makes 6 servings (about 3½ cups)*

Warm Lemon Sauce

⅓ cup sugar
2 tablespoons cornstarch
⅛ teaspoon salt
   Dash nutmeg (optional)
¾ cup water
   Grated peel of ½
      SUNKIST® lemon

Juice of 1 SUNKIST® lemon
1 tablespoon butter or
   margarine
Few drops yellow food
   coloring (optional)

In small saucepan, combine sugar, cornstarch, salt and nutmeg. Gradually blend in water, lemon peel and juice. Add butter. Cook over medium heat, stirring until thickened. Stir in food coloring. Serve warm.

Makes about 1 cup

◆ Walnut-Raisin Baked Apples ◆

6 large baking apples, such
   as Rome Beauty
1 cup plus 2 tablespoons
   packed light brown
   sugar, divided
1 cup (4 ounces) shredded
   ALPINE LACE® American
   Flavor Pasteurized
   Process Cheese Product

¾ cup golden raisins
⅓ cup chopped California
   walnuts, toasted
1 teaspoon ground
   cinnamon
3 tablespoons fresh lemon
   juice
2 cups apple cider

1. Preheat the oven to 375°F. Spray a shallow baking dish with nonstick cooking spray.

2. Core the apples, cutting almost through, but not through, the bottoms of the apples, leaving about a 2-inch-wide cavity in the centers. Pare apples one third of the way down from the top stem end, then place upright in the baking dish. If necessary, cut a thin slice off the bottoms of the apples so they stand firm.

3. In a small bowl, toss together the 1 cup of brown sugar, the cheese, raisins, walnuts and cinnamon. Using a small spoon, stuff one sixth of the cheese mixture into the cavity of each apple, mounding it in the center. Drizzle the lemon juice over the apples. Pour the cider in the baking dish around the apples.

4. Bake the apples, uncovered, for 35 minutes, basting every 10 minutes with the cider. Sprinkle with the remaining 2 tablespoons sugar and bake 10 minutes more or until the apples can be pierced easily with a fork. To serve, transfer each apple to a serving dish and spoon some of the cider sauce over each serving.

Makes 6 servings

◆ Blueberry Bread Pudding ◆

1 package BOB EVANS®
Frozen White Dinner
Roll Dough, prepared
according to package
directions (day old)
5 eggs
1 cup whipping cream
¾ cup milk
½ cup granulated sugar

Pinch salt
1 cup packed brown sugar
½ cup water
1 cup butter, melted
2 tablespoons vanilla
extract
1 teaspoon ground
cinnamon
1 cup fresh blueberries

Preheat oven to 350°F. Cut prepared dinner rolls into cubes; place in large bowl. Whisk together eggs, cream, milk, granulated sugar and salt; pour over bread cubes and toss to coat. Pour mixture into greased 11×7-inch baking dish; bake 1 hour.

To prepare sauce, stir brown sugar and water in medium saucepan until sugar is dissolved. Cook, uncovered, over medium heat until reduced by half. Remove from heat; stir in butter, vanilla and cinnamon until well blended. To serve, pour sauce over bread pudding and garnish with blueberries. Refrigerate leftovers.

Makes 9 servings

◆ Peanut Maple Triangle Puffs ◆

½ cup creamy peanut
    butter
1¼ cups powdered sugar,
    divided
¼ cup plus 3 tablespoons
    maple-flavored syrup,
    divided

1 package (17½ ounces)
    frozen puff pastry,
    thawed
1 to 2 tablespoons water

1. Preheat oven to 400°F. Combine peanut butter, ¼ cup powdered sugar and ¼ cup syrup in small bowl until well blended; set aside.

2. Cut each puff pastry dough sheet into 3-inch squares. Place rounded teaspoon peanut butter mixture in center of each square. Fold squares over to form triangle. Seal edges with fork.

3. Place triangles about 2 inches apart onto *ungreased* baking sheets; spray with cooking spray. Bake 6 to 8 minutes or until golden brown. Remove from baking sheets to wire rack to cool.

4. Combine remaining 1 cup powdered sugar, 3 tablespoons syrup and 1 to 2 tablespoons water in small bowl. Glaze puffs just before serving.

Makes 28 puffs

Note: *For longer storage, do not glaze cookies and store loosely covered so pastry dough remains crisp. Glaze before serving.*

Prep and Bake Time: 30 minutes

Peanut Maple Triangle Puffs

◆ Fresh Apricot Cobbler ◆

1 cup all-purpose flour
¼ cup granulated sugar
2 tablespoons instant
    nonfat dry milk
    powder
2 teaspoons baking powder
¼ teaspoon baking soda
¼ teaspoon salt
2 tablespoons canola oil

7 tablespoons buttermilk
½ cup firmly packed dark
    brown sugar
½ cup water
4½ teaspoons cornstarch
1½ pounds ripe apricots, pits
    removed, quartered
Frozen yogurt (optional)

1. Preheat oven to 400°F. Combine flour, granulated sugar, milk powder, baking powder, baking soda and salt in medium bowl. Stir in oil until mixture becomes crumbly. Add buttermilk and stir just until moistened.

2. Combine brown sugar, water and cornstarch in medium saucepan, stirring until cornstarch is dissolved. Cook over medium heat until thickened, stirring constantly. Add apricots; cook and stir about 3 minutes or until apricots are completely covered in sauce.

3. Pour into 8-inch square baking pan and immediately drop flour mixture in small spoonfuls on top of apricot mixture. Bake 25 minutes or until topping is lightly browned. Serve warm with frozen yogurt, if desired.

Makes 6 servings

◆ Cinnamon-Raisin Bread Pudding ◆

1 can (12 ounces)
    evaporated skim milk
⅓ cup cholesterol-free egg
    substitute
2 tablespoons sugar
3 teaspoons maple syrup,
    divided

¼ teaspoon vanilla
⅛ teaspoon ground
    cinnamon
4 slices cinnamon-raisin
    bread, torn into 1-inch
    pieces

1. Preheat oven to 350°F. Spray 4 custard cups with nonstick cooking spray. Pour 2 cups water into 8×8-inch baking pan; set aside.

2. Combine milk, egg substitute, sugar, 2 teaspoons maple syrup, vanilla and cinnamon in medium bowl. Stir in bread. Spoon evenly into prepared custard cups. Place cups in prepared pan.

3. Bake 40 minutes or until bread pudding is set. Drizzle remaining 1 teaspoon syrup over pudding. Serve immediately. *Makes 4 servings*

Fresh Apricot Cobbler

◆ Cherry Turnovers ◆

8 frozen phyllo dough
   sheets, thawed
¼ cup butter or margarine,
   melted
6 tablespoons no-sugar-
   added black cherry
   fruit spread

1½ tablespoons cherry-
   flavored liqueur
   (optional)
1 egg
1 teaspoon cold water

Preheat oven to 400°F. Lightly brush each phyllo sheet with butter; stack. Cut through all sheets to form six (5-inch) squares. Combine fruit spread and cherry liqueur, if desired. Place 1 tablespoon fruit spread mixture in center of each stack of eight phyllo squares; brush edges of phyllo with butter. Fold edges over to form triangle; gently press edges together to seal. Place on *ungreased* cookie sheet. Beat together egg and water; brush over phyllo triangles. Bake 10 minutes or until golden brown. Cool on wire rack. Serve warm or at room temperature.

Makes 6 turnovers

Mini Noodle Kugels with ◆ Raspberry Filling ◆

4 ounces uncooked medium
   or wide egg noodles
½ cup egg substitute
3 tablespoon sugar
¼ teaspoon ground
   cinnamon
   Pinch nutmeg
½ cup low-fat cottage
   cheese

⅓ cup applesauce
¼ cup chopped dried apples
   or raisins
   Vegetable oil cooking
   spray
6 tablespoons raspberry
   jam

Preheat oven to 350°F. Prepare egg noodles according to package directions. While noodles are cooking, beat egg substitute, sugar, cinnamon and nutmeg in large bowl until sugar is dissolved and mixture is foamy. Fold in cottage cheese, applesauce and apples. Lightly spray muffin tin (preferably nonstick) with cooking spray. (Do not use baking cups.)

Drain noodles and immediately add to egg mixture. Fill each muffin tin half full. Add 2 teaspoons raspberry jam to each, then fill muffin cups to full. Bake until firm and tops are golden brown, about 45 minutes. Serve warm.

Makes 9 servings

Favorite recipe from **National Pasta Association**

Cherry Turnovers

◆ Apple Cranberry Buckle ◆

6 medium Granny Smith apples, peeled, cored, thinly sliced

¾ cup dried cranberries or dried cherries

⅓ cup orange juice

⅔ cup packed light brown sugar

1½ cups plus 2 tablespoons all-purpose flour, divided

1¼ teaspoons ground cinnamon

¼ teaspoon ground cloves

¾ cup plus 1 teaspoon granulated sugar, divided

1½ teaspoons baking powder

1 egg

⅓ cup milk

¼ cup margarine or butter, melted

1 cup apple butter

2 tablespoons amaretto liqueur (optional)

Mint leaves (optional)

Preheat oven to 375°F. Place apples and cranberries in 11×7-inch baking dish. Drizzle orange juice over fruit.

Combine brown sugar, 2 tablespoons flour, cinnamon and cloves in small bowl. Pour over apple mixture; toss to coat.

Combine remaining 1½ cups flour, ¾ cup granulated sugar and baking powder in medium bowl. Add egg, milk and margarine; stir with mixing spoon to blend. Drop tablespoonfuls over top of apple mixture.

Sprinkle remaining 1 teaspoon granulated sugar over topping. Bake 35 minutes or until topping is lightly browned and apples are tender. Cool buckle slightly in pan on wire rack.

Combine apple butter and liqueur, if desired, in small microwavable bowl. Microwave at HIGH 1 minute or until warm. Spoon 1 to 2 tablespoonfuls sauce over each serving. Garnish with mint leaves, if desired.

Makes 8 servings

Apple Cranberry Buckle

◆ Smucker's® Double Apple Turnovers ◆

½ cup SMUCKER'S® Apple
    Butter
½ cup apple cider or juice
½ teaspoon ground
    cinnamon
    Grated peel of 1 orange
¼ cup golden raisins

4 large firm apples, peeled,
    cored and chopped
1 package frozen phyllo
    dough, thawed
    Nonstick cooking spray
    Granulated sugar for
    garnish

Preheat oven to 375°F. Place apple butter, cider, cinnamon and orange peel in saucepan and simmer 5 minutes. Add raisins and heat 2 minutes more. Add apples; cook over medium heat about 10 minutes or until apples begin to soften and most of liquid evaporates. Cool in refrigerator.

Unwrap phyllo dough. Remove one sheet of dough, keeping remaining sheets covered with damp cloth. Coat dough with cooking spray, then cover with second sheet of dough. Spray top sheet with cooking spray.

Spoon about ⅓ cup apple filling on lower right corner of dough. Fold dough over filling to form large rectangle. Then fold turnover as if it were a flag, making triangular packet with each turn. Repeat with remaining dough and filling to make 6 turnovers. Place turnovers on baking sheet. Sprinkle with granulated sugar before baking. Bake approximately 25 minutes or until turnovers are golden. *Makes 6 turnovers*

Prep Time: 30 minutes
Cook Time: 40 minutes

◆ Apple Strudel Tarts with Vanilla Sauce ◆

3 cups chopped, peeled,
  cored apples
¼ cup sugar
¼ cup raisins
2 tablespoons margarine or
  butter
1½ teaspoons ground
  cinnamon, divided

6 sheets phyllo dough,
  thawed
2 tablespoons margarine or
  butter, melted
2 cups milk
¼ cup vanilla pudding mix

For filling, combine apples, sugar, raisins, 2 tablespoons margarine and 1 teaspoon cinnamon in large skillet. Cook over medium heat, stirring frequently, until apples are tender.

Preheat oven to 350°F. Grease 6 custard cups or 6-cup muffin pan; set aside. Brush 1 sheet phyllo dough with melted margarine. Top with another phyllo dough sheet. Repeat brushing and layering with remaining phyllo dough and melted margarine. Cut phyllo stack lengthwise into 6 strips. Cut stack crosswise into thirds, making 18 pieces total. Press 3 pieces into each custard or muffin cup, placing pieces at angles so that each cup is covered with dough. Spoon apple mixture evenly into each cup. Bake 20 minutes or until golden brown. Cool 5 minutes in cups; carefully remove tarts to serving dishes.

For sauce, combine milk, pudding mix and remaining ½ teaspoon cinnamon in medium saucepan. Cook over medium-low heat, stirring frequently, until slightly thickened. Serve tarts warm with sauce.   *Makes 6 tarts*

Note: Prevent phyllo dough sheets from drying out by keeping extra sheets covered with slightly damp dish cloth or plastic wrap. Phyllo sheets are fragile and may tear during preparation; this will not affect final results.

Favorite recipe from **New York Apple Association, Inc.**

◆ Country Skillet Pudding ◆

2 cups boiling water
1 cup packed brown sugar
6 tablespoons butter, softened, divided
2 teaspoons vanilla extract, divided
½ cup granulated sugar
½ cup milk

⅛ teaspoon salt
1 cup all-purpose flour
1 teaspoon baking powder
½ cup raisins
½ cup chopped walnuts or pecans
Whipped cream

Preheat oven to 350°F. Combine boiling water, brown sugar, 2 tablespoons butter and 1 teaspoon vanilla in 10-inch ovenproof skillet or similar size shallow casserole dish until smooth. Beat granulated sugar and remaining 4 tablespoons butter in medium bowl until creamy. Beat in milk, remaining 1 teaspoon vanilla and salt. Add combined flour and baking powder; beat until smooth. Fold in raisins and nuts. Spoon mixture by heaping tablespoons evenly onto liquid in skillet; do not stir or spread. Bake 25 minutes or until set and liquid is bubbly. Serve warm with whipped cream. Refrigerate leftovers.

Makes 6 servings

Favorite recipe from **Bob Evans®**

◆ Honey Bread Pudding ◆

8 cups egg bread, cubed
1 cup raisins
3 cups 2% low-fat milk
1 cup evaporated low-fat milk
6 eggs, beaten

½ cup honey
1 tablespoon grated orange peel
1 teaspoon ground cinnamon
1 teaspoon vanilla

Arrange bread and raisins in bottom of lightly greased shallow 2-quart baking dish. Beat remaining ingredients in large bowl until well blended; pour over bread cubes in baking dish and let stand 1 hour or until liquid is absorbed. Bake at 375°F 45 to 50 minutes or until knife inserted near center comes out clean.

Makes 8 servings

Favorite recipe from **National Honey Board**

Country Skillet Pudding

◆ Almond-Pear Strudel ◆

¾ cup slivered almonds, divided

5 to 6 cups thinly sliced crisp pears (4 to 5 medium pears)

1 tablespoon grated lemon peel

1 tablespoon lemon juice

⅓ cup plus 1 teaspoon sugar, divided

2 teaspoons ground cinnamon

1 teaspoon ground nutmeg

6 sheets (¼ pound) phyllo dough

4 tablespoons melted butter or margarine, divided

½ teaspoon almond extract

1. Preheat oven to 300°F. Spread almonds in shallow baking pan. Bake 10 to 12 minutes or until lightly browned, stirring frequently; cool and cover. Place sliced pears in large microwavable container. Stir in lemon peel and lemon juice. Microwave on HIGH 6 minutes or until tender; cool. Combine ⅓ cup sugar, cinnamon and nutmeg in small bowl; cover. Cover pears and refrigerate overnight.

2. Lay 2 sheets plastic wrap on work surface to make 20-inch square. Place 1 phyllo sheet in middle of plastic wrap. (Cover remaining phyllo dough with damp kitchen towel to prevent dough from drying out.). Brush 1 teaspoon melted butter onto phyllo sheet. Place second phyllo sheet over first; brush with 1 teaspoon butter. Repeat layering with remaining sheets of phyllo. Cover with plastic wrap. Cover remaining butter. Refrigerate phyllo dough and butter overnight or up to 1 day.

3. Preheat oven to 400°F. Drain reserved pears in colander. Toss pears with reserved sugar mixture and almond extract. Melt reserved butter. Uncover phyllo dough and spread pear mixture evenly over phyllo, leaving 3-inch strip on far long side. Sprinkle pear mixture with ½ cup toasted almonds. Brush strip with 2 teaspoons melted butter. Beginning at long side of phyllo opposite 3-inch strip, carefully roll up jelly-roll style, using plastic wrap to gently lift, forming strudel. Place strudel, seam-side down, onto buttered baking sheet. Brush top with 1 teaspoon butter. Bake 20 minutes or until deep golden. Brush again with 1 teaspoon butter. Stir remaining ¼ cup toasted almonds with remaining butter; sprinkle on top of strudel. Sprinkle with remaining 1 teaspoon sugar. Bake an additional 5 minutes. Cool 10 minutes; sprinkle with powdered sugar, if desired.

Makes 8 servings

Almond-Pear Strudel

◆ Maple Caramel Bread Pudding ◆

8 slices cinnamon raisin bread

2 whole eggs

1 egg white

⅓ cup sugar

1½ cups reduced-fat (2%) milk

½ cup maple syrup

½ teaspoon ground cinnamon

¼ teaspoon ground nutmeg

¼ teaspoon salt

6 tablespoons fat-free caramel ice cream topping

1. Preheat oven to 350°F. Spray 8×8-inch baking dish with nonstick cooking spray. Cut bread into ¾-inch cubes; arrange in prepared dish.

2. Beat whole eggs, egg white and sugar in medium bowl. Beat in milk, syrup, cinnamon, nutmeg and salt; pour evenly over bread. Toss bread gently to coat.

3. Bake 45 minutes or until center is set. Transfer to wire cooling rack; let stand 20 minutes before serving. Serve warm with caramel topping.

Makes 6 servings

Maple Caramel Bread Pudding

◆ Grandma's Apple Crisp ◆

¾ **cup apple juice**
3½ **teaspoons EQUAL® FOR RECIPES *or* 12 packets EQUAL® sweetener *or* ½ cup EQUAL® SPOONFUL™**

1 **tablespoon cornstarch**
1 **teaspoon grated lemon peel**
4 **cups sliced peeled apples Crispy Topping (recipe follows)**

• Combine apple juice, Equal®, cornstarch and lemon peel in medium saucepan; add apples and heat to boiling. Reduce heat and simmer, uncovered, until juice is thickened and apples begin to lose their crispness, about 5 minutes.

• Arrange apples in 8-inch square baking pan; sprinkle Crispy Topping over apples. Bake in preheated 400°F oven until topping is browned and apples are tender, about 25 minutes. Serve warm.   *Makes 6 servings*

Crispy Topping

¼ **cup all-purpose flour**
2½ **teaspoons EQUAL® FOR RECIPES *or* 8 packets EQUAL® sweetener *or* ⅓ cup EQUAL® SPOONFUL™**
1 **teaspoon ground cinnamon**
½ **teaspoon ground nutmeg**

3 **dashes ground allspice**
4 **tablespoons cold margarine, cut into pieces**
¼ **cup uncooked quick-cooking oats**
¼ **cup unsweetened flaked coconut***

*Unsweetened coconut can be purchased in health food stores.

• Combine flour, Equal® and spices in small bowl; cut in margarine with pastry blender until mixture resembles coarse crumbs. Stir in oats and coconut.

Grandma's Apple Crisp

◆ Orange Bread Pudding with Rum Sauce ◆

Rum Sauce (recipe follows)
½ **loaf (1 pound) day-old French bread**
5 **eggs**
1 **egg white**
⅔ **cup granulated sugar**
⅓ **cup packed brown sugar**
¼ **teaspoon ground cinnamon**

2 **cups milk**
1 **cup orange juice**
½ **cup raisins**
¼ **cup pine nuts**
1 **tablespoon vanilla extract**
3 **tablespoons butter, divided**
Boiling water

Prepare Rum Sauce; refrigerate until ready to use. Preheat oven to 350°F. Cut bread into 1-inch slices; cut each slice, with crust, into 1-inch cubes to make 8 cups. Beat eggs and egg white in large bowl of electric mixer on medium speed until foamy. Gradually beat in granulated sugar, brown sugar and cinnamon. Stir in milk, orange juice, raisins, pine nuts and vanilla. Add bread cubes; mix well, pushing bread into liquid so each piece is moistened. Butter 3-quart baking dish or casserole with 1 tablespoon butter. Pour bread mixture into dish. Dot top with the remaining 2 tablespoons butter. Set dish in larger pan. Pour boiling water into larger pan to depth of 1½ inches. Bake, uncovered, 45 minutes or until top of pudding is golden brown and knife inserted in center comes out clean. Remove pudding from water bath and place on rack to cool 30 minutes. Serve warm with Rum Sauce. To reheat cake, bake, covered, in 350°F oven 15 minutes or until warmed.

Makes 8 servings

Rum Sauce

¼ **cup butter or margarine, softened**
1 **egg yolk**
1½ **cups powdered sugar**

2 **tablespoons rum**
1 **teaspoon grated orange peel**

Beat butter in small bowl of electric mixer on medium speed until creamy. Beat in egg yolk. Add powdered sugar; beat until light and fluffy. Add rum; beat until well blended. Stir in orange peel. Cover and refrigerate up to 2 days. Serve chilled sauce over warm pudding. *Makes about 1 cup*

◆ Cream Cheese Dessert Coffeecake ◆

¼ cup water
4 egg yolks
1 cup butter
1 tablespoon sugar
1 teaspoon salt

2½ cups all-purpose flour
2¼ teaspoons RED STAR®
   Active Dry Yeast
½ cup finely chopped nuts

FILLING
2 (8-ounce) packages
   cream cheese, softened

1 cup sugar
1 egg yolk

TOPPING
1 egg white

½ cup finely chopped nuts

GLAZE
1 cup powdered sugar
1 teaspoon vanilla

2 to 3 tablespoons water

Bread Machine Method
Place room temperature ingredients, except nuts, in pan in order listed. Select dough/manual cycle. At end of first kneading cycle, remove dough and follow shaping and baking instructions.

Traditional Method
In small bowl, dissolve yeast in water heated to 110° to 115°F with 1 teaspoon sugar. Let stand 5 minutes. Combine flour, remaining sugar and salt. With pastry blender, cut in butter until consistency of cornmeal. Add yeast mixture and egg yolks; mix lightly.

Shaping and Baking
Shape prepared dough into ball. Cover with plastic wrap; refrigerate 2 hours. Divide cold dough into halves. On lightly floured surface, roll each half into 15×10-inch rectangle. Transfer one rectangle to greased 15×10-inch jelly roll pan. In mixing bowl, beat Filling ingredients until smooth. Spread Filling over dough. Carefully place remaining rectangle over Filling. Brush dough with 1 lightly beaten egg white. Sprinkle with nuts. Cover; let rise in warm place 1 hour. Bake in preheated 350°F oven 25 minutes. Mix Glaze ingredients until smooth. Drizzle Glaze over warm coffeecake. When cool, cut into squares or bars. Store in refrigerator. *Makes 1 coffeecake (20 squares)*

◆ Crunch Peach Cobbler ◆

1 can (29 ounces) *or* 2 cans (16 ounces each) cling peach slices in syrup, undrained
⅓ cup plus 1 tablespoon granulated sugar, divided
1 tablespoon cornstarch
½ teaspoon vanilla
2 cups all-purpose flour, divided
½ cup packed brown sugar

⅓ cup uncooked rolled oats
¼ cup margarine or butter, melted
½ teaspoon ground cinnamon
½ teaspoon salt
½ cup shortening
4 to 5 tablespoons cold water
Sweetened whipped cream for garnish

1. Drain peach slices in fine-meshed sieve over 2-cup glass measure. Reserve ¾ cup syrup.

2. Combine ⅓ cup granulated sugar and cornstarch in small saucepan. Slowly add reserved syrup. Stir well. Add vanilla. Cook over low heat, stirring constantly, until thickened. Set aside.

3. Combine ½ cup flour, brown sugar, oats, margarine and cinnamon in small bowl; stir until mixture forms coarse crumbs. Set aside.

4. Preheat oven to 350°F. Combine remaining 1½ cups flour, 1 tablespoon granulated sugar and salt in small bowl. Cut in shortening with pastry blender or 2 knives until mixture forms pea-sized pieces. Sprinkle water, 1 tablespoon at a time, over flour mixture. Toss lightly with fork until mixture holds together. Press together to form ball.

5. Roll out dough into 10-inch square, ⅛ inch thick. Fold dough in half, then in half again. Carefully place folded dough in center of 8×8-inch baking dish. Unfold and press onto bottom and about 1 inch up sides of dish. Arrange peaches over crust. Pour sauce over peaches. Sprinkle with crumb topping.

6. Bake 45 minutes. Serve warm or at room temperature with sweetened whipped cream.   *Makes about 6 servings*

Crunch Peach Cobbler

◆ Apple-Cherry Crisp ◆

1 pound Granny Smith
   apples, peeled, cored
   and sliced ¼ inch thick
1 can (16 ounces) tart pie
   cherries packed in
   water, drained
1 can (16 ounces) dark
   sweet pitted cherries in
   heavy syrup, drained

2 teaspoons vanilla
1 teaspoon ground
   cinnamon
1 cup fruit-juice-sweetened
   granola without
   raisins*
⅓ cup sliced almonds
1 quart fat-free vanilla ice
   cream or frozen yogurt

Available in the health food section of supermarkets.

1. Preheat oven to 350°F. Spray an 11×7-inch glass baking dish with nonstick cooking spray; set aside.

2. Combine apples, cherries, vanilla and cinnamon in large bowl; stir until well blended. Spoon into prepared baking dish. Cover with foil; bake 30 minutes.

3. Remove from oven; stir to distribute juices. Sprinkle granola and almonds evenly over fruit. Bake, uncovered, 15 minutes more or until juice is bubbling and almonds are golden; serve warm or at room temperature topped with ice cream.   *Makes 8 servings*

Apple-Cherry Crisp

ACKNOWLEDGMENTS

The publishers would like to thank the companies and organizations listed below for the use of their recipes and photos in this publication.

BelGioioso® Cheese, Inc.

Birds Eye®

Blue Diamond Growers®

Bob Evans®

California Tree Fruit Agreement

Cherry Marketing Institute, Inc.

Colorado Potato Administrative Committee

Del Monte Corporation

Dole Food Company, Inc.

Duncan Hines

Equal® sweetener

Idaho Potato Commission

Kahlúa® Liqueur

Kellogg Company

Kraft Foods, Inc.

Land O' Lakes, Inc.

Lawry's® Foods, Inc.

M&M/MARS

McIlhenny Company (TABASCO® brand Pepper Sauce)

National Honey Board

National Pasta Association

New York Apple Association, Inc.

Norseland, Inc.

The Procter & Gamble Company

The Quaker® Kitchens

Reckitt & Colman Inc.

RED STAR® Yeast & Products, a Division of Universal Foods Corporation

Roman Meal® Company

Sargento® Foods Inc.

The J.M. Smucker Company

Sonoma® Dried Tomatoes

Sunkist Growers

Walnut Marketing Board

Washington Apple Commission

Wisconsin Milk Marketing Board

INDEX

METRIC CONVERSION CHART

VOLUME MEASUREMENTS (dry)

⅛ teaspoon = 0.5 mL
¼ teaspoon = 1 mL
½ teaspoon = 2 mL
¾ teaspoon = 4 mL
1 teaspoon = 5 mL
1 tablespoon = 15 mL
2 tablespoons = 30 mL
¼ cup = 60 mL
⅓ cup = 75 mL
½ cup = 125 mL
⅔ cup = 150 mL
¾ cup = 175 mL
1 cup = 250 mL
2 cups = 1 pint = 500 mL
3 cups = 750 mL
4 cups = 1 quart = 1 L

VOLUME MEASUREMENTS (fluid)

1 fluid ounce (2 tablespoons) = 30 mL
4 fluid ounces (½ cup) = 125 mL
8 fluid ounces (1 cup) = 250 mL
12 fluid ounces (1½ cups) = 375 mL
16 fluid ounces (2 cups) = 500 mL

WEIGHTS (mass)

½ ounce = 15 g
1 ounce = 30 g
3 ounces = 90 g
4 ounces = 120 g
8 ounces = 225 g
10 ounces = 285 g
12 ounces = 360 g
16 ounces = 1 pound = 450 g

DIMENSIONS

$\frac{1}{16}$ inch = 2 mm
⅛ inch = 3 mm
¼ inch = 6 mm
½ inch = 1.5 cm
¾ inch = 2 cm
1 inch = 2.5 cm

OVEN TEMPERATURES

250°F = 120°C
275°F = 140°C
300°F = 150°C
325°F = 160°C
350°F = 180°C
375°F = 190°C
400°F = 200°C
425°F = 220°C
450°F = 230°C

BAKING PAN SIZES

Utensil	Size in Inches/Quarts	Metric Volume	Size in Centimeters
Baking or Cake Pan (square or rectangular)	8×8×2	2 L	20×20×5
	9×9×2	2.5 L	23×23×5
	12×8×2	3 L	30×20×5
	13×9×2	3.5 L	33×23×5
Loaf Pan	8×4×3	1.5 L	20×10×7
	9×5×3	2 L	23×13×7
Round Layer Cake Pan	8×1½	1.2 L	20×4
	9×1½	1.5 L	23×4
Pie Plate	8×1¼	750 mL	20×3
	9×1¼	1 L	23×3
Baking Dish or Casserole	1 quart	1 L	—
	1½ quart	1.5 L	—
	2 quart	2 L	—